Advocacy Leadership

Educational leaders—and other school professionals—are experiencing a new work environment in which contracting, outsourcing, student recruitment, public relations, and an obsession with test scores are taking center stage. Leaders are pushed to be entrepreneurial managers, increasingly expected to act less like educators and more like MBAs. In this timely and important new book, Gary L. Anderson provides a devastating critique of why this managerial role is counterproductive, especially for improving opportunities for low-income students and students of color, and instead proposes ways of re-theorizing educational leadership to emphasize its *advocacy* role. *Advocacy Leadership* lays out a post-reform agenda that moves beyond the neo-liberal, competition framework to define a new accountability, a new pedagogy, and a new leadership role definition. Drawing on personal narrative, discourse analysis, and interdisciplinary scholarship, Anderson delivers a compelling argument for the need to move away from current inauthentic and inequitable approaches to school reform in order to jump-start a conversation about an alternative vision of education today.

Gary L. Anderson is a former teacher and principal, and is currently a Professor of Educational Leadership in the Steinhardt School of Culture, Education, and Human Development at New York University where he co-developed a new masters degree in Educational Leadership, Politics, and Advocacy.

The Critical Social Thought Series

Edited by Michael W. Apple,
University of Wisconsin—Madison

Advocacy Leadership
Toward a Post-Reform Agenda
in Education

Gary L. Anderson

Routledge
Taylor & Francis Group

NEW YORK AND LONDON

First published 2009
by Routledge
270 Madison Ave, New York, NY 10016

Simultaneously published in the UK
by Routledge
2 Park Square, Milton Park, Abingdon, Oxon OX14 4RN

Routledge is an imprint of the Taylor & Francis Group, an informa business

Typeset in Minion by EvS Communication Networx, Inc.
Printed and bound in the United States of America on acid-free paper by Walsworth Publishing Company, Marceline, MO.

Library of Congress Cataloging in Publication Data
Anderson, Gary L.
Advocacy leadership : toward a post-reform agenda in education / Gary L. Anderson.
p. cm. — (The critical social thought series)
Includes bibliographical references. [etc.]
1. School management and organization—Social aspects—United States. 2. Educational leadership—United States. 3. Critical pedagogy—United States. I. Title.
LB2805.A56 2009
371.200973—dc22
2008040082

ISBN 10: (hbk) 0-415-99427-6
ISBN 10: (pbk) 0-415-99428-4
ISBN 10: (ebk) 0-203-88061-7

ISBN 13: (hbk) 978-0-415-99427-9
ISBN 13: (pbk) 978-0-415-99428-6
ISBN 13: (ebk) 978-0-203-88061-6

Contents

Series Editor Introduction

My first day as a teacher taught me a good deal about one of the dangers of defining the role of the school administrator in strictly bureaucratic terms. I was teaching in an inner-city school in a very poor city on the East Coast. The school buildings were aged and in disrepair. Many of the windows didn't open, which proved to be a serious problem since it was over 100° degrees in my classroom. Given the oppressive conditions that I and the students were experiencing, I took off my jacket.

The principal walked by and looked in. She quickly entered my room and publicly berated me. In a stern voice that made it clear that I had broached a cardinal rule, she said "Mr. Apple, how can children learn if you do not dress appropriately?" This was a time of strict dress codes for teachers. In the minds of the central office and that principal there was a strong relationship between teachers wearing jackets and ties (for men) and skirts or dresses (for women) on the one hand and better performance on the mandatory yearly tests that the city gave on the other.

This experience now seems a bit quaint. But the correlation between bureaucratic leadership and control still exists in all too many schools systems throughout this nation and others. There are of course many models of leadership that now circulate within educational circles and in the government and corporate sectors. Indeed, it is nearly impossible to keep up with these multiple theories of leadership and with how each one will permanently "solve" all of our dilemmas. However, very little of this literature is expressly grounded in a deep concern for social equality and very few works are explicitly aimed at working to transform the institutions and power relations that dominate this society. These more socially conscious models do exist. But it is hard to hear them above the din of neoliberal and neoconservative attacks on social democratic goals and processes and on the people and policies that keep them alive.

As is visible all around us, the public sphere is under concerted attack, driven by a nearly religious commitment to privatization and marketization. For all too many people, private is now necessarily good and public is now necessarily bad. I consciously used the word *religious* in the previous sentence because neoliberal positions do indeed have something of a religious fervor to them. They seem to be impervious to empirical falsification. Yet, as I demonstrate in *Educating the "Right" Way* (Apple, 2006), neoliberalism with its commitment to markets, privatization, and commodification not only has not lived up to its rhetorical promises in education, but it has a number of profound, hidden, and negative effects as well. At the very moment when social movements that are organized to transform our institutions have never been more essential, neoliberalism's transformation of democracy into simply individual consumption practices is one of the most dangerous ideological tendencies I can think of. If it is social movements that have been and are the engines of what we might call "thick democracy" in education and elsewhere (Anyon, 2005; Apple, Au, & Gandin, in press), then what we do not need is the eviscerated "thin democracy" of marketization.

Of course, neoliberalism doesn't stand alone. Side by side with an emphasis on making schools act exactly like businesses or turning them into businesses themselves, there is also immense pressure on all educational institutions to "show results" on what are often very flawed measurement instruments. Somewhat cutely, we might say that the commitment here is, "If it moves in classrooms, measure it; and if it hasn't moved yet, measure it anyway in case it moves tomorrow." The results of what is known as "new managerialism" have all too often been a drastic narrowing of the curriculum, especially for poor children, the deskilling and intensification of teachers' work, ever increasing pressure on school administrators to show increased test scores at whatever cost, and a growing sense of frustration among many people who have devoted their lives to working in difficult conditions (Lipman, 2004; Valenzuela, 2005). When all of this is coupled with a neoconservative movement to curtail the voices, cultures, and histories of the "Others" in this society (e.g., Buras, 2008), this has made it even more essential that educators see the big picture of what is happening.

In *Advocacy Leadership*, Gary Anderson gives us the big picture. But he does more: He critically describes the current state of educational reforms in clear and cogent ways, by placing them in their social and ideological contexts. He shows what this means for educational leaders who take their educational, ethical, and political responsibilities seriously. And he outlines ways in which committed educational leaders who see their role as advocates for social justice can act on their commitments in an educationally and socially sound manner.

Anderson is not utopian. He is basing his proposals on many of the things we already know. As Deborah Meier has shown, for example, administrators who possess a powerful educational and social vision and who act on these principles can make a significant difference (Meier, 1995, 2002).

Anderson points to a number of examples of what he means, from successful urban schools that have formed deep and long-lasting connections between schools and their local communities in the United States to the exceptional transformations that are now firmly in place in Porto Alegre, Brazil (see Apple et al., 2003; Apple & Buras, 2006).

It should be clear—and Gary Anderson makes it even clearer—that we should not want to defend every existing school policy and practice. Much of what happens in urban schools, and not only there, is not defensible and the anger and the demands for large-scale transformations on the part of oppressed communities is fully understandable (Pedroni, 2007). But the choices we have are not only those of marketization and stronger control and testing. As Anderson indicates, there are more democratic alternatives that *work* (see also Apple & Beane, 2007). By combining a keen critical eye with a vision of committed leadership and then connecting that with a strategic sense of what needs to be and can be done, *Advocacy Leadership* challenges us to lead in ways that can assist all of us in building an education worthy of its name.

Michael W. Apple
*John Bascom Professor of
Curriculum and Instruction
and Educational Policy Studies
University of Wisconsin, Madison*

Foreword
Advocates, Managers, Leaders, and Social Entrepreneurs?
The Future of Educational Leadership

This book arrives at a critically important time in U.S. public education, especially within urban and segregated, suburban public school districts. As demographic, socioeconomic, and policy shifts increasingly isolate many of these school systems by race and poverty, policy makers, researchers, and advocates call for what are often conflicting approaches to ameliorating the persistent racial achievement gap found both within these systems and across school districts. Meanwhile, rural communities are becoming more stratified by race and poverty as well.

Some, like Anderson, ask school leaders to become culturally competent social advocates of the students and communities they serve, and to create high quality curricula that prepare students to critique social inequalities while also allowing them to engage on equal terms with their more privileged peers in higher education and the workplace. Other more dominant strategies ask superintendents, principals, and even teachers to embrace assumptions and practices informed by business and become more entrepreneurial; these approaches hold that school leadership and educational strategies be based exclusively on "objective," quantitative data.

Within this schema, educators in all parts of schooling systems are finding their roles redefined along corporate principles of accountability, management, data based decision making, and competition. Foundations are investing millions of dollars in initiatives aimed at developing leaders who come from nontraditional backgrounds, mostly eschewing longstanding university-based, education school preparation programs and those who matriculate from them. In their stead, recently developed alternative leadership preparation programs can be found housed in school system administrative offices and university-based business schools.

Meanwhile, in several large cities, school system leaders and city and state policy makers have embraced an array of market-based educational reforms such as charter schools, educational management organizations, and to some degree, small schools. Assuming that parents are consumers and schools are products, most of these reforms allow school leaders to exert some degree of autonomy over the teachers they hire and terminate, curricular approaches, and budgetary decisions while also asking them to produce measurable student achievement gains on standardized assessments. These new schools and organizational arrangements also frequently allow school staff to exert some selectivity about which students they will enroll and under which circumstances students will be expelled. At the macropolicy level, these market-based reforms coincide with a curtailment of traditional, equity-based school reform strategies and growing economic inequality. For example, in 2007, the Supreme Court placed limits on school districts' abilities to design student assignment plans that could result in racially diverse schools, and the federal No Child Left Behind Act's approaches to struggling schools and schooling systems deemphasizes redistribution of resources and instead largely focuses on sanctioning schools for lackluster performance.

While more managerial, corporate strategies have gained policy currency in recent years, they have developed in tandem with grassroots, community based, and multiracial social movements that have challenged these very approaches. Often operating locally and below the political radar, these movements embody an array of approaches and strategies that are less uniform around traditional progressive approaches to educational advocacy, but rather more strategic— seeking alliances across government, corporate, community, and philanthropic bases to achieve desired outcomes. In these efforts, schools are a central, but not exclusive concern of the reformers, who often align displeasure with educational inequality with that of inequities in labor, housing, criminal justice, and other social policies. It is within these social movements that Anderson finds hope for a post-reform agenda of educational reform and school leadership practice.

Within shifting political and professional climates, Anderson's book helps to frame a much-needed discussion through a close examination of the changing context of educational leadership and the implications of these changes in terms of the lives of leaders, teachers, students, and community members and their schools. In pushing for reconciliation between the advocacy leader and the managerial leader, his book makes at least three contributions to educational leadership and policy discourse. First, it asks readers to consider what it means to be a new public school leader in the current political, social, and economic climate. Students and faculty in traditional and alternative leadership preparation programs will benefit greatly from this book, which demands that future educational leaders become much more knowledgeable about the political and economic shifts that not only powerfully impact the lives of students, but also change the nature of the educational leadership practice. In an environment dominated by market approaches, educational leaders will need to become more adept at particular management capacities such as negotiation with and compliance with private educational contractors. Second, Anderson posits an alternative conceptualization of educational leadership that challenges the current emphasis on what he calls the managerial leader. Instead, Anderson proposes that leaders think of themselves as advocates—especially those who hold progressive views on issues of educational inequality. This vision of educational leaders requires them to become engaged in the political contexts that shape much of the schooling experiences of students in urban and segregated suburban schools. He argues that where managerial leaders might serve to preserve the status quo for the most part, advocacy leaders help to challenge it. Finally, this book makes a powerfully compelling case for the blending of educational leadership research and preparation with policy analysis. Too often study in these areas is bifurcated—with researchers publishing in different journals and with students reading work that falsely decouples micro- organizational analyses from macropolicy study. The result is that many newly minted and existing educational leaders may be woefully underprepared to challenge and operate in school system climates that ask them to be managers, advocates, leaders, *and* social entrepreneurs. In addition, those leaders prepared through alternative routes could be lacking in understanding of and commitment to issues of social and educational justice. Anderson's book, then, is sorely needed for educational leaders who have origins in traditional and market-oriented preparation programs.

Anderson ultimately calls for the adoption of an alternative vision of the state's role in providing high-quality and equitable education. This vision would blend the innovations that markets can provide with the social protections of a more empowering state. Unlike prevailing iterations of educational reforms, educators, community members, and school leaders are key levers for realizing this vision, and as such, must become attentive to and engaged in the political processes shaping the conditions under which students are educated in U.S. public schools.

Janelle Scott
University of California at Berkeley

Acknowledgments

I believe with Mikhail Bakhtin that our speech is filled with others' words, varying degrees of otherness, and varying degrees of "our-own-ness." My thinking has been shaped by a combination of my own personal and professional experiences and the ideas of many of the writers cited in this book. There were also friends and colleagues who read the manuscript at varying degrees of completion or engaged with me in many helpful conversations. Special thanks to Jean Anyon, Gustavo Fischman, Norm Fruchter, Jennifer Goldstein, Mike Johanek, Colleen Larson, Nancy Lesko, Pauline Lipman, Deborah Meier, Larry Parker, Monica Pini, Janelle Scott, Lois Weiner, and John Wenk. My doctoral students, particularly those in my Educational Leadership in the New Economy seminar, have also challenged my thinking in important ways. And as always, my partner and sometimes coauthor, Kathryn Herr, served as a captive reader and sounding board for new ideas. Finally, I want to thank Michael Apple, the series editor, and Catherine Bernard, the development editor at Routledge, who liked the initial draft and helped make it better. It is an honor to have a book published with such an impressive list of critical scholars.

Introduction

Globalization enters the education sector on an ideological horse, and its effects on education are largely the product of that financially driven, free-market ideology, not of a clear conception for improving education.

Martin Carnoy, 2000, p. 50

In spite of a call for evidence-based practices, current educational reform, as Martin Carnoy suggests above, has little empirical warrant in research. Instead, it is grounded in large part in a new global free-market ideology, the business model du jour, a shift in emphasis from inputs to outcomes, high-stakes account-ability measures, older notions of top-down social engineering, and a deficit view of educators. This is a hybrid approach to reform which no longer has any claim to being new. It already has its own track record, and it is not a good one. It is becoming increasingly apparent, for instance, that a high-stakes account-ability approach has resulted in massive unintended consequences, perverse incentives, and little real progress in raising student achievement or closing the achievement gap (Abernathy, 2007; Nichols & Berliner, 2007; Rothstein, 2004). Appropriating a civil rights era concern for social and racial equality, current reforms call on educators to raise test scores, absent a call to advocate for the social policies that an authentic concern for low-income students and students of color would require.

This book is not a call to "reform the reform" as many critics of No Child Left Behind (NCLB) recommend. No doubt, over the next few years, there will be plenty of tinkering. My intent is to challenge the underlying ideological assump-tions of the reforms and to expose which social sectors ultimately benefit from them. I will explore how current approaches to school reform, as Carnoy suggests, serve the needs of free-market social reforms rather than promote a balanced attempt to improve education and achieve a just and democratic society. In the final chapter, I will summarize the key areas of a post-reform agenda identified through an analysis of current interdisciplinary scholarship on school reform.

Those promoting evidence-based practices won't have to look far for evidence that market and test-driven educational reform is draining schools of authentic teaching and leading practices and making schools more racially segregated and unequal (Abernathy, 2005 ; Darling-Hammond & Wood, 2008; Lipman, 2004; McNeil, 2000; Orfield, 2001; Rothstein, 2004). In a society in which publicly controlled spaces are fast being absorbed into the private sphere, our public schools and our democracy are increasingly at risk.

Many might think I am overstating the threat, and in this period in which "hope" is the watchword, Chicken Littles who claim the sky is falling are not exactly popular. So in this book, I hope to amass evidence that will convince the skeptical reader that unless educators and supporters of public schools become a stronger countervailing force, a powerful alliance of business and conservative ideological interests will have their way.

Much ink has already been spilled criticizing current school reform and much more is needed to fully understand where things have gone wrong. While I will be contributing to this critique, my main focus in this book is on implications of school reform for educational leadership. Educational leaders, particularly in urban settings, are experiencing a new work environment in which contracting, outsourcing, recruiting students, public relations, private-sector partnerships, and an obsession with spreadsheets and test scores are taking center stage. Leaders are becoming entrepreneurial managers that are increasingly expected to develop a new "skill set" and act less like educators and more like MBAs.

While teachers increasingly teach to the test, leaders are expected to lead to the test. Since control is exercised though high-stakes tests that drive what goes on in classrooms, principals are being given more and more power to exercise leadership over less and less. At the school level the current popular term among researchers is *distributed leadership*, but, in fact, power is being distributed *upward* by centralizing policy over curriculum and instruction through high-stakes testing and mayoral control. So this book is ultimately about leadership and power, and the ways in which leadership in this context needs to be viewed as advocacy in alliance with other groups, such as teachers, parent and community leaders, unions, policy advocates, and other emerging civil society groups. This is particularly true for leaders in low-income communities of color, which wield the least amount of political power, have the most urgent needs, and receive the fewest resources.

But more importantly, educational leaders at all levels of the system are being asked to legitimate the slow dismantling of a Welfare State and potentially of a public school system that, while rife with imperfections, represents one of the few remaining public spaces in our largely privatized society. This book explores why this new entrepreneurial leadership role is counterproductive, especially for improving opportunities for low-income students and students of color. It also proposes retheorizing educational leadership away from its entrepreneurial and legitimation role and toward a more proactive advocacy role. My reference to a post-reform agenda refers not only to the end of a particular reform such as NCLB, but rather to the end of an extremist market ideology riding into our schools on a Trojan horse masquerading as educational reform.

Advocacy at Multiple Levels

Much of this book is premised on the notion that advocacy leaders think on multiple tracks at once. They think strategically and have short- and long-term goals. They have a broad social analysis, but are not paralyzed by it. They act in the present, but have, as the old civil rights saying goes, "their eyes on the prize," and the prize is much more than raising student achievement, important as that is.

One reason that advocacy leaders are relatively rare is that those of us who prepare and certify administrators have tended to provide apolitical and ahistorical accounts of school improvement and student achievement. There is certainly no lack of research on school improvement and student achievement. The cognitive sciences have contributed useful research on communities of practice, distributed leadership, teacher and student efficacy, stereotype threat, and organizational learning. Sociocultural studies have provided us with crucial ethnographic research on noncognitive sources of school failure. And yet, with notable exceptions, most of these studies of schools and classrooms are done as if the political economy hadn't radically changed. There is also a quest for so-called evidence-based practices as if such practices are like a cure for cancer, applicable to any time or place. That we are moving from a welfare state economy to a competition and security state that will continue to shrink public investment in social welfare is not even treated as a potential confounding variable in achieving student success.

In this book, I attempt to paint a multilevel portrait of leadership and school reform and suggest a multilevel post-reform agenda. I am only too aware of the trade-offs this entails between breadth and depth of analysis, and yet our current views of good scholarship discourage connecting dots at broader levels. To do so is to run the risk of making high-level inferences, which are anathema to both quantitative and qualitative researchers.

In order to do low-inference research, researchers fragment knowledge and confidently offer up their little brick to be placed in the wall of knowledge. Few education scholars read outside narrow disciplinary boundaries, or share a common bibliography. The field of educational leadership is probably more guilty than most of this tendency. The result is that earning a doctorate too often means knowing more and more about less and less. We each have a well-honed piece of a larger puzzle, but aren't sure where to put it, since the larger picture eludes us. Foucault (1972) called this tendency *dividing practices* that result in the depolitization of knowledge. And yet, a growing interest in broader notions of social justice has emerged in the field of educational leadership (Larson & Murtadha, 2002). For instance, school finance, a field once dominated by narrow production–function studies is leading advocacy movements for adequate school funding (Rebell & Wolf, 2008) and has begun to recognize that redistributive fiscal issues are as important outside the education sector, if not more, than within it (Berliner, 2007).

But in trying to paint a larger picture, scholars run the opposite risk. In attempting to capture shifts in political economy and link them to shifts at the community, school, classroom, and individual levels, we run the risk of making higher inference assertions than we might make within a more bounded area of analysis. So while I draw heavily on more empirical research to make assertions, I also draw on personal narrative and discourse analysis to contextualize my analysis and make my argument more grounded. I'm not sure what this type of scholarship is called, but I think connecting dots that are currently left unconnected is worth the risk of making somewhat higher-level inferences. This is especially true, given my goal of challenging the ideological nature of what attempts to pass for "evidence-based" reform.

Most reformers want us to believe that we live in a postideological world, and that current school reform is merely a pragmatic attempt to solve intractable problems. While I will argue that the current approach to school reform is more ideological than not, it is also true that ideologically inspired reforms are not monolithic, nor are they always successful: local contexts, resistances, and backlashes can modify their intent. This current reform, which has ridden to power by critiquing public schooling, has already built a record that reformers are finding difficult to defend.

Furthermore, current school reform is not ideologically coherent. Mixed in with these largely corporate-inspired reforms are some reforms, such as small high schools, that progressive educators have promoted for some time. Recently Joel Klein and Al Sharpton have exemplified this "hybrid" approach by creating the Equality project that promotes New York City reform as carrying on the legacy of the civil rights movement. Many thoughtful colleagues and friends both in universities and schools agree with former Secretary of Education Rod Page and others that school reform will attack the soft bigotry of low expectations and will force public schools to be more responsive to those communities that have been historically neglected.

While defending or critiquing the current reform model has become a small cottage industry of late, critics appear to have little to offer as an alternative. Most provide a laundry list of changes that would make the No Child Left Behind legislation less flawed, while others seem to implicitly suggest a return to past compensatory or remedial programs that failed to adequately educate low-income students and students of color. Without a new vision of what a "post-reform" agenda might look like and how we might get there, advocates for change will have few tools to work with.

While I respectfully disagree with defenders of the current reform paradigm, my proposal for a post-reform era will retain some potentially progressive aspects of the current reform. In creating my own hybrid of recommendations, I am not supporting current "third way" or "new Democrat" approaches. Such approaches have, whether out of political expediency or ideological backsliding, bought into neoliberal economic models and their extension to all social sectors, including education. It is at the ideological and paradigmatic levels that a post-reform agenda draws inspiration. We can have small high schools in both a progressive or reactionary social context, but they will look very different and have a very different curriculum (Ayres & Klonsky, 2006).

While some may see my proposal as "radical," I prefer to think of current market-based reforms as radical, just as they were viewed as radical when Milton Friedman proposed them five decades ago. I am in fact, not calling for radical change, but rather I am seeking to restore balance to a society and school system that appears on the verge of abdicating social responsibility to an untested free market ideology. In this book I describe how leadership and schooling is being redefined along corporate and free market lines, and how growing evidence of the failure of this approach presents an opportunity for rethinking reform by viewing educators as advocates for children and youth and a vibrant public sector. By outlining what a "post-reform" agenda might look like, and the type of new leadership it will require, I aim at jump-starting a conversation about an alternative vision of education for the 21st century.

And I am not the only one. While there are many proposals for tinkering with reform, there are several that are expanding the conversation beyond narrow versions of accountability and that challenge the erroneous assumptions of this reform. For instance, The Forum for Education and Democracy has released a report, *Democracy at Risk: The Need For a New Federal Policy in Education* written by prominent educators and policy experts who have launched effective alternative schools, charter schools, and school improvement networks, such as Linda Darling-Hammond, Carl Glickman, Gloria Ladson-Billings, Judith Browne-Dianis, Deborah Meier, Larry Myatt, Pedro Noguera, Wendy Puriefoy, Sharon Robinson, Nancy Sizer, Ted Sizer, Angela Valenzuela, and George Wood (Darling-Hammond & Wood, 2008). Their report not only documents the on-going deterioration of America's schools on the 25th anniversary of the report *A Nation at Risk* (National Commission on Excellence in Education, 1983), but suggests that we are on the wrong road to improving them. "While other countries are making strategic investments that have transformed schooling and produced results, we have demanded results without transforming schooling" (Darling-Hammond & Wood, 2008, p. 2).

The National Education Association's (NEA) "Positive Agenda" also attempts to expand the scope of school reform to include preschool and after-school programs, smaller class sizes, school-based health centers, more counselors and social work-ers in schools, and shared responsibility for appropriate school accountability by stakeholders at all levels. The problem is that addressing those things that would truly make a difference in the lives of low-income students cannot be done with cheap reforms that rely on bully pulpits, paper and pencil testing, and privatiza-tion. To address these fiscal issues, the NEA states that making taxes fair and eliminating inefficient and ineffective business subsidies are essential prerequisites to achieving adequacy, equity, and stability in school funding.

Reformers in education have long depended on a paradigm of social engineering with its primitive policy levers of incentives and punishments and its outside-in approach to changing "resistant" teachers and administrators. For this reason, a new paradigm is called for that locates a concern with *authenticity* at its center. While I will define authenticity in detail in chapter 2, for now, suffice it to say that I use it in the Deweyan sense of reconnecting education to real life experience and democracy. At a societal level, where a new individualism (Elliott & Lemert, 2006) is evident, authenticity means achieving greater congruence with cherished, but currently neglected goals of community, solidarity, and a common good. I use the term, *authenticity*, also because it has been appropriated by many teachers and administrators who complain that current high-stakes accountability measures and market-oriented policies are inauthentic in that they have undermined professional autonomy and judgment. The two primary concepts around which this book is organized, then, is the idea of moving educational leadership and school reform in the direction of greater *advocacy* for children at multiple levels of the system, and greater *authenticity* within the classroom, school, and society.

A Brief Critique of the Current Paradigm of School Reform

Some might wonder how our bureaucratic public school system could become any more inauthentic or inequitable than it has been for decades. Wouldn't *anything* be better? Don't we need to blow this system up and start over for the sake of low-income urban children of color? Don't lazy teachers, coddled by their unions, need a kick in the butt to place the welfare of students above their own? This notion that the current system is so bad that we need to "nuke" it and start over, seems pervasive among pundits. While it is true that public schools for low-income children of color have generally been deplorable, I will argue that the forces that make the current system inauthentic and inequitable will not go away through market-driven reforms that emphasize business principles and narrow accountability measures. In fact, we could end up with something that resembles our privatized health care system, one that virtually leaves out 50 million low-income Americans and one that everyone but well-heeled insurance and pharmaceutical companies deems a failure. The notion that a privatized or marketized school system will better serve low-income students and students of color lacks any empirical evidence.

Nor will more standardized tests cause teachers to provide more relevant, rigorous, and authentic academic experiences for kids. On the contrary, they tend to narrow the curriculum and eliminate more creative activities (McNeil, 2000). There is growing evidence that principals also are forced to spend less time with teachers and students and more time complying with NCLB mandates (Abernathy, 2007). As for equity; privileged groups in society, like myself and anyone reading this book, know how to use our economic, social, cultural, and political capital to bend social institutions to our will and get advantages for our own children. In fact, a school system based on choice policies and with an even greater dependence on standardized testing (which favors affluent and middle class kids) will ultimately make it even easier for relatively privileged groups to work the system for their children (on school choice, Andre-Bechely, 2004; Cooper, 2007; on standardized testing, Dorn, 2007; Lemann, 2000).

Ideologies of individual choice in a free market and personal responsibility for one's success or failure in school make it easier to rationalize what deep down we know is a system that is rigged against those without the economic, social, and cultural capital to compete effectively. Reaffirming our beliefs in a common good and dedicating ourselves to the creation of public schools that are both authentic and equitable is, in my view, a more dignified and doable project than giving up on them by turning them over to market forces, business management models, or profit-driven corporations like Edison schools (Saltman, 2005).

Reaffirming the common good does not involve a return to some elusive past glory. The system we have had for two centuries has been depressingly inequitable. Nor is the rigid choice between a separate and monolithic public and private sector a fair characterization of our problem: the line between private and public is always blurred in a mixed economy like ours (Minow, 2002). Furthermore, as we rebuild public schools, there is room for exit strategies from below in the form of means tested charter schools and vouchers. No one should have to tolerate public schools designed for neglected groups that our current economic model considers surplus populations.

Nor are individual striving and broad social structures and policies independent of each other. Nobody prospers without some level of individual striving and work ethic, but to the extent that the powerful have free rein to make policies to benefit themselves and their children, the system becomes upwardly mobile only for a relatively elite segment of the population. That is our current reality, and it is getting worse with the downturn in an economy built on speculation, housing bubbles, and cheap gas.

In state socialist societies, the state-controlled public sector overwhelmed and stifled the private, depriving those societies of the dynamism that a strong, but regulated, private sector can provide. Here we are seeing the opposite. In spite of talk of a public school "monopoly," we have a corporate-led private sector that is encroaching on every public space it can take over (Peters, 2001). A proper balance between the public and private sectors is key to any healthy society and is squarely within an American ethos that, until recently, valued checks and balances and was suspicious of concentrations of power.

New Leaders for the New Economy?

While critiques of NCLB have become increasingly common, what have not been closely analyzed are the implications for school leadership in such a system. The current state of school leadership and the preparation of leaders are in need of serious reevaluation according to critiques such as the Levine Report

(Education Schools Project, 2005). Future scenarios for school leadership seem to be pushing in two different directions, both espousing an equity agenda: One sees school leaders (superintendents and principals) as increasingly coming from noneducation sectors and viewing themselves as CEOs, borrowing heavily from private-sector management.[1] This trend is currently producing what is sometimes called the entrepreneurial, managerial, or "hybrid" leader, referring to leaders who can not only straddle the public and private sectors, but increasingly move back and forth between them (Ball, 2007; Gewirtz, 2002). In New York City, for instance, although principals remain middle management, they are increasingly modeled after CEOs who contract out services, are cut loose from traditional district supports, and are held directly accountable for test scores.

The other alternative is a cohort of leaders who see themselves as advocates for children and defenders of public schools. They are motivated primarily through their advocacy for children and their communities, especially in low-income communities and those that are stratified by race and social class. Many public school leaders already belong to this group, but find it difficult to stand up to or work around the onslaught of testing demands and market and business-oriented reforms that they feel are leaving many children more vulnerable (Fruchter, 2007; Larson & Murtadha, 2002; Meier, 2002; Shirley, 1997). These are what I refer to in this book as advocacy leaders.

The new cadre of managerial leaders modeled on CEOs see themselves as advocates against bureaucracy and bad teaching. One would think these new leaders, many of whom are young and noneducators, had just discovered the dysfunctionalities of public bureaucracies. However, anyone who has flown on our private airline carriers lately, read about our new privatized army (Scahill, 2007; Singer, 2003), or struggled with their health management organization, should have a more balanced view of whether public or private bureaucracies are more effective, efficient, or transparent. Public bureaucracies have been so vilified that there is little balanced discussion of their benefits and liabilities (see Goodsell, 2004, for a defense of bureaucracy).

Leaders like myself have struggled within and railed against the public school bureaucracy for decades. We also believe it needs to be shaken up, and many, including this author, see promise in some judicious versions of public school choice, greater school autonomy, breaking up large high schools into small schools, and working with some nonprofits. We believe teachers' unions also need to be reformed by being less rigid on some issues, more democratic, and engaging in social advocacy for more child and family friendly local, national, and international policies (Weiner, 2008). If these kinds of reforms are implemented with the genuine goal of creating a more equitable and democratic public system, they might lead to more authentic teaching and learning, more authentic community participation, and perhaps, down the road, more authentic forms of assessment. However, if they are implemented as part of an ideological strategy to marketize and privatize schools, we will end up forfeiting the last semisovereign public space we have within which to create a more just and democratic society.

As much as new school reformers want to see themselves as pragmatic and nonideological, I hope to demonstrate that they are, in fact, bringing an extremist ideology into the public education sector. Variously termed neoliberalism, the competition state, or privatization, this ideology is poised to transform public education in ways that will be largely irreversible. Throughout this book, I will refer to this ideology as *neoliberalism*. I will expand on a definition of the term throughout the book, but briefly, neoliberalism refers to the free-market economic models developed by Milton Friedman, Gary Becker, and other economists at the University of Chicago during the mid-20th century. Sometimes called *neoclassical* economics, these models have gone from being viewed as attempts by ideological extremists to thoroughly marketize society to being viewed in schools of economics as a dominant global ideology. The term *neoliberal* is gaining popularity in the United States. The term was largely used outside the United States to reference the Washington Consensus on international trade and the imposition of Chicago School economic models on developing countries through the World Bank and the International Monetary Fund.

Within the United States, *neoliberal* was first used in the 1980s to refer to a group of democrats—including Bill Clinton—who helped to establish the democratic leadership council, an organization within the Democratic Party that promoted free-trade policies (Rothenberg, 1984). While I will use the broader, global notion of neoliberalism, it is important to keep in mind that both Democrats and Republicans have implemented neoliberal policies. The North American Free Trade Agreement (NAFTA), supported by Bill Clinton and passed during his administration, is an example of a neoliberal policy. NCLB is a hybrid policy, but contains many neoliberal elements. Harvey (2005) points out that, as with most other ideologies, there is a large gap between the theory and the actual implementation of neoliberalism.

There is a growing body of data to show that where implemented, neoliberalism has not been successful. Chile, a country where neoliberal educational policies were imposed, is experiencing massive student walkouts and pressures to "republicize" its school system (Pinkney Pastrana, 2007). In the United States experiments with choice schemes (including vouchers) and charter schools has yet to produce impressive results. But, like all effective ideologies, standardizing, marketizing, and privatizing our public school system has taken on the ring of common sense.

In the absence of leadership preparation programs that provide an analysis of this global shift in political economy and its implications for public school systems, many school administrators tend to buy into what appears to be a logic of flexing up an overly bureaucratized system and appropriating the pragmatic logic of the entrepreneurial leader. Those who are more skeptical may feel pressure to go along for the sake of their careers, or to seek early retirement. However, voices of dissent are increasing in number and their ability to gain media attention has improved, and a deteriorating economy is beginning to call into question the hegemony of neoliberal ideology.

The Incredible Shrinking Life World of Schooling and the Colonizing System World

While neoliberals have appropriated the critique of bureaucracy, it is hardly new. Past reforms that created the factory model school batch-processed kids through monotonous classrooms that ignored their own life experience and the world around them. This particular view of schools as bureaucratic and inauthentic is an old complaint, most vividly made by John Dewey and educational progressives throughout the 20th century. Callahan (1962) and others have documented how business leaders in the early 20th century created the factory-model school that processed and measured children the way industry rolled out widgets and measured product quality. The promotion of bell curve distributions, an ideology of meritocracy, and White flight to the suburbs have resulted in a dual school system: One has well-resourced schools, well-qualified teachers, and enriched, authentic instruction for middle class children. The other has underresourced schools, less well-qualified teachers, and rote, inauthentic instruction for the poor and working class, groups that consist disproportionately of children of color.

To hear some neoliberal commentators on educational reform, one would think that the American public school system was designed by the Soviet Politboro, not influential businesspeople of the early 20th century (Callahan, 1962). Ironically, policy makers are once again being lobbied by the business community with policy solutions, but this time they seem to have a new toolkit. This alliance of the business community and policy makers has resulted in a plethora of business-oriented restructuring schemes involving merit pay, statistical quality control, site-based management, high-stakes assessments, incentive schemes, privatization, and marketization.

Though some of these business reforms might be useful if properly transferred between sectors, many believe the cure has so far been worse than the illness and has increased not decreased already high levels of inauthenticity in schools. Any attempt to thoughtfully reform schools will have to address the creation of schools as authentic social spaces in which students, their parents, school professionals, and the surrounding community are deeply understood, respected, and empowered.

Some scholars, like Cuban (2004), suggest I may be beating a dead horse. Cuban agrees that the track record of business reforms has not been good, and while believing business reformers will persist, does not think they will be particularly successful. He points out that many business-led innovations, such as vouchers, site-based management, total quality management (TQM), and experiments with school–business partnerships in the 1980s have either not been effective or popular or have not taken hold. However, there is growing evidence that we may not be looking in the right places for where these reforms are taking hold. Burch (2005) documents an unprecedented privatization that has already taken place in outsourcing of services in school districts around the country. Ball's (2007) and Gewirtz's (2002) research on marketization and public–private partnerships in Britain demonstrates an impressive incursion of the private sector on the public sector in Britain, and many of these British reformers are consulting with U.S. school districts.[2] Under what Naomi Klein (2007) calls "disaster capitalism," schools in post-Katrina New Orleans are being massively converted to charter schools. Furthermore, and perhaps for the first time ever, high-stakes testing linked to standardized curricula has effectively reached behind the classroom door to significantly undermine teachers' judgment and autonomy (McNeil, 2000).

Looking at the relative failure of specific business initiatives, such as school–business partnerships and TQM in the 1980s, fails to capture the ways ideology spreads among school professionals and the general population. Business and market ideology become taken-for-granted, commonsense notions, even when actual evidence is never presented for assertions. For instance, TQM may now be an artifact of another era, but many of its basic ideas, such as continuous improvement, statistical control of quality, internal customers, and elimination of variance, have crossed over into the realm of common sense in educational administration and policy. Some of what initially made high-stakes accountability measures so appealing to educators was that the ground had been laid for a business logic of outcomes-based measurement of product quality.

While promoted as an antidote to bureaucracy, current high-stakes accountability systems have resulted in the cancerlike growth of the system world, and the shrinking of the life world of schools (Habermas, 1987; Sergiovanni, 2000). Briefly, the system world is the set of rules, procedures, accountability measures, and other structures required for the effective and efficient functioning of an educational organization. The life world is made up of the lives of the students, their relationships with each other and with adults in the school, and the teaching and learning that occur in classrooms and throughout the school and community. At present, in too many schools, these two dimensions of our schools are out of balance, causing a diminution of authentic activities in classrooms and of authentic relationships among students, teachers, and communities.

Authentic schools that serve low-income children have a developed sense of internal accountability that functions within the life world of the schools. According to Carnoy, Elmore, and Siskin, (2003) these internal forms of accountability include,

> Individual teachers' and administrators' beliefs about teaching and learning, their shared understanding of who their students are, the routines they develop for getting their work done, and the external expectations from parents, communities, and administrative agencies under which they work. (p. 3)

This life world level of accountability is where authentic forms of accountability operate, because they are the spaces in which a community of professionals, parents, and community members come to agreement about the well-being of their students/children. Achieving this common agreement has always been the central challenge of educational leadership. There have always been external or formal forms of accountability as well; policy handbooks, union contracts, state regulations, legal procedures, report cards, supervisors, and even a certain amount of standardized testing. Good schools have always been those that bring coherence to these various forms of accountability, and the best leaders have known how to maintain balance and coherence among them.

The current reform movement has added new external forms of accountability, including high-stakes testing, the discipline of the market, school reconstitution, and the threat of public humiliation if annual targets are not achieved. This new system world of high-stakes formal accountability measures has made it more difficult to achieve coherence and balance among the various forms of account-ability. Teaching staffs, principals, and often parents are finding that their shared understandings of good teaching and learning and other aspects of the life world of the school clash with the demands of the formal accountability system. While it is true that authentic schools are hard to sustain over time, sustainability depends on a certain amount of stability. The current frenetic churn of policy changes makes sustaining good schools more difficulty. While high-stakes accountability targets underperforming schools in an attempt to "motivate" teachers to teach better, it does so with a punitive, zero tolerance policy that lacks an understand-ing of what motivates professionals.

This imbalance between the system and life world of schools is not new; the overbureaucratization of schooling has had a similar effect over the years. Current reforms claim to eliminate bureaucracy, and indeed in cities like Chicago, New York, and others, we have seen infamous bureaucracies reduced dramatically. However, these bureaucracies have largely been replaced by a system of "steering from a distance" in which high-stakes testing and incentive systems drive the life world of schools in more effective, but also more distorting ways. Whereas, school professionals found the old bureaucracy to be maddening, they could usually—for good or ill—keep it from encroaching into the classroom. This is no longer the case, as curriculum standardization and high-stakes testing regimes force teachers to use scripted curricula and gear their teaching more closely to the test, which often leads to "gaming" the system.

Furthermore, as nonprofit and for-profit partnerships and educational man-agement organizations (EMOs) grow, they are creating their own bureaucracies that are far less accountable to the public than the old public bureaucracies were. What's more, their corporate headquarters may be thousands of miles away. The new system world is increasingly faceless and impersonal, but more powerful and controlling and less publicly accountable. Through the rhetoric of increasing school autonomy, principals and teachers are brought under greater control. The new business model has a new system world that more efficiently colonizes the life world without appearing to do so. The unsubstantiated premise of these systems of accountability and control is that incompetent or lazy teachers and principals are the reason millions of low-income students do poorly in school.

What is Advocacy Leadership?

The premise of this book is that bringing greater authenticity to schools cannot be separated from bringing greater social justice to low-income schools and communities. Both will require a focus on leadership. Traditionally, the idea of school leaders engaging in advocacy has been viewed as the occasional trip to the state legislature to lobby for increased resources or specific policies (Fowler, 2008; Whitaker, 2007). However, while advocacy leaders enact these traditional advocacy and policy roles, I am calling here for a much broader reorientation of leadership as inherently focused on advocacy for one's clients.

Leadership theory has had an explosion of popularity in recent years. My purpose here is not to review this extensive literature. I agree with those who see leadership as a more diffuse concept in which leadership can emerge at all levels of an organization. I also agree that a single individual may at times be a leader and at other times a follower. But, in this book, I will tend to focus more on formal school leaders, such as principals and superintendents, since they are key players, either as catalysts for greater advocacy for children or—as is too often the case—as obstacles. Teachers also are increasingly taking on leadership roles in schools, as are leaders of community organizations. I view the emergence of leadership development in community organizing and nonprofit, community based organizations as potentially changing the kinds of alliances that advocacy-oriented school leaders might form. At New York University, we have inaugurated a new master's degree program in educational leadership, politics, and advocacy in tandem with our master's degree program that certifies aspiring principals and superintendents. We see many parallels between the kinds of leadership training that professional advocates receive and the training we provide to aspiring principals and superintendents.

While there is much writing on "distributed," "shared," "collaborative," or "participatory" leadership, such theories tend to be limited to a human relations school of management, in which inclusion is used as a strategy to raise morale and productivity, build capacity, and perhaps make more locally grounded decisions. Such approaches, when authentic, can lead to better decisions, but they do not tend to come out of traditions of direct democracy that expand participation beyond school professionals. I will take up this issue in more detail in chapter 5.

I use the term *advocacy leadership* because I believe that a more politicized notion of leadership is needed that acknowledges that schools are sites of struggle over material and cultural resources and ideological commitments. Political alliances of leaders may have to be built among superintendents, principals, teacher leaders, union leaders, student leaders, and community leaders in order to defend the democratic goals of public schooling against those who wish to replace political democracy with a logic of the marketplace.

Michael Apple (1996) has identified four overlapping groups that have successfully shifted the American discourse to the political right since the late 1970s:

(1) neoliberals inspired by Milton Friedman's free-market ideology; (2) economic and cultural conservatives who promote a return to high standards, discipline, and personal responsibility; (3) a group of "authoritarian populists" associated with the religious right who want prayer in schools, traditional family values, and who, like conservatives, are suspicious of "big government"; and (4) middle-class professionals "whose own professional interests and advancement depend on the expanded use of accountability, efficiency, and management procedures that are their own cultural capital" (p. 6).

Current leadership theories in education fail to take up or even discuss the challenge that this political coalition represents for public schooling. With few exceptions, leadership theories in education, even those that claim to distribute leadership, are limited to viewing leadership as "reengineering" and "reculturing" schools to build capacity and make them more productive, not expand democratic participation. Throughout the book, I will try to use narrative examples of how leadership, authenticity, and advocacy must be explicitly linked if we are ever to make schools and society more equitable.

So what do advocacy leaders do? An advocacy leader believes in the basic principles of a high quality and equitable public education for all children and is willing to take risks to make it happen. Advocacy leaders tend to be skilled at getting beneath high-sounding rhetoric to the devil in the details. They are skeptical by nature. They know the difference between the trappings of democracy and the real thing. They refuse to collude in so-called collaborative teams or distributed leadership endeavors that are inauthentic. For instance, they know when a site-based leadership team is rigged against low-income parents. They know when parents of children with disabilities are being railroaded by school professionals in individual educational plan (IEP) meetings. They know the hard ball politics of influential parents and the ways they work the system to get privileges for their children at the expense of others. They are not seduced by business models yet they don't close off any avenue of new ideas. They are skeptical of the idea that we can avoid the difficult give-and-take of politics by replacing politics with market-based choice policies.

They find time to read widely, and have a well-developed social analysis, but do not agree on all issues, and do not follow a "party line." They are learners, much like their students, and they are constantly pushing their comfort zone. They create learning communities in their schools. They use multiple forms of data to monitor the progress of students and programs. Testing data are used diagnostically, but not allowed to distort curriculum and instruction. They are intolerant of racist, sexist, and homophobic language or actions and work to build a culture of tolerance. They expose their students to multiple career options, and provide alternatives to the military recruiters' pitch. They understand the stressors on low-income parents, the time constraints on teachers, and the anxieties parents have around the success and well-being of their children. And yet, they draw an ethical line that cannot be crossed—not to be authoritarian, but to defend against the powerful using their power against the powerless. While being prounion, they are not afraid to fight the union when it is supporting policies that put the needs of teachers above those of children.

Advocacy leaders know that they must operate on multiple levels. At the individual level, good teachers and administrators have always seen themselves as advocates for the child who was made fun of, discriminated against, or lacked sufficient resources to be successful in school. But an advocacy leader also sees the systemic problems that exist in a classroom, a school, a district, a community, and they seek solutions that address causes, not just symptoms. At a broader level, they know that some causes, such as inequitable social policies, may be beyond their immediate control, but they have a deep belief in the power of education to foster not just kids with high tests scores, but also powerful and informed democratic citizens with influence over those very policies in the future.

The reason that advocacy and authenticity are twin themes in this book is because a post-reform agenda cannot merely address the ways that current reforms are hollowing out authentic practices and relationships from schools. However, important, solutions limited to the development of learning communities, authentic forms of assessment, culturally responsive pedagogies, and distributed leadership will not address in any significant way how resources and opportunities are redistributed within and between schools. Nor will they address the vast inequities in resources and opportunities in American society.

By the same token, preparing school professionals to be advocacy leaders will do no good if they neglect the life world of the school. There are many practices these days that pass for advocacy, and many are well-intended, but to the extent they overrely on test scores, they may contribute to the hollowing out of schools through pedagogies that fail to view students holistically. For instance, while the disaggregation of test scores by race, socioeconomic status, and other areas was a well-intended first step toward addressing inequalities in schools, it has proven to be a blunt instrument that has too often had the unintended consequence of dumbing down the curriculum for the very groups it was meant to shine a light on. It has provoked endless strategizing over focusing on "bubble kids," or those who require the least effort to help pass minimum competency exams. This "gaming" of the system has too often shifted resources away from those who are furthest behind.

I view this book itself as a form of advocacy. I am not interested in writing a neutral book. The well-funded dominant argument for school reform has millions of outlets; the counterargument has few. Although I do not believe this period is big business's finest hour, I am also not interested in writing an antibusiness book. I have actually owned two (not very successful) small businesses myself, and believe in a vibrant private sector economy. The book does, however, argue against the inappropriate transfer of ideas from one sector to another (see Cuban, 2004, for a more extensive discussion of this). While the book is scholarly, I do not believe that scholars have to be neutral when making an argument for or against something. Ultimately the reader will determine whether I have effectively made my case.

Summary of Chapters

In chapter 1, "School Reform, Authenticity, and Advocacy," I provide a discussion of the two key concepts that frame the book, authenticity and advocacy, and why they are useful in rethinking the role of educational leaders. I discuss the implications of advocacy at the individual, relational, and societal levels and how current reforms, including No Child Left Behind, have created greater levels of inauthenticity at all three levels. This lack of authenticity undermines its equity agenda, which many argue is itself inauthentic. I also attempt to demonstrate why NCLB is neither an authentic reform, nor, in spite of its name, one that advocates for poor and minority children.

In chapter 2, "Authentic Leadership," I describe in greater detail a growing erosion of authenticity in society and educational reform as well as the assault on authenticity at the level of the individual, the organization, and society. In this chapter, I also describe, using my experience growing up in a factory town, the economic and social changes that occurred from a Keynesian, "welfare" state to a neoliberal "competition" state inspired by Milton Friedman's free market and human capital theories. I link this economic shift since the late 1970s to aspects of recent reforms that promote the marketization and semiprivatization of the public sector, along with managerial concepts borrowed from business that have created an "audit culture" in schools that has increased levels of inauthenticity.

In chapter 3, "The New Economy of Schooling," I present an overview of the neoliberal agenda and the "competition state" with an emphasis on corporatization, marketization, and privatization. I begin the chapter with a description of New York's Tweed Hall (the new Department of Education) and the new cadre of MBAs that Mayor Bloomberg and Chancellor Klein have hired to implement their new business-inspired reforms. I include here a discussion of how public–private partnerships are becoming a "third way" of blurring the public and private/corporate sectors. Since both Republicans and "new" Democrats promote neoliberal, free market policies, I discuss the difference between more progressive "third way" approaches with more neoclassical third way approaches that focus more on vouchers and charter schools.

Then, I provide a brief history of the American corporation and how it moved from being an entity chartered by the state for specific projects for the common good (building public projects) to becoming a "private" enterprise with the same rights as individuals. I review literature on the impact of corporations on the cities they locate in, including tax breaks, as well as the influence of such entities as chambers of commerce, and business roundtables. I also describe how the corporation and the factory became a model for schooling in the late 19th and early 20th centuries.

In the next section, I discuss marketization and the importation of business principles into the public sector. I discuss British research on the new "managerial" school in which principals become marketers of their schools, as well as similar trends in the United States. I also discuss the impact of choice policies on school leadership. In a section on privatization, I discuss in more detail public–private partnerships and the advent of outsourcing of services by school districts as well as educational management organizations (EMOs). I make some distinctions between the nonprofit and for-profit sectors and discuss appropriate and inappropriate participation by the private sector in the public sector. I draw here on Stephen Ball's (2007) analysis of the public–private blurring that is more advanced in the education sector in Britain than in the United States.

In chapter 4, "Disciplining Leaders: Mediating the New Economy," I discuss research that demonstrates that a major role of school leaders is the *management of meaning*. Because a large part of administrative work is talk, leaders tend to manage schools through the discourses they take up (and those they don't). I present a mediation model that I developed out of my dissertation data many years ago, but that I never had a chance to further develop. This model, based on institutional theory, Meyer and Rowan (1977), shows how school leaders mediate the various levels of the organization and its social environment and how they mediate ideologies, both within schools and within themselves. School administrators become a nexus between the new neoliberal state and teachers and students. They are managers of meaning and the new accountants for the new audit culture. To demonstrate how these expectations are set up for administrators, I present a critical discourse analysis of the new national standards and certification exam for educational administrators to demonstrate the enforcement of the new neoliberal common sense.

In chapter 5, "Toward an Authentic Distribution of Leadership," I provide an argument for shifting from inauthentic forms of "distributed" leadership to authentic reforms of democratic leadership. Since the 1980s, notions of school autonomy and shared decision making were promoted as a way to improve schools. Borrowed from management models linked to "quality circles" and total quality management popular at the time, these forms of "distributed leadership" are part of an older human relations movement attempt to raise productivity through the use of theories of what motivates employees. Such innovations did not come from democratic traditions of decision making. Democratic traditions are more authentic in that they expand the parameters of decision making and link means to ends, drawing on what Webber called substantive forms of rationality. In other words, business models, as well as those that come from psychological notions of distributed cognition, are largely limited to theories of increasing productivity. Employees tend to have autonomy over trivial decisions, but seldom are consulted about such important decisions as investment of resources, salaries, benefits, or outsourcing of jobs. More authentic forms of democratic decision making extend participation beyond school professionals and empower students, their families, and communities to have more influence on educational and social policies.

In chapter 6, "Toward a Post-Reform Agenda," I argue that educators cannot merely resist neoliberal reforms, but rather they need to develop a counterproposal. In this chapter I present the outline of a post-reform agenda. By "post-reform" I refer to what has become, at least since the 1983 *Nation at Risk* report a reform "industry." This industry has systematically pathologized public schooling in an attempt to discredit it or to retool public schooling in ways to make it more effectively produce human capital for a global economy. Thus, throughout the book, I refer to a shift to a new paradigm that returns balance to public schooling, and takes seriously its multiple goals.

1
School Reform, Authenticity, and Advocacy

As a young, idealistic teacher in Harlem in the late 1970s, like many urban teachers I struggled with how to integrate my political commitments to poor and working class students with my teaching. Having myself grown up working class and having struggled academically in school, I saw myself in many of my students. The alternative school I taught in was located in the old Hotel Theresa in New York City, a high rise building in central Harlem that at one time was an elegant hotel where jazz greats like Duke Ellington and political figures like Fidel Castro stayed. In those days it housed mostly city offices and our community-based school called College Adapter Program (CAP). It was a "second chance" school for youth who had dropped out of their high schools but showed promise. Our job was to get them ready for nearby City College, which at the time had open admissions and free tuition.

In those years as a teacher in Harlem, I struggled with the age-old problem of rigor and relevance. I knew I needed to teach students the skills to succeed in college. At the same time, I wanted them to have a relevant and empowering education. In the five years I taught there, I learned that students can be taught rigorous skills using an empowering curriculum, and Harlem was alive with relevant history. I remember teaching *The Autobiography of Malcolm X* in a classroom that was rumored to have once been Malcolm's office.

I hadn't chosen to teach in Harlem. Newly arrived in New York City, I didn't even know I was in Harlem until someone told me during my interview. I wondered how my mainly African-American and Puerto Rican students would view me. I was young, White, and from the Midwest, with only two years of teaching experience. I had read about the need to put on a tough front for so-called "inner-city" kids. I was never good at posturing and was far from "hip," so I decided to just be myself, hoping that being authentic would set a tone in which my students could be authentic with me. I used a lot of humor, poking fun at myself and joking about my lack of urban sophistication. As one of the few White teachers in this alternative school, I think I was a bit of a curiosity.

These were not only kids of color; they were uptown kids who felt out of place downtown (where they seldom ventured). In the Manhattan of the 1970s, the designations "uptown" and "downtown" had class and race implications. As I laced my teaching with stories of my own struggles in school and with a sense of not measuring up, my students, especially the male students' tough fronts (necessary body armor for urban survival) melted away. As they saw my vulnerabilities, they also began showing me theirs. They laughed at my stories about growing up in Iowa, and their own stories flowed into the journals they kept for class. In many ways, I was their conduit to the mysterious White world they had little contact with, other than through the media. It was during those years in the old Hotel Theresa that I fell in love with my students and with teaching.

During those years, I learned how to teach a rigorous and empowering curriculum in spite of standardized tests. I taught English and knew that their success in college would depend on their ability to write competent papers. But since most of my students also had to pass the GED exam, a standardized test of high school academic skills, I learned how to help them demystify the exam and taught them the skills they would need to pass it. I told them not to confuse test prep with education, and we bonded around our plot to outwit the test. Together we were "getting over" on the system. Though at the tender age of 25, I was, in many ways, naïve and paternalistic, I saw myself as their advocate in a world in which few were looking out for their welfare. But, at a broader level, I had only a partial understanding of the vast economic and political changes that were occurring around us during the 1970s and 1980s, changes we would later refer to with terms like the *new economy, new capitalism,* and *neoliberalism.*

As a political activist and veteran of Students for a Democratic Society (SDS) and the anti-Vietnam war movement, I knew that the country was moving to the political right. New York City went bankrupt during this time, and while the financiers were bailed out, the city took a huge hit (Harvey, 2005). Nationally resources were being reallocated away from Great Society programs. This tendency culminated in Reagan's massive tax cuts for corporations and individuals as part of a "revolution" that resulted in the most massive reallocation of wealth upward, the country had seen since the 1920s. The top tax rate for individuals was reduced from 78 to 28% and tax adjustments on depreciations on investments for corporations allowed many corporations to pay no taxes at all. Just as African Americans were finally beginning to enjoy the benefits of the welfare state, including programs like CAP, it was coming under attack.

During the years I was teaching, I also worked some evenings with an organization led by Michael Harrington, author of *The Other America*, a book that helped inspire John Kennedy's war on poverty in the early 60s and later Lyndon Johnson's Great Society programs. In the 1970s his Democratic Socialist Organizing Committee (DSOC), which was also led by Cornel West and Gloria Steinem, worked within the Democratic Party to bring about prolabor policies. But I was never able to understand the connections between my work with DSOC and my work with my students in Harlem. I saw them as two separate worlds. By day, I tried to provide my students with the skills and cultural capital they would need to have any chance of success in an unequal system; by night, I worked to try to stop the unraveling of social gains achieved by decades of social activism, an unraveling that would leave an even more unequal society. Little did I know then how unequal we would become as a nation.

Around 1980, the funders of CAP mandated a shift from college preparation to vocational training and our funding was severely cut. The CAP acronym stayed the same, but instead of College Adapter Program, we became Career Advancement Program. Instead of teaching English classes to prepare students for college, I began teaching business English. We prepared keypunch operators just as the job was becoming obsolete. At CAP we had worked hard to "pump up" students psychically for a future that included a college education. Now, that excitement was gone. I left CAP to direct a program in the South Bronx, but the America that I had grown up in was changing in ways few of us grasped at the time.

Authenticity and Advocacy are Inseparable

I had struggled in those years with the twin themes of *authenticity* and *advocacy* that are central to this book—themes that seem lacking in our current discourse on teaching, leading, and reforming schools. I learned that authentic teaching wasn't essentially about cognition, learning theory, and teaching methods, though good teachers know these things. It was essentially about relationality and connecting in authentic ways with students. It was both the cognitive and noncognitive dimensions of teaching that were essential. Good teachers figure out how to relate to kids in authentic ways—despite differences of class, race, or gender, and without giving up their authority as teachers.

But I also sensed that building authentic relationships with students was not enough. Authentic teaching could not make up for inauthentic institutions or an inauthentic society in which discourses of equity contradicted vast and growing inequities. To paraphrase Paulo Freire (1970), being authentic with students means helping them to read the word *and* the world. To be authentic with low-income students, teachers needed to help them develop curiosity about the world, including why some struggle while others enjoy obscene privilege. As Freire has argued, this cannot be a pedagogy of answers. Such a pedagogy is indoctrination, no matter what side of the political spectrum it is taught from.

Beware of the leader who has lots of answers and few questions. Many administrators are taught to problem *solve*, not problem *pose*. There are entire courses in educational administration programs in universities on "decision making," which is largely an exercise in solving problems. But seldom are the skills of problem posing taught. And yet we know that how a problem is framed or understood will determine the way we go about resolving it. And even when problem posing is taught, problems are seldom understood in a social or historical context.

The moral of these stories is that it is hard to separate authenticity and advocacy. Authenticity at the interpersonal level is exceedingly difficult unless we create authentic institutions and an authentic society in which the values of equity and democracy can be practiced. Building relationships in schools, whether with students or teachers, becomes more difficult as reforms demand more scripted classrooms and more stressful workplaces.

Zero tolerance policies are a good example of divorcing authenticity from advocacy. We think we can solve problems by "getting tough" instead of doing the hard work of using teachable moments with children and youth. Increasingly in schools, incidents that in the past would have been handled with a meeting of principals, parents, teachers, and the students involved, are too often handled by the juvenile justice system. Once the police are on the scene—and their presence is ubiquitous in urban schools—the principal's authority is usurped. Not only do students miss out on the opportunity to be taught moral and ethical lessons by caring adults, they are getting criminal records at earlier ages, entering what is now being called the pipeline to prison. These youth are also disproportionately poor and of color.

I myself have struggled and continue to struggle with how to link authenticity and advocacy. My own teaching and leadership in Harlem was aimed at helping individual students become upwardly mobile, and our program was successful in sending many struggling students to college. Yet political forces occurring at another level were chipping away at the collective gains of 40 years of social struggle, and our program became a victim of those very forces.

Today as we struggle to get more students to graduate from high school, public funding for higher education is decreasing, leaving fewer affordable seats for low-income students. The average public subsidy for higher education has plummeted from over 30% to an average of 12%. State subsidies have dropped so low that what we used to call state-funded universities are now referred to as state-assisted, and in cases like Virginia, where state subsidies represent a mere 7% of budgets, some are referring to them as "state-located" universities.

While I tried to teach an empowering curriculum in Harlem, exposing students to writers of the Harlem Renaissance and the history of the civil rights movement, I'm not sure how well I got across the notion of becoming empowered democratic citizens in the political context in which my students were living. Juggling teaching, leadership, and advocacy is an ongoing puzzle to solve, and is best done collectively with other professionals struggling with the same issues.

We didn't have participatory action research or learning communities in those days, and many of these teacher and principal support groups today are more about feeding the system than challenging it. But the potential is there. Once leaders decide to take seriously the challenge of being an authentic advocate for low-income children of color, they will need the support of other colleagues to work through the complex dilemmas such advocacy will unearth.

Authenticity, Advocacy, and School Reform

In Harlem, my teaching experience ultimately morphed into administration as I became a bilingual coordinator, a program director in the Bronx, and ultimately took a principalship elsewhere. As an administrator, as in the classroom, I found I was sometimes able to create authentic spaces with teachers and students and advocate for the things I cared about. I learned to recognize when a window of opportunity opened up in the bureaucracy, and I could slip through some policy or practice that supported the kids with the least power. Later, I went on to do a doctorate, and in my early years working as a professor in the ivory tower, I often missed the adrenaline rush of being in a school with all of the sense of busy accomplishment one felt at the end of the day. Sometimes I had secret fantasies of returning to work in schools. As a professor I have spent a lot of time with aspiring and practicing principals, enviously listening in my classes to their stories about their teaching and leadership dilemmas, interviewing them for research projects, or visiting them as they interned in schools.

About seven or eight years ago though, when I was teaching at a university in Los Angeles, I began to notice a shift in the dilemmas I was hearing from my students. Both teachers (who were aspiring principals) and practicing administrators were beginning to frame their dilemmas differently. Whereas before they were confident that they could transform their schools along a vision that they believed in strongly, now they seemed discouraged and less hopeful—even cynical. This was particularly true of those teachers and administrators who saw themselves as advocates for those in the system who were most marginalized. Despite the rhetoric of decentralization and school autonomy, teachers reported that new reforms were forcing them to eliminate those activities they and their students most enjoyed and around which they were able to bond. I found my own fantasies of returning to work in schools dissipate. It didn't look like fun anymore, and the few authentic spaces in schools where one could create a true learning community seemed to be drying up. These teachers and principals, mostly in low-income schools in the Los Angeles Unified School district, were struggling with mandated reforms that involved scripted curricula, constant testing and an obsession with test scores, greater surveillance of their work, fewer opportunities for creativity, overcrowded schools, and the constant implementation of new policies, often through ballot initiatives.

For the most part, these students of mine were overachievers who were highly committed to their students. Most of them chose to work in low-income areas where their students' lack of access to social, cultural, and economic forms of capital made their work overwhelming but rewarding. Now it seemed that society was exclusively holding them accountable for low student performance. They expected to be held accountable and wanted all mediocre teachers and principals to be held accountable as well. But this new system was not accountability in the authentic sense that any professional expects to be held accountable; rather it was a kind of accountability that was punitive and humiliating, like an angry mob searching for a scapegoat. How did school reform so effectively reach behind the classroom door, and with such problematic results?

Scapegoating School Professionals

Public schools for low-income kids have never been very good, and being a teacher or administrator in such schools was never easy. Teachers, principals, and superintendents are generally known for their resilience and their famous "high tolerance for ambiguity." Teachers survive a succession of principals—some good, some bad. They've seen many reforms and innovations come and go—some useful, most not. While some teachers are incompetent, even racist, and should be removed, the vast majority do the best they can under circumstances that are often less than ideal. In low-income neighborhoods, some of their students are homeless, have serious health problems, are recruited by gangs, or are victims of other forms of violence. Teachers in those schools often have children with special needs and English language learners in their classes. Even teachers in middle- and upper-class neighborhoods endure many privileged students and parents who treat teachers with disdain, and problems of drugs and stress-related illnesses are prevalent among students in these communities as well. In addition, teachers work under the anonymity of a profession with low status and low pay. While the range of good and not-so-good teachers is probably similar to the range of good and not-so-good doctors, nurses, CEOs, and lawyers, good teachers manage to do amazing things with children and youth in their classrooms.

Principals and superintendents are also resilient. They live in the crossfire of multiple constituencies, all with different needs and demands. They are expected to mediate these conflicting demands on a daily basis. They are middle managers, increasingly getting their marching orders from city, state, and federal-level mandates. In spite of layers of bureaucracy and limited autonomy, good principals have always somehow managed to create amenable work environments for teachers, a welcoming atmosphere for parents, and a safe and stimulating school culture for students.

But it has always been a given that this good work of teachers and administrators was done in spite of, not because of the largely problematic institutions they worked in. For decades reformers have decried "a grammar of schooling" that creates a dysfunctional workplace for teachers and administrators and a fragmented, monotonous, and tracked educational experience for students, especially in middle and high schools, and especially in low-income schools (Tyack & Cuban, 1997). Reforms that have attempted to "restructure" schools or target the inequities of the system through such policies as compensatory education, more equitable financing formulas, and desegregation plans have had only limited success.

Our best scholars and practitioners have worked long and hard to understand how to break open the grammar of schooling in ways that would create more effective and equitable public schools. Many critical scholars, including this author, have argued over the years that public schools not only could not ameliorate social inequalities, but that in fact, they may contribute to them though practices, such as tracking, that helped to reproduce an inequitable social order.

But everyone, from Left to Right, from the academy to the school house, was optimistic that public schools could be made to work better for teachers and for children and that they could be changed. In fact, a whole new field of study, "educational change," was created to better understand how to break the code of the seemingly intractable grammar of schooling. But until recently, it was assumed that however we succeeded in improving schooling, it would be in the context of core values of a system of public schooling aimed at making opportunity available to all American children. There were some groups that favored deschooling society, free schools, Afrocentric schools, and other experiments outside of the public bureaucracy, but none of those were pushing privatization per se. Whether you railed at the public schools from the left, the right, or the center, the core value of a rigorous, equitable, and *public* school system open to all was largely assumed.

During the 1980s and into the 1990s, school reforms continued along two parallel tracks that often coexisted in considerable tension; one harking back to John Dewey and the other to Edward Thorndike (Donmoyer, 2005). The Dewey track moved toward "authentic" reforms involving authentic assessments, participatory decision making, teaching the whole child, project methods, learning communities, small schools, and child-centered teaching. Reforms such as the Coalition of Essential Schools exemplified this approach. The Thorndike track found these reforms too unstructured and fragmented and sought more "systemic" change, relying on more centralized pressures for change, more standardized accountability systems, and more teacher directed learning.

Many scholars of color felt that neither the Deweyian nor the Thorndike approach was effective for low-income children and children of color. Delpit (1995) and others argued that so-called progressive reforms often failed to understand the needs of children who were not White or middle class. More importantly, these scholars of color felt left out of the school reform conversation.

Most teachers and administrators were also left out of these academic and policy conversations, or were having conversations of their own that were more focused on how they were coping with the day-to-day implications of school reform policies. But mostly, they didn't pay too much attention to these early debates over reform, since many were already suffering from policy overload. Teachers could usually hunker down and wait out the worst effects within the enclaves of their classrooms. Principals became experts at buffering good teachers from the latest innovation. They had seen so many reforms come and go that the skepticism was often palpable. They went to the workshops and retreats, used what they could, but were largely absorbed by the day-to-day work that anyone who has taught in or led a school knows is all consuming. Besides, teachers who work together all day need to get along, and many of these debates, particularly concerning teaching methods, were seen as divisive.

Then during the second half of the 1990s something changed. It's hard to pinpoint the exact moment. A few scholars and some practitioners had warned the change was coming, but because the changes were taking place largely over the heads and outside the typical education discourse, few people noticed. Early warnings came from a shift to outcomes-based assessment. This shift in focus from inputs to the statistical measurement of outputs, a concept borrowed from business management, became a centerpiece of the Goals 2000: Educate America Act passed in 1994. In Texas, there was some debate about the Texas accountability system before it was essentially transferred to Washington under former Texas governor, George W. Bush. This debate had more to do with how the TAAS test and the use of scores to punish schools were viewed (Anderson, 2001; McNeil, 2000, Skrla & Scheurich, 2004). Other early warnings came from British scholars' experiences under Thatcherism and the increasing marketization of schools under a neoliberal economic system (Gewirtz, Ball, & Bowe, 1995). There were rumblings about the Business Roundtable and local and national chambers of commerce taking a larger role in reform, but little of this made its way into a fragmented educational discourse. Some finance scholars had noticed that a new breed of school business managers with MBAs were shifting to out-sourcing and privatizing of services, but again, few others were paying attention. There were debates over school vouchers, but vouchers didn't seem politically viable since the public had voted them down in ballot initiatives in several states. So there was a sense that as long as voucher legislation was held at bay, we were safe from a massive marketization of the public school system.

On January 8, 2002, George W. Bush signed the reauthorization of the Elementary and Secondary Education Act, known as No Child Left Behind, and did a photo op with liberal Senator Ted Kennedy. Even at that stage most educators were not too wary since it was a bipartisan bill, and George Bush was still seen as a moderate Republican in some education circles. Furthermore, the legislation had some seemingly progressive touches, like the disaggregation of test scores by race and socioeconomic status so that to be "high performing" a school had to be successful with all subgroups of students. And anyway, who could argue against schools being accountable to the public. Most educational researchers, teachers, and administrators went along without too much fuss. Nobody, including most politicians, knew what landmines lurked within the over 700 pages of dense legislation.

An accountability system that had only been experienced intensely in some states, such as Texas and North Carolina, was now a national phenomenon, and it soon became apparent that this reform was different. After many false starts, the change experts had figured out how to get behind the classroom door, and they did it, through high-stakes testing. Seemingly overnight, teachers had scripted curricula, test preparation booklets, and instructional "coaches" to make sure they did it the right way. Based on studies using randomized assignment to ex-perimental and control groups, these "evidence-based" instructional programs had to be implemented in a particular way, using all of the components that vendors made available at considerable cost. Principals were taught to do "walk throughs" of classrooms as yet another layer of surveillance.

On the positive side, some principals were able to use the leverage NCLB gave them to selectively implement some good programs. Others were able to protect those teachers whose students always did well from the worst excesses of the reform. And some newer teachers found the scripted lessons helpful, since they didn't have to prepare their own materials (or learn how to teach for that matter). Undoubtedly some bad teachers disliked the extra attention because now they actually had to do something. Many teachers—generally, not the bad ones—retired early in disgust; others persevered, finding ways to work in the interstices of the reform. Some good principals with good teachers were able to raise test scores without throwing out authentic teaching practices. But one thing was certain, teaching and administration in schools would never be the same.

Finally, change experts had succeeded, but teachers were not celebrating. The Harvard Civil Rights Project did a study in 2004 of teachers in Virginia and California and reported that.

> Teachers confirm that the NCLB accountability system is influencing the instructional and curricular practices of teachers, but it is producing unintended and possibly negative consequences. They reported that, in response to NCLB accountability, they ignored important aspects of the curriculum, de-emphasized or neglected untested topics, and focused instruction on the tested subjects, probably excessively. Teachers rejected the idea that the NCLB testing requirements would focus teacher's instruction or improve the curriculum. (Sunderman, Tracey, Kim, & Orfield, 2004, p. 2)

While many teachers were teaching to the tests, many principals were "leading to the tests." Abernathy (2007) quotes a principal in his study who discusses how the reform has reallocated his time and priorities away from authentic time with teachers and students.

> I would estimate that exploring data takes at least five extra days each year. Testing takes about ten days out of my year. Staff development issues consume another three days. The service time I spend and additional time writing the district Title grant add another ten days. Additional state reports, all in one way or another tying into AYP, add about thirty days time in total taken away from other duties I used to perform. Some do not get done; some are shortchanged, and some I do by adding on to my day or year. (p. 104)

But this reform also had an airtight discursive strategy. Anyone who voiced any criticism of the reform was accused of not believing that poor kids could learn. Poverty didn't seem to be the problem; the problem, we were told, were the teachers and administrators.

Is No Child Left Behind an Authentic Form of Advocacy?

Most scholars, even those critical of NCLB, praise the legislation for its insistence on, not just calling for equal access to quality schooling, but to equality of achievement outcomes. While researchers at the Civil Rights Project at Harvard University have taken NCLB to task for its results, they have praised the legislation for its "inspiring vision." (Sunderman & Kim, 2004) Many of these researchers see the limitations of NCLB, not in its goals, but rather as a lack of funding for its mandates, a flawed theory of implementation resulting in various unintended consequences, or its primitive top-down/bottom-up mix of sticks and carrots (Abernathy, 2007). While my argument in this book includes a critique of these limitations, I am much more skeptical about the authenticity of its espoused equity agenda.

NCLB had widespread support among both political parties, and many conservatives and progressives shared former Secretary of Education, Rod Paige's view that holding schools accountable through high-stakes testing and the disaggregation of test scores by race and SES is a way to advocate for children. In fact, the title No Child Left Behind was taken from a politically liberal child advocacy group, the Children's Defense Fund, headed by Marian Wright Edelman. Some, even now, view the act as a form of advocacy and part of the legacy of the Civil Rights Movement. They point out that before NCLB, the only thing that mattered in many American school districts was whether the high school football team was winning, not how low-income kids, English language learners, or kids of color were doing in school. With No Child Left Behind and the disaggregation of test scores, all subgroups had to achieve at a higher level. Suddenly, they argue, principals began to give a damn about kids of color and low-income kids—or at least their test scores (Anderson, 2001).

Besides, supporters argue, it would be one thing if we were going back to some better time, some panacea of the past, but they point out that public schools have never served poor students and students of color well. They characterize critics of NCLB as the *education establishment*—also a code word for unions—wanting to protect a system that serves their interests, not those of the children. In fact, they point out that many members of the public education establishment don't even send their own children to public schools, and certainly not the inner-city schools many of them work in.

These are sincere arguments and on the surface appear reasonable, but they are fundamentally flawed for reasons I will outline in this book. For one thing, they fail to understand how progressive social change is accomplished through authentic forms of democratic participation, not top-down mandates, however well intended. These mandates, even when they have teeth, as they do in NCLB, usually fail, especially in education, because they create inauthentic reforms.

Their arguments also fail to locate NCLB in the larger context of a growing neoliberal, free market agenda, one broadly supported by Republicans and "new" Democrats. Increasingly public schools are known as "government schools" or "public monopolies," a page taken directly from neoliberal economist Milton Friedman's (1962) *Capitalism and Freedom*. Neoliberal or neoclassical economists advocate the marketization of all social sectors. While neoliberals did not succeed this time in getting vouchers included in the NCLB legislation, there are many routes to the same end.

Finally, if it is true that NCLB represents advocacy at the federal level for low-income children, as some supporters argue, then how do we explain why a federal government that claims to care for poor and disenfranchised families had not raised the minimum wage of $5.15 since 1996, while corporate profits skyrocketed, or why it has reallocated wealth upward to such an extent that the country is more unequal today than at any time since the 1920s? Or how do we explain the fact that roughly 50 million Americans, mostly low-income, have no health insurance, or that, as *Business Week* reports, the average American worker makes $33,000 a year, while the average chief executive officer (CEO) makes $9.6 million (Lavelle, 2005). It seems ingenuous to see an authentic concern for the poor in a policy surrounded by other social policies that maintain, rather than challenge, poverty (Children's Defense Fund, 2004).

Taking a page from institutional theory (Meyer & Rowan, 1977; W. R. Scott, 2001), I want to suggest that school reform itself has become a legitimating ritual for a larger restructuring of the state from a welfare state to a competition state characterized by neoliberal economic policies. We are headed into a period in which the use of school reform language becomes a way to introduce new forms of governance. At the level of the state, these new forms of governance mean that the state moves from being a provider of services, to becoming an overseer and regulator of nonprofit and for-profit private service providers. In the British context, Ball (2007) describes a complex merging of the public and private sectors that includes a growing education service industry, new forms of ideological philanthropy, new social entrepreneurs, and new privatizing discourses. Similar changes are occurring in the U.S. context. Regardless of what we think about these changes, they are moving forward with little public deliberation. This lack of authentic deliberation makes such changes less likely to respond to public needs and more likely to respond to bottom lines and special interests.

Perhaps the most devastating critique of NCLB comes from The National Council of Churches' (2003) Committee on Public Education which has felt a need to speak out from an ethical, moral, and social justice perspective, objecting to NCLB on the following grounds.

1. The law will discredit public education. Undermining support for public schooling threatens our democracy.
2. The annual yearly progress component fails to acknowledge significant improvements students have made, too many are labeled failures even when they are making strides. Those labeled failures are disproportionately poor children and children of color.

3. Schools are ranked by test scores of children in demographic subgroups, a "failing group of children" will know when they are the ones who made their school a "failing" school.
4. Children in special education are required to pass tests designated for children without disabilities.
5. English language learners are required to take tests in English before they learn English.
6. Schools and teachers are blamed for many challenges that are neither of their own making nor within their capacity to change.
7. An emphasis on testing basic skills obscures the role of the humanities, the arts, and child and adolescent development. Children are treated as products to be tested, measured, and made more uniform.
8. The law operates through sanctions, it takes Federal Title I funding away from educational programming in already overstressed schools and uses funds to bus students to other schools or to pay for private tutoring firms.
9. The law exacerbates racial and economic segregation in urban areas. Because urban schools have more subgroups and more complex demands, they are more likely to be labeled "in need of improvement" than more affluent districts. This labeling of schools and districts encourages families with means to move to wealthy, homogeneous school districts.
10. Demands are made on states and school districts without fully funding those reforms to build the capacity to close achievement gaps. (pp. 2–3)

While we could debate some of these assertions, the fact that a national ecumenical Christian organization would endorse such a strong moral objection to NCLB, suggests that NCLB's claim to be advocacy for low-income students and students of color should be viewed with some skepticism. The National Council of Churches in their 1999 policy statement, *Churches and the Public Schools at the Close of the Twentieth Century*, contains a claim that is becoming ever more obvious to more and more Americans,

> Too often, criticism of the public schools fails to reflect our present societal complexity. At a moment when childhood poverty is shamefully widespread, when many families are under constant stress, when schools are often limited by lack of funds or resources, criticism of the public schools often ignores an essential truth: we cannot believe that we can improve public schools by concentrating on the schools alone. They alone can neither cause nor cure the problems we face. In this context, we must address with prayerful determination the issues of race and class, which threaten both public education and democracy in America.

But perhaps most importantly, politically negotiated policies that fail to include the views of those most affected tend to lack both internal coherence and congruence with the lived reality of teachers, principals, superintendents, parents, and especially that constituency that is never heard from—students. In a word, such policies lack authenticity. This lack of authenticity is due to a lack of congruence between espoused equity goals and the reality on the ground, but is also due to a failure to locate school reform in its larger context of social policies that increase social inequality.

Redefining the Role of School Leaders

While some advocacy leaders may find ways to use some of NCLB's mandates to advance an equity agenda, I believe that overall, the legislation makes it more difficult to do so. Some may balk at the idea that teachers and administrators should take on an advocacy role of any kind. After all, aren't teachers and administrators supposed to be apolitical? This has been a chronic misconception of the role of professionals generally. Many researchers have documented the many ways the cards in education and society at large are stacked in both overt and subtle ways against those with the least power (Anyon, 2005; Rothstein, 2004). Educators often have only two choices: collude with a status quo that leaves poor children and children of color behind or be an advocate for those very children. Not everyone may agree on the form advocacy for children should take, but the notion that educators should advocate for children is taken for granted among many educators who work with low-income children and families of color.

Many school leaders are effective politicians, building political bases and garnering resources for their schools. This is not what I mean by being an advocacy leader. Typically, leaders who are politically savvy use their political capital to get promoted out of their current position. Those who acquire extra resources for their schools are often not creating new resources for low-income kids, but rather successfully winning the resources away from other equally deserving schools. Here's a brief example of what I mean by calling for school professionals to see themselves as advocates for children in schools.

When our daughter was in the second grade, she attended an elementary school in New Mexico in an urban neighborhood in which roughly half of the students were from middle-class families and the other half were from largely Latino lower-income families. In August the school posted the class lists for the fall on one of the doors to the school, and children and parents would drop by to find out which class they were placed in. My daughter saw her name on one of the lists and remarked how relieved she was that she hadn't been placed in the "dumb" class. I was familiar with the notion of tracking in high schools, and knew that within-class tracking occurred in elementary schools through assignment to reading groups, special education, and gifted programs, but I was unaware that there were whole classes that were considered "dumb" or "smart" classes. I noticed that the "dumb" class also had a larger percentage of Spanish surname students than the "smart" classes.

Since I taught at the nearby university, I had a mole in the school, a student of mine that taught fourth grade. I asked her in confidence about this and without skipping a beat she explained how many middle class parents would negotiate with the teachers and principal to get their children into the classes they wanted. In fact, she implied that some teachers were proactive in this, assuring parents—mostly what she called "soccer moms"—that they would see to it that their child got the best teacher for the following year. She told me that there was a high track through the school, and that these high track teachers would pass certain children along through this track. In fact, she said, one year when one of the middle-class students graduated from elementary school, the high track teachers could be identified because they all wore orchids, gifts of the mother whose child had moved smoothly up through the high track classes.

This teacher's observations were later confirmed as I attended community parent meetings, in which parents openly discussed the ways they worked the teachers and principal on behalf of their kids. These "tracks" were not formally structured, but rather came about through the micropolitics among principals, teachers, and parents, with either the indifference or tacit approval of the administrator.

Of course, these teachers and principals didn't think they were doing anything wrong—nor did the parents for that matter. In fact, the parents likely felt they were "advocating" for their children, and the teachers perhaps saw their behavior as advocacy for their students and parents. After all, this tracking system had its rationales. The high track teachers were more skilled and could integrate the more gifted students we were told. The slower students wouldn't be able to keep up and would hold other students back. (Why these skilled teachers could integrate the "gifted" kids but not the "slower" ones was never explained.) The low track had more bilingual teachers and so bilingual students were better off there. However, what was generally not acknowledged was that the middle class parents and the largely middle class teachers shared a common view of the destiny of "their" children. And if a teacher or administrator didn't have such a tacit understanding, then middle class parents knew how to apply pressure all the way up the system.

Sometimes middle-class parents don't even have to advocate. Our own daughter did not go through the high track; There was a middle range track that was less academically driven, but, in our view, more holistic. The mere perception that we might complain though, likely kept our daughter out of the lowest track. The parents of students in the "dumb classes" were largely lower-income parents who were less likely to be aware of this tracking system, and even if they were, many would not have had the social networks or the cultural capital to effectively contest their child's placement (Lareau, 1989).

More recently in New York City, a local community organization called the Center for Immigrant Families (CIF) challenged a similar situation in the rapidly gentrifying Upper West Side of Manhattan. The *New York Times* reports a feverish growth in demand for private schools in Manhattan, with tuitions hovering around $30,000 a year for preschool through high school (Hu, 2008). For those without access to $400,000 per child for a private school education, there are other ways to get a privileged education for your child. CIF describes the subtle and not so subtle ways principals admitted middle class condo owners to their schools over the children of immigrant families who lived in the neighborhood, including asking for a financial contribution to the school. Their participatory action research with local immigrant families exposed the worst excesses of these schools, and they protested to the New York City Department of Education. Through their advocacy, they were able to get the DOE to allocate spaces at these schools through a lottery system.

While these are examples of advocacy leadership exercised by community groups or individuals, they represent missed opportunities for principals who may have seen their professional star hitched to the more powerful middle class parents. Unfortunately most parents see advocacy only as linked to self-interest. Parents rightly advocate for their children, and this is unlikely to change in our individualistic culture and school choice policy environment. But parents with more economic, social, and cultural capital will generally be more effective. So who advocates for those low track students who end up in the "dumb classes" or the leftover schools, if not teachers, counselors, school social workers, school psychologists, principals, and superintendents. Unless school professionals see themselves as advocates for more equitable placement of children in classes or schools, they are colluding in a tracking system that is unjust.

This example of how educators can be advocates for equity is relevant to many schools in socioeconomically mixed, gentrifying, or middle class communities. Unfortunately, in too many American schools tracking occurs not within schools, but through neighborhoods sharply segregated by income and race. Ironically, racial segregation nationally has increased not decreased since the passing of desegregation laws. As Americans continue to become less equal in socioeconomic terms, segregation by class has also become more pronounced. Anyone who works in an urban school knows that it is not uncommon for schools to have well over 90% of their students on free and reduced lunch programs. Under these circumstances, how do administrators exercise advocacy in schools in which internal tracking by class and race is less relevant because all of their students are low-income students and more often students of color.

The policy response to this problem through NCLB has been largely limited to school choice policies and a call for higher expectations and higher test scores for everyone. There may be some truth in former secretary of education, Rod Paige's claim that the soft bigotry of school professionals' low expectations may be partly to blame for the underachievement of low-income children and children of color. No one escapes the subtle forms of classism and racism that circulate among us on a daily basis. But the solution is not to make teachers the enemy and subject them and their students to high-stakes testing and public humiliation as the policies Paige promoted do.

While raising expectations is necessary in specific cases, a broader solution involves a new way of conceptualizing the role of school professionals. While I will discuss this in more detail in chapter 4, it partly involves linking forms of advocacy within the school to forms of advocacy outside the school. Not all of the principals rebuffed the Center for Immigrant Families' attempt to open up schools to their children. Some principals were allies and supported their work. These principals were not merely concerned with getting more donations from parents, but were motivated by a sense of social justice. While calls for social justice have become far too abstract of late, social justice consists of the kinds of courageous and concrete decisions that some teachers and principals make everyday.

Advocacy principals and teachers attempt to build alliances with existing community groups to leverage power and foster public forms of accountability grounded in empowered communities (Gold, Simon, & Brown, 2004; Shirley, 1997). As school professionals more closely interact with communities, they develop a greater understanding of the constraints under which low-income parents operate on a daily basis. What leaves children behind is more than mediocre education. Children are successful in school to the extent that they have good teachers, but their success also depends on what they experience or don't experience outside of school. In a word, it depends on their economic welfare and their access to mainstream social and cultural capital.

Social inequities are primarily caused by social and economic policies—not school-related factors. Cuban (1990) in his classic article on why school reforms seem to recycle every few decades speculates on why Americans turn to schools for solutions in times of social turmoil. One of the reasons offered by historians, according to Cuban, is

> that elite classes or dominant groups in the society that set directions for major social policies charge the public schools with the responsibility for solving national ills. These elite groups do so because the sources of those ills are deeply rooted in the structures of the society and, if the major problems of poverty, racism, drug addictions, and environmental destruction were addressed directly, grave upheavals in economic, social, and political institutions would occur. (p. 2)

Anyon (2005) takes this observation a step further in arguing that if we really want to improve the lot of poor children, we need to give them the same access to economic resources that the middle class currently enjoys. This means more equitable redistribution of wealth, not merely educational opportunity, tutorial services, or cultural capital. Student achievement improves as family resources increase. Anyon cites various studies that show the many ways that poverty is the result of macroeconomic policies, not low academic achievement. Anyon writes, "I believe that in the long run we would do better to increase the access of the urban poor to economic resources so they, too, can afford the time, money, and inclination to prepare their children for school success" (p. 71).

Somehow, we have been convinced that teachers and administrators should not and cannot influence social policy. A brief example drawn from our professional colleagues in nursing may be instructive. In 2005 several ballot initiatives, propositions 86, 87, and 89 were defeated in California in spite of a heroic effort by the California Nurses Association to get them passed. The nurses supported Proposition 86, which would have added a tax to cigarettes to fund health care and Proposition 87, which would have more heavily taxed oil companies. Proposition 89, or the clean elections proposition, was sponsored by the nurses union, and was an attempt to curb the influence of corporate money in politics. The tobacco and oil industries, along with a long list of other corporations lined up against the initiatives to the tune of a record $190 million. In a press release, Rose Ann DeMoro, executive director of the California Nurses Association, said

> CNA will also step up efforts for reform on other critical issues facing Californians, "especially the growing collapse of our healthcare system and the disgrace of having 6.5 million uninsured and millions more underinsured residents. We will transform healthcare in California, soon." (California Nurses Association, 2006)

Among these health professionals, there is a growing realization that they cannot be effective in doing their job unless they are supported by social policies that redirect resources to public health.

Meanwhile, the California teachers unions, with the notable exception of United Teachers of Los Angeles (UTLA), the Los Angeles local, largely sat on the sidelines and even fought the nurses on one of the propositions. Ironically, nurses are trying to call attention to the crises of our already privatized health care system, while associations that represent educators seem largely unconcerned about the growing privatization of our educational system.

The year before in 2004, governor Schwarzenegger promoted proposition 75 that would have required public employee unions to obtain annual written consent from each member in order to use a portion of that member's dues for political activity. In case anyone doubts that this represents an ideological struggle, Milton Friedman, the father of neoliberal, free-market policies was a signatory on official ballot arguments supporting the initiative. This initiative, which already exists in some states, has drastically reduced the political power of labor with respect to corporate support of social policies.

Opponents pointed out that corporate shareholders do not have to sign off for permission of their corporations to support political issues and candidates. Furthermore union members can already opt out of having their dues used for political activity if they choose to do so. Thanks to massive union organizing statewide, the initiative was defeated and once again, the nurses were at the forefront, fighting political battles that transcended their important, but narrower issues, such as salaries and nurse–patient ratios.

While structural change is always achieved collectively, in the absence of universal health care, individual advocacy educators have found ways to use data on students eligible for free and reduced lunch programs to get their parents signed up for free or low cost health insurance through Medicaid (Cohen Ross, 1999). This reduces the number of uninsured students in the school and represents another way of linking to the community. So educators can support those "finger in the dike" local solutions until real universal and affordable health care is available to all Americans. But educators will have to be trained to operate on two levels; one micro and short term; the other macro and long term. This dual approach is the bread and butter of advocacy movements. What is certain is that when it comes to insuring our students, insurance and pharmaceutical company lobbyists will win the day unless professionals who care about the well-being of children and their families provide a countervailing force.

While America has changed many times throughout its history, we are today experiencing one of those epochal shifts on a grand scale. The country will look very different as technology continues to develop, capital flows through cyberspace in real time, and the dividing line between the public and the private continues to blur. Whether we can harness these changes in a way that preserves a sense of democratic principles, a common good, a public sphere, and an authentic self, remains to be seen. For now, these democratic ideals seem increasingly like quaint concepts from a distance past—noble ideas, but not realistic in the current climate of crisis. Neoliberal policies in education and other social sectors seem inevitable. How often do we hear the expressions, "That train has already left the station" or "That genie is already out of the bottle"? We are swept along in a current that seems too strong to resist. But there are signs that we are getting clearer about what the real implications are for our educational system if current trends continue. In the next chapter, I will focus in greater detail on one casualty of the new economy: authenticity.

2
Authentic Leadership

I am not the first to call for more authentic leadership. There is a vast literature that links leadership and authenticity. In fact, I have contributed to it myself. Its definition of authenticity tends to be limited to building more open, ethical, caring, and trusting relations in schools. These are not unimportant goals, but I have come to believe they are insufficient, and can even end up making an unjust status quo more palatable. This definition of authentic leadership focuses on turning bureaucratic institutions into caring "communities" in which all of the school professionals develop a strong sense of belonging (Sergiovanni, 1999). In this chapter, I will use this notion of authenticity as a starting point, but will argue that inauthenticity in educational leadership is a far more significant problem than failing to build trust and community in schools. In fact, the main problem with literature that calls for greater trust and community in schools is that it fails to analyze those broader sources of inauthenticity that make trust and community in schools less likely. I will discuss these broader sources of inauthenticity in some detail in this chapter.

Research, beginning with the human relations movement of the mid-20th century through current research on trust and community, has found that teachers, students, and administrators are more productive professionally in schools where norms of collegiality and trust are cultivated. In schools of business, public management, and education, the fields of leadership and organizational theory have tended to view authenticity as an important element of effective leadership and of a productive work environment. In general, this line of research is driven by a logic of improving the culture of schools as a means to greater productivity. In some cases, it includes a recognition that viewing authenticity as an ethical issue requires viewing individuals as more than means to more productive organizations, pointing out the need to place human regard and decency above the bottom line (Begley, 2001; Gardner, Avolio, & Walumbwa, 2005; George, 2003; Novicevic, Harvey, Buckley, Brown, & Evans, 2006: Sweetland, 2001; Terry, 1993).

In a post-Enron world, some business literature on leadership has thankfully refocused on issues of authenticity and ethics that Barnard (1938) addressed decades ago. Nevertheless, few discussions of leader authenticity place it in the context of social advocacy or political economy. Instead, a lack of authenticity is related to the nature of hierarchical organizations resulting in depersonalized and unjust relationships among individuals and groups. Such studies have shown that when asked to identify the key characteristics of effective leaders, "such qualities as honesty, integrity, credibility, being fair-minded, straightforward and dependable head the list" (Duignan & Bhindi, 1997, p. 206). But as I will discuss below, these qualities can be used to maintain an inequitable status quo or they can lead to a collective will that challenges unjust practices.

Such behaviors and dispositions are clearly justified as ends in themselves. After all, no one wants to work in an inauthentic environment, and it is nearly impossible to build professional capacity in an atmosphere of distrust. When injustices against students are occurring, having an authentic workplace may even be a precondition for effective advocacy, but it doesn't guarantee it. *Authenticity*, as I am using the term in this book, requires building social trust as a way to leverage more equitable schools and communities and a more equitable society (see Gold, Simon, & Brown, 2004, for a discussion of social trust in school community relations).

My own involvement in this research began in the 1980s through a line of research that focused on school micropolitics or the behind-the-scenes negotiations that occurred over resources, professional status, and ideological commitments (Ball, 1987). Based on research on how principals, teachers, students, and parents negotiated politics in schools, Joseph Blase and this author (Blase & Anderson, 1995) developed a leadership matrix based on two continua of leadership (see Figure 2.1).

The horizontal continuum ranged from open to closed leadership styles. An *open leadership style* is characterized by a willingness to share power. Respondents also reported that open principals were more honest, communicative, participatory, and collegial than closed principals. A *closed leadership style* is characterized by an unwillingness to share power. Respondents reported that closed principals were less accessible, less supportive, more defensive, more egocentric, and seemed more insecure than open leaders.

The vertical continuum ranged from a transactional to transformative orientation toward the goals and direction of the organization. These terms were borrowed from James McGregor Burns's (1982) classic book *Leadership*. Transactional leadership is based on exchange relationships among leaders and followers. In return for effort, productivity, and loyalty, leaders offer tangible and intangible rewards to followers. This orientation can be pursued with an open or closed style, but tends to create a relatively static environment that seldom disrupts the status quo.

On the other hand, transformative leadership is oriented toward bringing about fundamental change, the object of which is the raising of the consciousness of leader and follower alike around end values of the organization. Transformative leadership tends to be dynamic as it challenges certain aspects of the status quo, and can also be done with an open or closed style (see Figure 2.1).

In his study of school micropolitics, Blase (1989) found that more closed, control-oriented principals spawned an inauthentic culture in which teachers,

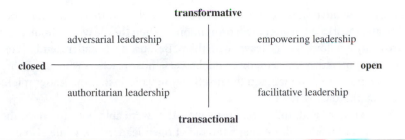

Figure 2.1 Micropolitical leadership matrix.

students, and parents felt a need to be deceptive and manipulative to get what they needed. Since authentic communication was difficult if not impossible, behind the scenes maneuvering became commonplace and distrust permeated the school. On the other hand, open principals, who were out and about in the school, maintaining constant and authentic communication with teachers, students, and parents created and fostered a culture of trust and diplomacy. It wasn't that differences, disagreements, and conflict didn't exist, but rather that they were handled openly and authentically. This allowed teachers to make their case in open forums rather than behind the back maneuvering or face-to-face dissimulation. Teachers reported winning some battles and losing others, but they appreciated the sense of trust, fairness, and authenticity that reigned.

Our matrix did muddy the waters a bit in ways that have to do with the advocacy theme of this book. Many leaders who fostered authentic schools were what Burns referred to as transactional leaders. They maintained a pleasant environment in which authentic communication was possible, but as transactional leaders they often saw themselves as largely maintaining the status quo. While their schools were pleasanter and more productive places to work, from an advocacy standpoint they often were little different from those of authoritarian leaders. This is partly because equity issues are often divisive and messy, and such schools may prefer to maintain good relations over taking on what they may view as risky and controversial issues. Research on educational leadership is only beginning to understand the importance of risk-taking for effective leadership (Brunner, 1999; Ylimaki 2005).

On the transformative end of our matrix are leaders who view themselves as advocates. Some advocate using a more closed, go-it-alone style and others with a more inclusive and open style. The former often engage in advocacy outside the school, being very effective at dealing with the politics of the larger school environment. They are often able to garner resources for the school and they are often charismatic, building a loyal following among a sector of the teaching staff and even of the school community. They are transformative rather than merely authoritarian, in the sense that they want the school to transcend its current ways of thinking and operating, and often surround themselves with a cadre of talented teachers. While such leaders can be powerful advocates for children, they are often advocates for their own careers as well, and their ambitions and political networks often gain them promotions. When they leave a school, their cadre of loyal followers often leaves with them. Because such leaders tend to create dependent, rather than empowered followers, those teachers who remain are seldom empowered to maintain the positive innovations that the leader might have brought to the school.

On the other hand, there were principals that were able both to create the caring and authentic culture characteristic of open leadership, while also empowering teachers, students, and parents to engage together in transformative leadership. These leaders were advocacy leaders, but they did so by calling attention to inequities and motivating multiple stakeholders to engage together in confronting the conditions leading to such inequities. For instance, if a disproportionate number of Black males were being referred to special education, it is less likely that the transactional leaders, whether open or closed in their leadership style, would confront, or perhaps even notice the issue. This is because school communities tend to find an equilibrium in which the status quo seems to be more or less working for everyone. Unfortunately, there may be constituencies for whom the status quo is not working well, but such constituencies may have little power or access to information.

Transformational leaders—both adversarial ones and empowering ones—are more likely to be willing to upset the status quo to challenge inequities. However, the control-oriented adversarial leader advocates in an authoritarian and paternalistic manner that often fails to garner the support and empowerment of multiple constituencies. Empowering leaders, on the other hand, can more easily achieve the goals of advocacy while also achieving greater inclusiveness and more authentic relations. Thus, authenticity involves more than authentic relations in a school, but also greater inclusion of voices and an advocacy stance against unjust practices. In this sense, the empowering leader who exhibits both an open leadership style and a transformative orientation comes closest to being an advocacy leader, combining both authenticity and advocacy.

In many ways, this book builds on these early insights about the relationship between authentic leadership and what we then called "empowering" leadership. But our insights about empowering leaders failed to grapple with how leaders might impact broader changes that were underway at the time. That failure to conceive of leadership as advocacy within a larger framework led to a continuing view of leadership as being largely limited to organizational leadership. But as I discussed in chapter 2, advocacy leaders have a strong sense of a larger cause, and see their work as ultimately making a contribution to a more just society. As Murtadha and Watts (2005) document, many African-American leaders took for granted this sense of being part of a larger movement for justice. But they point out that,

> Through socially critical writings, oratorical power, and activism, many leaders succeeded in making a difference in the educational settings that

served Black people. Their narratives and critiques, however, have not been incorporated as a central element in the literature of school administration, leadership, reform, and change. (p. 591)

In the current context of inauthentic schemes to reform schools, advocacy leaders are struggling with how to make a difference, in spite of mandates to implement what many consider inauthentic, and often unjust, policies and practices.

A Multilevel Approach to Restoring Authenticity to Schooling

A library search for *authenticity* will net several specialized uses of the term ranging from linguistic authenticity to philosophical ruminations on the authentic life. For the purposes of this book, authenticity, at an *individual* level, is living a life, whether in personal or professional terms, that is congruent with one's espoused values. It also assumes that constructing a self is a social process, best done through collective and interactive endeavors. Our identities are constructed in social institutions like families and organizations like schools.

At the *organizational* level, authenticity has to do with viewing human beings as ends in themselves, rather than as means to other ends. Corporate CEO George Soros (1998) has observed that *transactions* have replaced *relationships* in human affairs. In schools, it means that the pedagogical relation, the interaction between teacher and student, is essentially a social relation that requires emotional commitment, caring, and a view that one's students deserve as high a quality education as one's own children receive. The current reality of middle class teachers in low-income schools populated by children of color is a result of historical and continuing social segregation by class and race. Within these unacceptable social arrangements, authentic teaching is not likely unless a symbiotic relationship exists with local communities. Authenticity at the organizational level also means that so-called distributed leadership is not engaged in merely as a human relations strategy to raise productivity, however that is defined, but also because it respects others' views and their right to participate in making decisions that affect their lives.

At a *societal* level, it is a state of affairs that is congruent with the shared political and cultural values of a society. In a country with ideals of equal opportunity, we become less authentic to the extent that we become less equal. We become less authentic to the extent that we do not share in society's risks and responsibilities. Authenticity also requires engagement with society as educated and empowered citizens, not merely as consumers with choices. Adam Smith, who is often evoked as the father of market capitalism, was also a moral philosopher who argued that enlightened self-interest was acceptable and desirable in society, but mere greed was not. Collective survival, whether at the national or global level, requires a highly developed sense of the common good. Table 2.1 provides a summary of areas of schooling in which authenticity is threatened.

Table 2.1 Characteristics of authenticity

Congruence	Congruence between individual and societally espoused beliefs and individual and societal actions/policies
Experience/community-based	To what extent are practices (especially teaching) and policies connected to the life world of the students and their communities?
Social justice/inclusion	To what extent are all students receiving a quality education that is culturally responsive and inclusive?
Nested practices	Acknowledges that practices at the classroom level are nested within practices and policies at other levels of the system and society (including social policies that affect children)
Socially constructed selves	Acknowledges that selves are constructed relationally within institutional and social contexts
Honesty/integrity	To what extent do educators perceive a need to "game" the system, and behave dishonestly in order to serve students needs?
Balance of system and life world	To what extent is the system world and life world of the school in balance and work together synergistically

Given the tendency of individuals to pursue their self-interest, advocacy at all three levels is needed to ensure that the powerful do not oppress the powerless. This notion was written into our Constitution by those who had fought the British monarchy and were obsessed with creating a nation in which formal power was dispersed through democratic principles. While their notion of democracy was limited to propertied White males at the time, the Constitution and the amendments they wrote were subsequently used to gain rights for other groups. An authentic democracy requires leaders to uphold laws and policies against discrimination and to challenge those who discriminate— defending the powerless from the powerful is the essence of advocacy leadership.

Shifts at any one of these three levels of authenticity—individual, organizational, societal—will tend to provoke shifts at other levels. Inauthentic social institutions do not nurture authentic individuals. Authenticity in social institutions is limited in an inauthentic, nondemocratic society. Authentic relationships are the first casualty of a dictatorship because fear and distrust reduce authentic social interactions to inauthentic public performances (Scott, 1990). The loss of authentic public space, as public spaces are either taken over militarily or are auctioned off to the highest bidder, whether through dictatorship or privatization, means the demise of a sovereign people.

This interconnectedness of authenticity and advocacy at different levels will form a framework I will use throughout the rest of the book. Attempts to understand authenticity in social institutions and human relationships cannot be successful unless all levels of society are taken into account. For educators, it means that high academic achievement is tied to what goes on outside schools as well as inside schools. It means that children who lack resources outside of school have as much right to those resources as children who lack resources inside schools. Few teachers or principals would knowingly withhold needed resources from a child in school. The same indignation should be felt for those same children when they are not provided with adequate access to health care, food, or shelter outside of school. Authentic education cannot exist unless all children—as a human right—have access to basic social welfare (Berliner, 2006). This will require more than indignation. It will require advocacy.

By advocacy, I am not suggesting that principals need to lead broad social movements in their spare time, and yet we underestimate the extent to which, in the aggregate, local actions evolve into social movements. The civil rights movement didn't begin in the 1950s. The groundwork was laid decades before. Siddle Walker (2005) has documented how Black teachers in Georgia in the early 20th century, who could not engage openly in activism under Jim Crow, nevertheless prepared the ground for social change though their professional associations.

Ways of being an advocate may seem more obvious at the organizational level where unjust social arrangements can be challenged more directly, but because injustice is so often embedded in the taken-for-granted practices of schooling, teachers and leaders have to first learn to *see* injustice when it occurs. The elementary school tracking system I described in the previous chapter was hidden in plain sight. Nevertheless, the principal and teachers not only failed to address it, but also in many instances collaborated with it. These are the times when an advocate leader might truly make a difference at the organizational level. But one thing is clear: To the extent that school leaders are not also asking broader social questions and are buying into their role as scapegoats for society's ills, the status quo will march on with slight fluctuations in test scores. These slight fluctuations will be seized upon by reform advocates to make exaggerated claims of advocacy for low-income children.

Because too often research about educational leadership limits leadership to the organizational level, I will begin my discussion of authenticity at the societal level.

AUTHENTICITY AT THE SOCIETAL LEVEL

Authenticity at the societal level requires congruence between our cherished ideals and the way we live out our collective lives. Americans have always believed in progress and the notion that one's children would live in a more humane, democratic, equitable, and prosperous society than their parents. These beliefs were at the heart of the liberalism espoused by the first leaders of our republic, along with the notion, seldom realized, that these opportunities should be available to all Americans regardless of their race or gender. Women, African-Americans, and the poor have led social movements to gain inclusion into society's opportunities. The New Deal policies of the Roosevelt administration in the 1930s were the result of a social movement brought on by the Great Depression and led to the development of a social safety net for citizens and a fairer distribution of risks and responsibilities among the population. Few Americans alive today remember a world without Social Security, unemployment insurance, and employee contributions to pensions and health insurance; and following World War II there were low-interest mortgages and the G.I. bill which enabled former members of the armed forces to go on to postsecondary school education. Many of these policies were successful because they responded to the demands of authentic grassroots movements that have continued to advocate for them over the years.

Perhaps the most important element was that after many years of a bloody labor movement, capital and labor came to a historic agreement. In exchange for management's acceptance of unions and higher wages, labor agreed to be less aggressive. Business and labor negotiated these agreements largely because of a more even balance of power between them, but also because industry recognized that unless it paid workers better wages, there would be few people to purchase their products. This agreement, however, has slowly unraveled over the years as unions became more conservative and receded in size and influence, and capital, responding to shareholder pressures went in search of lower wages. These trends became most notable during the1970s, the decade most historians see as pivotal in our shift to globalization and neoliberal, free market policies.

Nevertheless, those of us who lived during the post-World War II years, remember how New Deal policies helped cushion those who lost their jobs and those over 65 who were no longer able to work. The GI bill and low cost mortgages led to upward social mobility for a large segment of the American working class. These policies provided a generation with the opportunity to attend postsecondary education in numbers previously unheard of, and to raise their families in affordable housing in which they grew equity over the life of the mortgage. Today, in a world of global competition, these hard won social gains have long been considered too costly, artifacts of the welfare state which has given away to the competitive state. However, some of us remember that even before globalization, capital was doing what it always does when there is no countervailing force—seeking greater profit for a small minority through paying lower wages to the vast majority.

Life at the End of the Welfare State

I was born in LaPorte, Indiana, a small factory town between Gary and South Bend. For the working class descendents of Polish, German, and Scandinavian immigrants there, the large Allis Chalmers plant and two other smaller factories made for a decent livelihood in the years before and after the Second World War. These were primarily union jobs that paid decent wages and included good benefits and pensions. I recall a solid working class childhood in which most of my relatives worked in one or another of these factories, sent their children to public schools, were prounion, and expected their lives and their children's lives to improve.

Returning from World War II as a young man, my father bought a modest home with government low-interest loans made available to returning service-men. Later, in his old age, his Social Security and pension made his life relatively comfortable. He was proud of his economic independence and spoke often of a time when old people who could no longer work either lived in poverty or at the mercy of family members. He ultimately became a staunch Democrat, but when I was a child, he was a supporter of Dwight Eisenhower, a war hero who received the votes of most returning servicemen. Although Eisenhower was a Republican, his politics were more liberal than most of today's Democrats, and it was he who warned Americans of an incipient military–industrial complex that could amass inordinate power and usurp the power of a sovereign people.

The 1950s and 1960s saw strong economic growth and upward social mobil-ity. Many welfare state policies of Roosevelt's New Deal were extended during Lyndon Johnson's Great Society. But there were early signs that in spite of an apparent business–labor agreement, business was seeking ways to avoid sharing power with unions. In a period of a few years in the late 1950s and early 1960s all of the factories in LaPorte closed their doors. In those days, they did not move overseas, they merely moved to nonunion states. The factory where my father worked moved to a small town in Iowa. He was one of the lucky ones, as they were willing to transfer him there to help with the new factory. So he packed up his family and, like so many Americans in those years, we were uprooted from the supports of our communities and extended families. It was in that small Iowa town that I ultimately grew into adolescence.

When we arrived, Iowa was beginning the transition from the family farm to corporate agribusiness. Farmers could no longer survive on 150 acres and their wives were forced into wage labor to pay the bills. The factory that employed my father moved there explicitly because they could pay women half of what they were paying men in LaPorte, and they knew the farmers' wives needed to work to save the family farm. Women were what Marx called the reserve army of labor that could be tapped to drive down wages. Today businesses use immigrant labor or seek cheaper labor overseas; in the 1950s they found cheaper labor among women and in nonunion states in the South and West.

Meanwhile, back in LaPorte, Indiana where the large Allis Chalmers plant was now a vacant and rusting shell, my uncles and cousins were suffering mas-sive unemployment. In and out of work over the years, many began to drink too much. Wives entered the workforce, not as liberated professionals, but as pink-collar minimum wage earners. The economic stress affected marriages; their kids got pregnant and began to drift off to Florida, California, or Texas; some dropped out of school to work to help support their families. Few went to any kind of postsecondary institution. My misfortune of not growing up with extended family was in another sense my salvation, as my father had stable employment and my sister and I ended up going to college. For many working class youth, academic and economic success is bought at the cost of alienation from one's family and community.

LaPorte in the 1960s was a harbinger of things to come in other communities in ensuing decades. By the decades of the 1980s and 1990s, two incomes per family began replacing the family wage of the postwar years. Union membership plummeted to its current private sector low of 7%. Social inequality grew, and for the first time, children were no longer expected to do better economically than their parents. The shifts my family lived through demonstrate both the gains of the New Deal and limitations of the American welfare state. Unlike in Europe, where welfare states were developed under a system of social democracy that more effectively regulated capital, in the United States there were few incentives for industry to behave in a socially responsible way. In our rush to dump "big government," labor unions, and even public education on the trash bin of history, we should learn the lessons of countries where big government and big labor formed a triangle of checks and balances with big business.

In many European social democracies, when industries such as textiles became unviable due to foreign competition, corporate CEOs, government representatives, and union leaders would sit down together to make a plan that would avoid the massive dislocations and misery that accompanies the closing of a large factory. In such a situation, the Allis Chalmers plant in LaPorte might have been retooled into a more viable industry. In such a process, the CEO would negotiate for government subsidies to aid in the transition. The union would be at the table to look out for the workers' interests, and the government would represent the interests of the commonwealth. The savings to society of such collaboration would be significant in terms of mental health, alcoholism, divorce, unemployment insurance, and the tangible and intangible benefits of saving an intact community. It is social policies like these, not mere academic achievement, that provide the conditions for social advancement. Academic achievement improves as the lives of children, families, and communities improve, not the other way around, as human capital theory and NCLB implicitly argue.

What the American welfare state did, in all of its bureaucratic imperfection, was to try to bring some stability to people's lives, which were exposed to the vagaries of cycles of boom and bust or the whim of factories that closed down and moved to where profits could be increased for the short-term benefit of shareholders. Outsourcing jobs and moving factories overseas wasn't invented in the 1970s and 1980s, it was a union busting tactic even in the 1950s. While what happened to LaPorte went largely unnoticed, this process repeated itself in larger Midwestern and Eastern cities like Pittsburg, Detroit, Cleveland, Flint, Buffalo, St Louis, Baltimore, and many others. But what is less known is that it also devastated rural America, where the family farm has all but disappeared.

In my Iowa high school, there were two groups: the townies and the farm kids. Among the townies, there were two sides of the track, those who were sons and daughters of local merchants and professionals and those who were sons and daughters of factory workers or those with more menial jobs. Among the farm kids, there were those few from relatively successful, large farms, and the rest from small, increasingly less viable farms. In school, I often found myself in classes with the sons and daughter of factory workers and small farmers. The higher track classes consisted largely of the more affluent town kids and kids from the more successful farms. Such was the social class tracking in rural schools.

I remember conversations with farm kids who talked endlessly of the advantages of one brand of tractor over another, or the best time to plant corn. These were young men with a love of farming who opted for the agriculture curriculum instead of industrial arts or courses for the college bound (their female equivalents were tracked into the secretarial curriculum). When I returned to my hometown years later and ran into my old classmates who grew up on farms, I discovered that virtually none of them had gone into farming. Without the requisite courses to enter college, most were driving trucks or working at the local factory. Ironically, their schooling provided them with no tools to understand how their world had changed around them. Many had become evangelical Christians and voted Republican.

Like the destruction of New Orleans by Hurricane Katrina, the demise of the family farm was not a natural phenomenon, but was rather the result of social policies. New Orleans was a casualty of a failure to fund the public sector infrastructure, such as the levies that protected the lowlands where mostly low-income families lived. The demise of the family farm was the result of federal subsidies for agribusiness. Over the years, farm bills in the legislature have provided what Timothy Egan (2007) calls red state welfare,

> The Red State welfare program, also known as the farm subsidy system, showers most of its tax dollars on the richest farmers, often people with no dirt under their fingernails, at the expense of everybody else trying to work the land. (p. A23)

These agribusiness subsidies also affect the U.S. diet as they support large commodity crops like corn, soybeans, and wheat, the foundation for junk foods and obesity, instead of fruits and healthier vegetables.

Ironically, the schooling my old Iowa classmates received did not provide them with the information or analytic skills to understand the ways in which the world was changing around them and stealing their futures. Scripted and depoliticized teaching today ensures that another generation will lack a social analysis that would provide them with the tools to defend democracy and work to ensure that our society is living out an authentic allegiance to its cherished ideals.

So while Americans were largely upwardly mobile in the postwar years, it is clear that not everyone prospered. This period was especially unkind to African Americans (and, as we saw above, working class women). In order for African Americans to receive the benefits of the welfare state that Whites took for granted, a civil rights struggle was necessary, resulting in the various civil rights laws that didn't take effect until the 1960s. Once again, like the labor movement that preceded the civil rights movement, social gains were the result of a social movement, not social engineering schemes like NCLB. It is also important to emphasize that, while these movements had formal and informal leaders, they could not have been successful without the everyday heroism of average people, including many teachers and principals, many of whom took tremendous political risks in supporting these movements (Siddle Walker, 2005).

It is a tragic irony that at the point when African Americans were beginning to enjoy the fruits of the welfare state, it was beginning to be dismantled. The brunt of the shift from welfare state to neoliberal competition state has been disproportionately borne by African Americans who had used welfare state institutions as their route to upward social mobility. Over the same period, massive immigration has helped drive down wages in the private service sector, where many African Americans also had found work. Whether working class African Americans or immigrants fleeing economic exploitation, the competition state leaves the most vulnerable without the protection of a labor union or a political infrastructure that can defend their interests. Without a new social movement, there is no reason to believe that the plight of millions of low-income Americans will improve.

The Grand Canyon: Authenticity and Inequality

In the movie *Grand Canyon*, Mack, a white middle class protagonist takes a wrong turn and gets lost at night in South Central Los Angeles. He is rescued from a mugging by Simon, an African American auto mechanic who lives in the neighborhood. Mack, days later, is drawn back to Simon, with whom he shared a fleeting but profound experience of solidarity. These two protagonists would otherwise have little occasion to meet in a Los Angeles segregated by race and class. The movie is an exploration of the Grand Canyon of social distances we have created across racial and social class lines, and it is this divide that is played out daily in schools, either through the creation of within school tracking or the absence of any race or class diversity in many schools. The United States is certainly not the only country in the world experiencing such problems. In fact, some countries have dissolved into class warfare and ethnic cleansing. My point is not to single out the United States so much as it is to call attention to how far our social reality has strayed from our social ideals, and how our social policies have contributed to this distance.

The late Christopher Lasch in *The Revolt of the Elites* describes an America in which professional and corporate elites seldom have any reason to have a conversation with an auto mechanic unless he is working on their car. Lasch saw this increasing social segregation by class and race as a betrayal of American democracy. Like Mack from *Grand Canyon,* most Americans have a deep-seated desire to live in an equitable and racially integrated society. The reality, however, is quite different and getting worse. Whether one measures income or wealth (income plus assets), differences between the haves and have-nots are greater than at any time since the 1920s, the decade before the Great Depression. The central fallacy of the No Child Left Behind Act is the notion that we can improve the lives of children in schools without recourse to social policies that address the massive reallocation of wealth away from poor children and their families.

Robert Reich, in his influential 1991 book, *The Work of Nations: Preparing Ourselves for 21st Century Capitalism*, argued that a new class of Americans was emerging that he called "symbolic analysts." These highly paid professionals and executives and their families are a product of our new high-tech, information society, and represent roughly one fifth of the working population. Often working as consultants, engineers, lawyers, bankers, real estate developers, systems analysts, entertainment professionals, and advertising executives, they increasingly inter-marry and see themselves as a group apart. They share social networks, friendships, neighborhoods, and their incomes allow them to purchase other people's labor. Their children are likely to attend private schools or public schools in affluent suburbs, and are unlikely to serve in the military. Whereas previous generations of wealthy Americans were heavily taxed to help provide for the national infrastruc-ture and the needs of the bottom one fifth, the tax structure currently insulates this new elite from contributing to the common good (Soros, 1998).

Furthermore, as economies are globalized the well-being of a country no longer depends on the performance of national industries, and national elites' loyalties are no longer national, but international. Over 15 years ago, Reich projected a 2020 scenario that is fast becoming reality.

> Distinguished from the rest of the population by their global linkages, good schools, comfortable lifestyles, excellent health care, and abundance of security guards, symbolic analysts will complete their secession from the union. The townships and urban enclaves where they reside and the symbolic analytic zones where they work will bear no resemblance to the rest of America; nor will there be any direct connections between the two. America's poorest citizens, meanwhile, will be isolated within their own enclaves of urban and rural desperation; an ever-larger portion of their young men will fill the nation's prisons. The remainder of the American population, growing gradually poorer, will feel powerless to alter any of these trends. (Reich, 1991, pp. 302–303)

This scenario supports the notion of the economically squeezed middle class described by Ehrenreich (1990) and Barlow (2003). Some members of the middle class have moved into this affluent one fifth, but many more are at risk of slipping back into the working class, out of which many of them emerged a generation or two ago. A large segment of this tenuous middle class, with its generally politically liberal values, struggles with the anxiety parents feel about providing advantages for their own children.

Brantlinger (2003) has documented how liberal, middle class parents man-age to maintain espoused theories of equity and social justice while deftly using the system to pass their privileges on to their children. This often creates a gap between our espoused theories of opportunity and public schooling with our need to work the system for our own children. Such gaps are related to the ways that inauthenticity plays out in our daily lives. Many resolve this tension by moving into the conservative, neoliberal camp. While such a move resolves the tension, it results in more neoliberal social policies and greater social inequality. The perception of an us vs. them world is partly the result of a lack of authentic options which leaves parents to seek individual solutions for what should be a collective endeavor.

Inauthenticity, then, whether at the individual, organizational, or societal level is linked to this growing gap between our cherished ideals and the realities of our lives. In many cases ideals like liberty and equality have come into conflict with each other as well, with equality often losing out to an invigorated belief in individual liberty. When Christopher Lasch referred to the revolt of the elites, he wasn't just referring to Reich's (1991) top one fifth of Americans. He also took on left-leaning liberals, who have also isolated themselves from working class Americans, and use their education and cultural capital to work the system. This is the same group that Michael Apple (2006) argues often allies itself with neoconservatives and neoliberals in support of high-stakes testing and other educational policies that draw on their expertise and favor their children's cultural and social capital. Thomas Frank (2000) has made a similar point, arguing that political liberals have abandoned the American working class to the political right.

This conflict of values between liberty and equality were also in tension during the social movements of the 1960s as individual-oriented, countercultural movements lived in uneasy tension with democratic socialist movements that stressed social inequalities and collectivist struggles around class, race, and gender. As Duggan (2003), Lakoff (2004), and others have documented, many of these tensions continue to keep political progressives from developing a unified critique of neoliberal and neoconservative movements. The libertarian, autonomous individual of the 1960s and the neoliberal focus on the individual, property rights, and free markets merged in the election of Ronald Reagan and a significant shift in society from the 1970s to the present. Later, it was a "new" democrat, not a Republican who gave us free trade agreements like NAFTA and rolled back welfare benefits for single mothers. In the contemporary "risk" society, the individual bears greater responsibility for personal and social choices. The idea that an authentic self and authentic society is achieved through democratic social interaction among diverse equals is at risk of becoming viewed as hopelessly utopian. In the next section, I will discuss how this growing gap between our cherished democratic ideals and our current reality has been reflected in a historic shift in the goals of schooling in the United States.

The New Economy and the Goals of Schooling

Educational historians have documented the multiple goals of public schooling over the years. The functions of our educational system have ranged from provid-

Table 2.2 Goals of schooling

	Humanistic	Economic
Individual	Personal fulfillment and enhancement	Individual self-interest
Social	Democratic citizenship	Social efficiency

ing literacy in order that children might be able to read the Bible and thus, save their souls, to the formation of human capital to enhance our competitiveness in a global economy. Along the way, it has served, among other goals, to "Americanize" millions of immigrants, transmit a common set of values, provide homemaking and vocational skills, and socialize the young into our political system.

Labaree (1997) has documented a contemporary shift in how Americans view the goals of schooling. Table 2.2, adapted from Labaree's work, shows four goals for American schools from an economic and humanistic perspective and with a focus on the individual or the social. As a neoliberal economic model has become more dominant, humanistic goals for schools have receded in importance. A notion of education for personal fulfillment and enhancement is currently viewed as elitist by many and appropriate only for affluent children whose vocational concerns are viewed as less salient. Education for *democratic citizenship*, or what we once called "civics," has largely been eliminated or replaced by the teaching of authoritarian forms of patriotism in many schools. In many cases, especially when the country is at war, teaching the skills of public debate on current issues is viewed as risky and controversial in many schools (Westheimer, 2007). While one could argue that the humanistic goals of education were never dominant, the economic goals have undeniably become front and center in the wake of the ascendancy of neoliberalism with its emphasis on the individual as human capital and its promotion of a competition state that has intensified competition among individuals.

On the economic side, the goal of *social efficiency* and its link to education has become a rallying cry for school reform since the Soviet Union put Sputnik, the first satellite, into space. The link between schooling and the economy, again, came to the fore when the U.S. economy was perceived as falling behind that of Japan and Germany in the late 1970s (National Commission on Excellence in Education, 1983). More recently, a report of the new Commission on the Skills of the American Workforce, *Tough Choices or Tough Times* (2006), makes a similar argument, replacing competition from Japan and Germany with competition from India and China.[1] It is hard to find any commissioned report that doesn't include international comparisons of America's test scores, linking them to international competitiveness. America's public schools have been blamed during economic bust times, but seldom praised when the economy performs well. The school–economy link is tenuous at best (Levin, 1998), but it does provide a useful argument for the continued funding of public schools. Whether true or not, the rationale that we should provide resources to low-income schools to improve the economy appears to be a more powerful argument to the American public than one merely based on equity arguments.

Social efficiency as a goal of schooling is grounded in human capital theory, which argued that education was more than an expenditure, it was an investment in human capital with a return in increased productivity. The notion that what's good for business is good for America has always informed the social efficiency notion, and for a period of time from the 1930s though the 1960s, the national economic welfare was shared to a great extent among business, unions, and government agencies, ensuring that all would share in the benefits of a strong economy. Since the 1970s, the unions' power has receded, while business has increasingly gained what many consider inappropriate levels of influence in Washington. This has caused increases in productivity and profitability to be less evenly distributed among the general population.

Human capital theory and school-to-work programs continue to link schooling and economic growth, as well as argue that the "new" economy will produce a need for more highly skilled workers. What is becoming increasingly clearer is that the promise of an increase in demand for highly skilled workers in an information age society has not materialized largely because of automation and outsourcing. According to economist James K. Galbraith (1998),

> What the existing economy needs is a fairly small number of first-rate technical talents combined with a small super class of managers and financiers, on top of a vast substructure of nominally literate and politically apathetic working people. (pp. 34–35)

So while social efficiency goals may not increase national productivity, nor lead to better jobs, they have served as a way to make schools a scapegoat for national ills as well as a way for educators to argue for greater investment in education. In other words, regardless of who appropriates the human capital discourse, it has largely been used as a legitimating ritual for either supporting education funding or scapegoating schools when the economy performs poorly. While human capital theory has been a useful tool for both liberals and conservatives, some have suggested replacing it with a discourse of human rights, which emphasizes humans as ends in themselves rather than means to greater productivity (Spring, 2000; Tomasevski, 2003).

The individual version of the social efficiency goal of schooling is what Labaree called *individual self-interest,* which he argues has become the central motivating force of Americans. But individual self-interest cannot serve as a national ideal to inspire young people and, while it was always a force in American society, it was tempered by larger ideals of democracy and equity. In a world in which students in elementary school are already building resumes for college, education has, according to Pope (2001), become "doing school, where they learn a hidden curriculum that includes manipulating the system, lying, sucking up, and doing whatever else it takes to keep a high grade point average" (p. 4). As these students take their places as leaders in the neoliberal, competition state, they will find little incentive to change their behaviors.

A similar phenomenon is modeled by middle and upper class parents. The loss of a sense of the common good has resulted in a growing dissociation between the well-being of one's own and other people's children. It may well be natural that parents should make the welfare of their own children their primary concern. All parents want the best for their children. What we are witnessing, however, is a shift in which parents aren't simply demanding that schools provide a quality education for their children. Instead they are demanding that schools provide their children with more than other children are getting (McGrath & Kurillof, 1999). While upper class parents have always been able to buy a superior education for their children, economically squeezed middle class parents are left to fight each other and the working class for privileges for their children.

While academic tracking may be in part due to a belief that students at the same level are best taught together, McGrath and Kurillof (1999) found that many middle class parents are adamant that their children not be mixed in with other people's children, unless those children are at similar academic levels. Because academic level tends to correlate so closely with socioeconomic level and race, it is often hard to sort out the real concerns. Regardless of whether middle class parents are classist, racist, or simply want their child to be competitive in the job market, the result is a society segregated by class and race, even when kids spend the day in the same school.

A society, in which individual self-interest becomes a dominant goal, cannot also claim to truly support goals of social equality. Because race is so often absent from discussions of neoliberalism and education, I want to make the link between the two as clearly as possible. We now know that racism is not merely an attitude; it is structured into the very fabric of American society. To take New York City as an example, the creation of White suburbs during the 1950s and 1960s had dire consequences for people of color in the city. Because African Americans were excluded from many welfare state benefits, including affordable, low-interest suburban housing, they remained in the city as White New Yorkers moved to the suburbs. Not only did this increase racial segregation, but it meant that home ownership and its economic benefits were out of reach for African Americans who remained as renters in the city. After the civil rights movement helped to remove these formal obstacles, African Americans began to move to the suburbs only to find more White flight from their neighborhoods and a consequent lack of appreciation in the price of their homes. Meanwhile manufacturing also left the city for the suburbs and the flight of higher-income residents from New York City sapped the tax base, leading to fiscal austerity, the deterioration of the city's public schools, and the depletion of public health programs during the 1970s.

The new white suburban communities could now use their political influence and tax base to develop good jobs, good schools, and public services, high-end stores, and rising property values without the use of legal racial barriers. The result was the creation of a new and powerful cycle of privilege…. (Barlow, 2003, p. 41)

In the wake of this structured racism, it no longer was necessary for Whites to appeal to a Jim Crow-like legal and state apparatus. Given the inherently unfair competition, it was possible to defend racial privilege merely by appealing to local control of schools, and "neutral," meritocratic practices like high-stakes standardized test scores.

Barlow (2003) provides an explanation for why individual self-interest has become such a central goal of the middle class and its implications for race. He argues that the growing inequality that neoliberalism has created has produced an American middle class that is seeing its standard of living decline. This decline is not so much because of falling incomes—though they are working more hours to maintain them—but rather the rising cost of housing, college tuition, and health care. As they experience downward pressures, job insecurity, and high levels of debt, they mobilize whatever social and cultural resources they have. This has created greater opposition to policies like affirmative action, along with a growing anti-immigrant sentiment. During times when the middle class feels relatively secure, it will support social welfare policies and racial equality, but in times of insecurity and fear, it embraces more narrow policies that reflect individual self-interest.

The goals of schooling, then, seem to be shifting under the competition state to a greater emphasis on the maximization of individual advantage for one's own children. The ripple effect of this shift is a pulling back from policies that benefit the common good, and toward policies that allow the middle and upper classes to cash in their relative advantage in economic, social, and cultural capital. But this begs the questions: How do they get away with it? Why don't those who are left out of the system push back? After all, we have a political system in which theoretically groups can organize to demand more authentic, equitable social policies. Some political scientists believe that politics take place less through political deliberation or political organizing, than by controlling hearts and minds though political spectacle.

Political Spectacle Replaces Political Deliberation

According to Edelman (1988), American society has increasingly replaced rational discussion about policy with political spectacle. Here's an example of political spectacle from school reform: In 2005, the Department of Education got its hand slapped by the General Accounting Office (GAO) because it paid $186,000 to a public relations firm to produce favorable news coverage of President Bush's education policies. The GAO described the activities engaged in by the Bush administration as "covert propaganda." What did the Education Department get for the money it paid the public relations firm Ketchum, Inc.? According to a front page *New York Times* story (Pear, 2005),

The auditors denounced a prepackaged television story disseminated by the education department. The segment, a "video news release" narrated by a woman named Karen Ryan, said that President Bush's program for providing remedial instruction and tutoring to children "gets an A-plus." (p. A13)

The narrator ended the news video by saying, "In Washington, I'm Karen Ryan reporting," giving the unsuspecting public the impression that this was a network news report, not government-sponsored propaganda, paid for by taxpayer dollars.

In a further blow to campaign finance reform and media authenticity, on June 25, 2007, the Supreme Court, encouraged this kind of deception by upholding the right of corporations and unions to run phony "issue ads" that promoted a particular candidate's views or attacked those of another. It is increasingly difficult for the average viewer to tell what looks like a public service ad or a news report from political propaganda.

The Iraq war provides a tragic list of inauthentic government sponsored hype: The famous aluminum tubes discovered in Iraq that were purportedly part of a program to build nuclear weapons, the media attention to Jessica Lynch's staged rescue, and all-American athlete Pat Tillman's heroic death, which we later learned was from friendly fire. As examples of political spectacle produced by a codependent relationship between a government committed to deception and a compliant media, these may appear to be extreme examples of inauthentic behavior. However, they set the tone for the American public's increasing levels of cynicism toward American institutions, including our public schools.

While Karl Rove is credited with masterminding the election of George Bush and the promotion of myriad conservative social policies through "swiftboating" and the creation of political spectacle, political manipulation and the dissemination of misinformation have a long and documented history in the United States and elsewhere. In *Constructing the Political Spectacle,* Edelman (1988) discusses the elements that make up the spectacle. As citizens gain greater sophistication in decoding it, they may initially become more cynical. Cynicism is fast becoming the emblem of our political culture. Nevertheless, the skill of demystifying these modern elements of political deception is a necessary precondition, along with reforming how political campaigns are funded, for bringing greater rationality to our political system. While the media are central in the creation of spectacle, it is also created in state and local political arenas, as Smith, Miller-Kahn, Heinecke, and Jarvis (2004) have demonstrated. Edelman argues that an understanding of the following elements is crucial for an analysis of current social policy formation:

1. *The importance of language and discourse.* Perhaps more than any other political scientist, Edelman (1978) focused on the relationship between language and politics and what he called "the linguistic structuring of

social problems" (p. 26). He provides a methodology for studying policy based on the notion that "how the problem is named involves alternative scenarios, each with its own facts, value judgments, and emotions" (p. 29). In chapter 3, I will provide an example of how critical discourse analysis can be used to demonstrate how ideological agendas are embedded in seemingly neutral language.

2. *The definition of events as crises.* "A crisis, like all new developments, is a creation of the language used to depict it; the appearance of a crisis is a political act, not a recognition of a fact or a rare situation" (p. 31). Crises, according to Edelman, "typically rationalize policies that are especially harmful to those who are already disadvantaged" (p. 31). Berliner and Biddle (1995) describe in great detail how a "manufactured crisis" was needed to jump-start our current school reform policies that date back at least to *The Nation at Risk* report in 1983.[2] Naomi Klein (2007) in her book, *The Shock Doctrine: The Rise of Disaster Capitalism* argues that alliances between the corporate sector and neoliberal governments use crisis and disaster to gain financial profit and undermine the public sector.

3. *A tendency to cover political interests with a discourse of rational policy analysis.* A crisis is often created through an appeal to scientific, rational, neutral discourses. For example, political advantage on the right has been gained not only through political rhetoric, but also through privately funded, ideologically driven think tanks that sponsor and disseminate so-called objective research.

4. *The linguistic evocation of enemies and the displacement of targets.* Those with the power to manage meaning can cast tenured radicals, the welfare state, social promotion, progressive teaching methods, and teachers unions as the villains of educational reform. All displace attention from other possible actors and events. Perhaps the most notable displacement of a target is laying the blame on the education sector for poor economic performance instead of on the state and the corporate sector. NCLB itself displaces these targets by calling for closing the education gap, while failing to call for closing the growing social and economic gaps. According to Apple (2006), "this is not surprising since the State is shifting the blame for the very evident inequalities in access and income it has promised to reduce, from itself on to individual schools, parents, and children. This is also part of a larger process in which dominant economic groups shift the blame for the massive and unequal effects of their own misguided decisions from themselves on to the state. The state is then faced with a very real crisis in legitimacy. Given this, we should not be at all surprised that the state will then seek to export this crisis outside itself." (p. 416)

5. *The public as political spectators.* Democratic participation is limited to such reactive rituals as voting or being polled: "…An individual vote is more nearly a form of self-expression and of legitimation than of influ-

ence..." (p. 97). For instance, in Argentina, where voting is compulsory, a large percentage of voters in 2002, disgusted with the lack of real political options, turned in blank votes as a way to demonstrate their disgust with both candidates and their refusal to participate in the political spectacle.

6. *The media as mediators of the political spectacle.* Edelman gave news reporting and other forms of media a central place in the construction of the political spectacle. Debord's (1995) "society of the spectacle" explored the influence of the media on social life more generally. As with the example above of the Houston School district scandal, by the time a news story is debunked, it has already had its political effect.

All of the elements of Edelman's description of the construction of a political spectacle are present in current school reform efforts. Although I will return to these elements throughout the book, a few examples should suffice here to illustrate some of the ways in which the current school reform spectacle is being constructed:

1. A crisis is constructed whereby the nation is defined as economically "at-risk" and blame is displaced from the corporate sector onto schools. *A Nation at Risk* (National Commission on Excellence in Education, 1983) reported, "If an unfriendly foreign power had attempted to impose on America the mediocre educational performance that exists today, we might well have viewed it as an act of war" (p. 5).[3] Think tanks release so-called commissioned reports with titles like *Tough Choices or Tough Times,* or *Rising Above the Gathering Storm* that use crisis language to scapegoat our educational system.

2. Language is used to create heroes and villains; for instance, by elevating "education entrepreneurs" and "parental choice" over the "educational establishment" and "educrats." Metaphors often stand in for public debate, such as when we use terms like *customer* or *consumer* of education as a way to make education into a commodity. This sleight of hand creates the internal logic for the marketization, corporatization, and commercialization of schools. In this way the social goals of schooling are shifted without public debate.

3. There is the promotion of neoliberal ideology as "objective research" produced by right-wing think tanks.

4. There is the tendency of the media to uncritically use this "research" in their reporting on education.

5. Finally, the move to replace genuine political participation with choice in an educational marketplace reduces the public to being spectators of politics instead of participants, and passive consumers instead of active citizens.

There are many other signs of an erosion of authenticity in American society that are less directly related to media spectacle. In baseball, Barry Bonds, Sammy

Sosa, and Mark McGuire blasted more home runs than legendary hitters like Babe Ruth, Roger Maris, and Hank Aaron, not merely through hard work or talent, but allegedly through the aid of muscles bulked up by illegal steroids. Disney movie sets used to imitate towns; now towns, like the town of Celebration in Florida, imitate Disney movie sets. Movies like *The Truman Show* spoof a social world increasingly saturated by phoniness and round-the-clock media, in which television "reality" shows appeal to a craving for some semblance of authentic life even if it isn't one's own. Meanwhile, private shopping malls have replaced the public square where shopping wasn't the only thing that brought citizens together.

Schools have not escaped these tendencies as, increasingly administrators are pressured to engage in impression management and teachers feel pressured to teach to standardized tests and use scripted curricula they have had no hand in developing. These tests and curricula are mandated by distant noneducators and produced and marketed by multinational corporations. In schools, as in the rest of society, it is increasingly difficult to figure out what is real and what is simulated, what is real debate and what is political spectacle, what is real experience and what is a "reality show."

So while we tend to think of authenticity as something that occurs between individuals or groups, societies can also become inauthentic. And when this happens, it has a ripple effect at other levels. Given the extent to which social policies of the last 40 years have led to vast social inequalities, how can Americans believe the equity discourse of Leave No Child Behind? Politicians who have shifted welfare from single mothers and their children to wealthy corporations have little credibility in claiming that they care about children left behind (Abramowitz, 2001). To the extent that authenticity is lacking at the societal level, it is less likely that it will be achieved at the organizational and individual levels.

AUTHENTICITY AT THE ORGANIZATIONAL LEVEL

Much new policy language contrasts old bureaucracy with new entrepreneurial approaches that claim to have flattened hierarchies and debureaucratized organizations. We still tend to blame bureaucracy for inauthenicity, and the critique of bureaucracy is embedded today in coded language like the term *educrats*. As discussed in chapter 1, one of the sources of this critique was Max Webber's distinction between instrumental and substantive rationality. Max Webber focused heavily on the threat that the instrumental rationality of bureaucracies represented for an authentic society. In such organizations, people tend to be means to ends, rather than ends in themselves. Human relations theories tend to call for treating people well and including them in decisions, not so much because this is the way people should be treated, but rather, because "empowered" employees tend to be more productive. Organizational theorists also warn of goal displacement, in which the real goals of an organization—in schools, educating children—often get displaced by more self-serving goals of organizational members or clients. This is why schools must repeat the mantra that "at our school, kids come first," since in many schools they clearly don't.

Webber sought more substantive forms of rationality in which people were ends in themselves and in which social ends took precedent over individual goals. Newer "network" organizations have changed in form, but as we will see, they continue to operate on the basis of instrumental rationality, a tendency exacerbated in public organizations as they increasingly operate in a marketized environment.

While new business models attempt to manage through network organization, rather than through bureaucratic hierarchies, there is some evidence that this has intensified instrumental rationality, not reduced it. These new flexible organizations are part of a growing neoliberal business model to which some social theorists attribute a growing inauthenticity in organizations (Sennett, 1998). They have developed to respond to markets, not to meet the human needs of those who work in them.

A central thesis of this book is that neoliberal economic shifts at the global and national levels of the last 40 years are creating significant social and cultural shifts at all levels of society, leading to greater levels of inauthenticity. Because of the ways we have thought about authenticity in the past—either limited to more authentic forms of instruction and assessment or more authentic relationships within organizations—new forms of inauthenticity can easily escape our attention. If the cost of getting rid of the ills of bureaucracy is the loss of a democratic public sphere, then the cost may be too high. Only by deepening our critique to include these new forms of inauthenticity can educators effectively contest the current dominance of neoliberal, market ideology in education.

As market relations become dominant in all aspects of our lives, it becomes increasingly difficult to think beyond individual competition toward any sense of a common good. While most people think of neoliberalism as a purely economic model, it has important social and cultural consequences that we are only beginning to understand. Richard Sennett (2006) provides perhaps the most eloquent account of the ways that shifts in political economy have resulted in cultural shifts in our workplaces and in the ways we live our lives. Since the corporate workplace is increasingly the model for schools, Sennett's work has important implications for 21st century school leaders. In his qualitative study of several corporations, Sennett has identified characteristics of work in what he calls the new capitalism. I will provide a condensed version of his argument here.

Sennett (2006) traces the recent phenomenon of globalization back to the breakdown in 1973 of the Bretton Woods controls over the global circulation of money. After Bretton Woods, there were large amounts of new capital seeking short-term investments. Later, stock prices began to replace profit as a goal for many businesses. Money was made, not by owning and producing, but by trading, and later speculation. This new speculative and flexible approach to capital has changed work life and institutional structures, particularly in sectors of capitalism such as finance, insurance, real estate, media, communications, and high technology, where short-term exchange replaces long-term relationships. In order to fit into this new "fast" capitalism, workers have to give up notions of stability of employment and become flexible, mobile workers in a constantly changing global economy.

Furthermore, workers become disposable as capital continuously seeks to cut labor costs though automation and outsourcing. A neoliberal management book, the best selling *Who Moved the Cheese?* used a childlike allegory about mice who embrace change to prepare the ideological terrain for the new entrepreneurial worker. The lesson is that it is better to see losing one's job as an opportunity for some better entrepreneurial opportunity that surely lies around the corner. The new entrepreneurial culture that is promoted in all sectors of society prepares employees for this new world of unstable employment in the new "risk" society. Along with this new instability of work comes intensification of work leading to longer work hours and greater levels of stress and anxiety.

However, Sennett (1998) argues that such trends are actually counterproductive for business, since the cost to business of the resulting short-term employment is that it reduces employee loyalty and organizational memory. Moreover, with shorter contracts, work in teams, and a highly competitive internal work environment, authentic relationships are less likely to form because of short timelines. This continual employee turnover and the tendency to use temporary workers and outside consultants weaken institutional knowledge. He argues that these new tendencies are good for the bottom line and stock prices, but are not good for the long-term health of businesses, national productivity, or the building of relationships and personal character. In fact, he titled one book in his trilogy, *The Corrosion of Character: The Personal Consequences of Work in the New Capitalism* (1998).

The creation of authentic human ties cannot easily occur in transient workplaces and communities. As principals in schools are moved from school to school and teacher turnover, especially in urban districts grows, a similar phenomenon occurs in education. Flexible organizations in a choice environment means teachers, administrators, and students will be more mobile, leading to less stability and a weakening of organizational learning. New, younger teachers may tolerate increased intensification and standardization of work, but many experienced teachers with families and a strong professional culture are tending to change careers or retire early. The very notion of teaching or administration as a lifelong career is becoming a thing of the past. In the long run, this will have devastating effects on the quality of schooling.

Sennett (2006) also identifies other personal deficits associated with this new neoliberal culture. The first is the demise of the work ethic. Only a fool would delay gratification in the new flexible workplace. Employees report feeling a sense of personal betrayal as companies trade loyalty to workers for short-term profits. Second, this loss of long-term employment with its associated benefits and pensions makes it more difficult for newer generations of employees to create life narratives. While much welfare state employment was not exciting, it provided people with a life narrative in which they could pay a mortgage over 30 years, look forward to a pension and Social Security, and plan for vacations. There is an absence of any way to think strategically about one's life, one's sense of purpose, future goals, and economic security.

In flattened hierarchies or network organizations, pyramidal hierarchy is replaced by a horizontal elite core and a mass periphery with minimal mediation and communication between the two. It represents a new concentration of power without centralization of authority. According to Sennett (1998), "this absence of authority frees those in control to shift, adapt, reorganize without having to justify themselves or their acts. In other words, it permits the freedom of the moment, a focus just on the present. Change is the responsible agent; change is not a person" (p. 115).

Internal units are created to compete with each other for contracts. Outside consultants are brought in to do the dirty work that management used to do. Senior management can claim it is taking its cue from the expert consultants who come in and leave quickly. In this impersonal environment, no relationships are built because no one has to take responsibility for decisions. Upper management with its stronger networks moves more often as new opportunities arise. Personnel records take the place of humans who are being standardized so "performance" can be compared (just as high-stakes testing in education allows students, teachers, and schools to be compared as a prerequisite for a marketized system). Flexibility to adjust to changes in the market is gained. This is perhaps good news for stockholders seeking short term profits, upper level executives, and consultancy firms, but it isn't clear who else benefits, or what it contributes to the common good. It also, according to Sennett, makes long term, authentic relationships less likely.

This new model is being intentionally implemented in school districts across the country. Today in New York City, a corporate model is taking shape. Upper level public administrators are contracting out to private companies or taking private sector positions in the burgeoning education services industry. Public–private partnerships are the vehicle for this shift in work culture. This restructuring of the institutional environment will dramatically change the work culture of schools. Whether this will make schools more authentic places for children and teachers remains to be seen. If Sennett's analysis of the new corporate culture is any indication, we can expect to see less employee loyalty, more work stress, and a new performance culture.

Accountability and the New Performance Culture

I'm all for school improvement, using research-based methodology, and analyzing test data, [but] schools are not factories. When I hear the phrase "No Child Left Behind," my staff and I cringe. For those of us from Minnesota, NCLB is a step backwards. We spend way too much time testing, doing paperwork, and trying to figure out what we are supposed to do. It has created more work for secretaries, business managers, paraprofessionals, teachers, and administrators. I'm talking hours. I spend more time with data and accountability; yet have to pull from my family to do it. The only way to keep up is to work longer and longer. If this would lead to higher achievement, it may be worthwhile. However, we need to have time working with instructional aspects too. We simply don't have time to hold teachers accountable for instruction. (Abernathy, 2007; participant in Abernathy's study of the impact of NCLB on school leadership in Minnesota)

It is ironic that a system designed to pressure schools to improve instruction has, in fact, diverted administrator time away from interacting with teachers and students. The problem is not limited to diverting time from instruction or time with families; NCLB's accountability system has created an audit culture in schools with a vast array of perverse incentives. School practitioners have devised forms of "creative compliance" with an accountability system that distorts authentic teaching and learning. Their creative compliance—now well known to most educators and researchers—involves what Elliott (2002) calls "the cynical production of auditable performances" (p. 202) such as teaching to the test, manipulating student dropout rates, recruiting "low-maintenance" students, focusing attention on the "bubble" students who are near the cut-off level, and many more. Such behaviors are clearly inauthentic and, in most cases, unethical, but they are predictable based on historical evidence.

Welch (1998) documents parallels between today's reforms and business-led reforms of the 19th and early 20th century when forms of efficiency were imposed on schooling through the imposition of a business ethos. In his analysis of the British Revised Code of 1860 whose centerpiece was "payment by results," he documents the audit culture of the time, which, like today, resulted in creative compliance. According to Welch,

> …teachers "stuffed and almost roasted" their pupils on test items once the teachers knew that the visit of the inspector was imminent. Other teachers secretly trained their pupils so that when they were asked questions they raised their right hands if they knew the correct answer but their left if they did not, thus creating a more favourable impression upon the visiting inspector. (p. 161)

Nearly 150 years later, such pressures are having a similar effect. The following is from the *Columbus Dispatch* in Columbus, Ohio, but newspapers across the country are full of similar stories.

> Answer sheets and test booklets arrive at districts in securely taped boxes, shipped by FedEx or UPS. Packets are shrink-wrapped and are supposed to be stored in a locked room until test time. But in some districts, teachers got access last school year. Some made copies. Others shared the ques-

tions with students ahead of time, or gave answers during the test. And a few devised nonverbal signals to cue children that their answers were incomplete. For all the lock-and-key procedures and explicit rules, more teachers cheated on Ohio standardized tests than ever before. (Smith Richards, 2006, p. 4)

Using data from the Chicago Public Schools, Jacob and Levitt (2002) have demonstrated that serious cases of teacher or administrator cheating on standardized tests occur in 4 to 5% of elementary school classrooms annually, and that frequency of cheating responds to relatively minor changes in incentives. They suggest that without appropriate safeguards, widespread cheating can be predicted to accompany high-stakes testing.

Audit cultures not only result in inauthentic practices, they are incapable of achieving real instructional improvement, much less stem the tide of growing class and racial inequalities. What makes No Child Left Behind more insidious than the British Revised Code, is that in 1860, teachers only had to perform for the intermittent arrival of state inspectors. In the past teachers could close the classroom door and ignore or modify reforms that failed to understand their local context, and administrators had considerable autonomy. The life world of schools was often buffered from the constant demands of reforms that came and went. In the new context of high-stakes testing, instructional coaches, administrative "walk throughs," and school report cards published in local papers, surveillance of teachers is constant and decisions about instruction and testing are made over the heads of principals and superintendents. In an era in which zero tolerance policies are popular, laying out unrealistic goals for students' annual yearly progress makes many politicians, goaded on by their business partners, score points by appearing to get tough with "failing" public schools, and presenting themselves as advocates for the poor. But this constant demand for forms of accountability that are unrealistic and fail to reflect the nature of authentic teaching and learning have left many educators demoralized and cynical.

Outcomes-based education has created a culture of accountability based on performance indicators. As Ball (2001) points out, a culture of accountability becomes a performance culture. The need to be constantly accountable increases our visibility and requires that we align our performances with external accountability criteria. Ball calls this ongoing requirement to perform for others, *fabrication*, and argues that a culture of performativity creates a need for fabricating performances.

Ironically, a performance culture often lessens efficiency rather than increases it. As anyone who has been involved in an elaborate external evaluation can attest, the generation of performance information, rituals like interviews and exhibit room documents, and coding of lesson plans diverts energy from the core pursuits of the organization, like teaching and spending time with students. Likewise a testing culture in schools often decreases rather than increases the amount of authentic (i.e., nonscripted) learning that takes place in classrooms. Of equal importance for Ball (2001), is the impact that a performance culture has on the possibility of authentic institutions and an authentic self. The reduction of persons to "databases" and the constant effort devoted to fabrication empties institutions of authentic practices and relationships. Management becomes,

> ubiquitous, invisible, inescapable—part of, embedded in everything we do. We choose and judge our actions and they are judged by others on the basis of their contribution to organizational performance. And in all this the demands of performativity dramatically close down the possibilities for metaphysical discourses, for relating practice to philosophical principles like social justice and equity. (Ball, 2001, p. 216)

By setting up a relationship in which teachers and administrators are viewed as the sources of poor student achievement, their position as subordinates in an overtly punitive system is intensified. Scott's (1990) descriptions of the public and hidden transcripts that are generated whenever unequal relations of power exist, is helpful in illustrating how mandated performativity impacts teachers and administrators. The public transcript refers to the tendency of both groups to act out behaviors and attitudes expected of them and which often purposely misrepresent their true feelings or intentions. According to Scott,

> ...the public performance of the subordinate will, out of prudence, fear, and the desire to curry favor, be shaped to appeal to the expectation of the powerful. I shall use the term public transcript as a shorthand way of describing the open interaction between subordinates and those who dominate. (Scott, 1990, p. 2)

In other words, social interactions become public performances, and the public transcript fixes the parameters of exchanges between the powerful and the powerless, making authentic communication less likely.

Such performances, according to Scott, also took a psychic toll, and many members of subordinate groups, such as peasants or slaves paid with their lives when they could no longer sustain the performance. While recognizing that teachers are hardly in a situation comparable to slaves, something similar happens to teachers when fabrication invades their professional culture. We are seeing an increase in early retirements and workplace stress among some teachers and a comparable sense of emotional stress among students who are also subjected to a testing regimen that requires more performativity in the classroom than authentic teaching and learning. Reports of students crying and vomiting around test time are common in schools throughout the country. As teachers and administrators make calculations about how to allocate time in order to feed an audit culture, the quality of relationships with students is often neglected, which results in a "hollowing out" of schools.

The Hollow School

The new managerial school, in which administrators become accountants in an audit culture, is being hollowed out of anything belonging to the noncognitive realm. It is, in Cummins's (1986) term *subtractive* rather than *additive*. An example might help here. New York City requires that schools have inquiry teams, which appears to be a great idea. A student of mine who is a high school teacher in a low-income school described to me her experience with her school's inquiry team.

The teachers were alarmed at how many African-American males were dropping out during or after their freshman year. The teachers in the inquiry group decided to interview and shadow a group of 15 9th grade African-American males to better understand in some holistic way what was causing these boys to abandon school. However, in this era of academic coaches, the inquiry group "coach" from downtown, told them that that was not exactly what inquiry groups were supposed to do. They were supposed to base decisions on "data" and data meant mainly test scores. So if the ninth grade students were the focus of their inquiry, the teachers were encouraged to look more closely at the scores of the ninth grade students to see which skills they had and hadn't been taught, and to focus on those skill areas that needed remediation. So the socioemotional life of these students was rendered irrelevant, and the intersection of their lives in and out of schools was ignored. The solution was to be found solely in doing more of what apparently was not working.

Now, this is just one anecdote and maybe an extreme one, since the New York City Department of Education claims that inquiry groups have greater autonomy over the focus and methods of their inquiry than what I have described. One could also reasonably argue that perhaps these students' teachers were not currently paying attention to their particular academic deficits, and that a closer look at test data might help to identify some areas to work on. Furthermore the Department of Education should be commended on its attempt to foster learning communities in its schools.

And yet, as Rothstein, Jacobson, and Wilder (2008) have documented, students are increasingly being seen as one-dimensional cognitive beings who can be summed up in a set of test scores. Ironically, to interview and shadow these ninth grade students would not only unearth dimensions of their lives that schools ignore at their peril, but also would represent an intervention that could in itself keep them in school. Wexler, Crichlow, Kern, and Martusewicz (1992) view a lack of authentic student–adult relationships, especially in low-income schools, as creating a sense in students that "nobody cares." In the absence of authentic relations with adults, students are left to forge identities that are institutionally structured, rather than relationally constructed. As teaching and learning are increasingly defined as measurable cognitive learning, there is an emptying out of socioemotional connection and a neglect of important aspects of education such as the construction of social identities and social solidarities. Students come to school hoping to "become somebody" in the eyes of their peers and the adults who they look to, albeit, often reluctantly, for guidance in this endeavor. As Wexler et al. put it, "For many students, school is a disappointment of socio-emotional hope" (p. 136).

In the absence of such authentic relations, students are left to form the institutionally structured identities offered by school subcultures of jocks, rads, gothics, skaters, sluts—all of which boil down in social class terms in one way or another to "loser" or "winner." They are often provided routes to identity in schools, such as JROTC, that have dire implications for their futures. These institutional identities are supplemented by the substitute, compensatory identities supplied by the mass cultural images of the entertainment industry or branding options like Abercrombie and Fitch or American Apparel. On the surface, youth are busy, with places to go and people to see. They multitask with cell phones, laptops, and text messaging, and yet underneath all the busy relating, there is too often a lack of authentic, stable adult relationships or any sense of a stable occupational future.

Hollow schools are created when we empty schools of authentic social interaction, viewing students as a series of subskills on spreadsheets. By interviewing students, we send a message that we want to get to know them and help figure out with them what they need to stay in school and become motivated. Such interventions should not ignore the importance of instruction, but improving instruction will not help students who have dropped out or who attend class only sporadically, a common problem in low-income urban schools.

Hollow schools are also created when we replace stern but caring educators who handle discipline with police officers who are not trained to deal effectively with youth and who too often provoke "situations" that would otherwise not occur. Hollow schools are the result of teachers who are not trusted to exercise their creative professionalism and are made to feel like replaceable understudies in a scripted curriculum. In hollow schools students and teachers alike learn to game a system that is hardly more than a series of high-stakes tests that privilege middle class kids. Of course hollow schools are not a creation of our high-stakes accountability system; they have been around for a long time. But the emphasis that NCLB places on test scores and its privileging of cognitive over noncognitive learning has not proven to make schools more authentic places for students to thrive.[4]

AUTHENTICITY AND THE INDIVIDUAL

Psychologists have always been fascinated by feral children, allegedly raised by animals such as wolves. Such situations raise the question, if the child thoroughly behaves like a wolf, is she a wolf or a human? Sociocultural theorists like Lev Vygotsky, who argue that the individual and society are inseparable, might say that she is a wolf. By the same token, our sense of who we are is intimately tied up with the kinds of institutions we inhabit and the kind of society we live in. Because humans are essentially relational, we construct our identities through interactions in families, among peers, in schools, workplaces, and other organizations, in our role as citizens in a democracy and in our sense of social solidarity with various groups. Therefore, the authenticity of this social environment is important in the construction of our social selves.

The predicament of the individual in an inauthentic society is not a new complaint. Anyone who has followed major league baseball over the years knows that scandals are not new, nor is the Iraq war the first war that garnered support through deception and untruths. And yet, we live in an age in which new technologies make it easier to distort, manipulate, and spin information (while at the same time providing possibilities for grassroots resistance). These same technologies and the corporate money and culture that has grown up around them, have also created a society in which flexibility, transiency, and mobility are prized over stability and community (Sennett, 2006). The line from the old Carole King song, "Doesn't anybody stay in one place anymore," seems quaint in an age in which chat rooms, text messaging, and e-mail threaten to replace face-to-face communication—an age in which "brick and mortar" institutions are moving into cyberspace. While technology has saved millions of lives and made our daily lives more comfortable, it can also divorce people from reality. While a real war rages, many upper and middle class young people spend hours a day fighting cyber wars on computers, only vaguely aware that their mostly poor and working class peers are real soldiers, fighting a real war in Iraq and Afghanistan.

While the scope of inauthenticity in our society and institutions seems greater than ever to some, it is difficult to provide empirical evidence of such an elusive phenomenon. The search for an authentic self or "human nature" has long been a project of philosophers as distinct as Rousseau, Freud, Marx, and Kierkegaard. But we can, at least, say with some authority that authenticity has been a social theme for many during the second half of the 20th century, though sometimes for different reasons. David Riesman's *The Lonely Crowd* (Riesman, Glazer, & Denny, 1954) and William Whyte's *The Organization Man* (1956), both books published in the mid-1950s, documented a new outer-directed, organizational way of life in postwar America that was replacing tradition and personal autonomy. Existential and Marxist accounts of alienation, particularly the work of Jean-Paul Sartre, were immensely popular during the 1960s as was J. D. Salinger's *The Catcher in the Rye* (1951) and Marcuse's *One Dimensional Man* (1964). All expressed a concern with how to live an authentic life in a society becoming increasingly inauthentic.

Authenticity became a central theme of the 1960s youth movement, in which many young people criticized what they perceived to be an inauthentic and even hypocritical society that failed to live up to its espoused values. Many youth, mostly White, middle class, and suburban, pursued "authentic lifestyles" through an emphasis on being natural: less makeup for women, more informal dress, beards and long hair for men. Authenticity also meant organic farming, a reconnection to the land, and a return to breast-feeding and herbal remedies, and in many cases breaking out of perceived repression and social constraints through free love and the use of drugs. Compulsory schooling came in for special scorn from education progressives and those who sought to deschool society (Illich, 1972).

While the sons and daughters of ethnic, hyphenated Europeans were becoming "White," many African Americans, Latino/as, American Indians, and Asian Americans were attempting to seek authenticity by recapturing a largely lost ethnic and cultural past. Angela Davis's large "Afro," besides being a political symbol of Black power, became part of a quest for an authentic self. While postmodernists have critiqued the notion of authentic identities of any kind, there was a strong impulse in the counterculture movement to expose the incongruence between cherished ideals and modern realities, including historical racial, gender, and class oppressions.

The result of these political and cultural movements was that many individuals could lead more authentic lives. Spanish speakers were no longer punished for speaking the language of their parents. Gays and lesbians could more easily show affection in public. The physically disabled were able to move about more easily. Many groups have achieved greater authenticity through social struggle. But as we have seen with movements like labor, the gains can be rolled back if citizens become complacent and fail to protect those public and democratic spaces in which political redress can be obtained. The defense of public schools is not so much a defense of public schools as they currently exist, as much as it is a defense of a public though imperfect social space that is fast being eroded.

Erosions of authentic democracy and community life are well documented by communitarians (Barber, 1984; Bellah, Madson, Sullivan, Swidler, & Tipton, 1985; Putnam, 2000) and philosophers (West, 2005). Movements for greater authenticity in education have occurred throughout the 20th century. Perhaps the most important was led by John Dewey's call for experience-based, child-centered education that taught children to live in an *authentic* democracy, which he contrasted with *formal* democracy with its emphasis on voting. He wanted schools to create citizens that infused the notion of democratic participation into our everyday activities. While Dewey's progressive education became popular during the counterculture movement of the 1960s, it was never as prevalent in public school classrooms as some believed (Goodlad, 1970).

But Dewey's (1929) call for authenticity transcended the classroom and the school. Writing in the late 1920s, a period much like our own, with large disparities of wealth and the dominance of a business culture, he warned that schools were leaving young people ill-prepared to encounter a utilitarian, business culture. He used the term *infantilism* to describe the basic, depoliticized education of Americans as compared to European school systems of the time.

> ...Such an education is at best extremely one-sided; it operates to create the specialized "business mind" and this, in turn, is manifested in leisure as well as in business itself. The one-sidedness is accentuated because of the tragic irrelevancy of prior schooling to the controlling realities of

social life. There is little preparation to induce either hearty resistance, discriminating criticism, or the vision or desire to direct economic forces in new channels. (p. 41)

Many scholars on the political right, left, and center, armed with empirical research, battle each other over how to close the achievement gap, without ever stopping to ask what it is rich and poor, Black and White students are actually learning. While closing the achievement gap is important as an equity issue, the test scores that are fought over represent a largely inauthentic education devoid of controversy, as testing and scripted curricula banish the last remnants of experiential learning and critical thought from the classroom.

Of course, public schools have never done a good job of engaging students in experiential learning or fomenting critical thought. While it is easy to defend public schooling as a hypothetical public space in which to construct well educated individuals to be advocates for democracy, it is much more difficult to defend actual existing public schools, especially in low-income, urban settings. This failure of our public schools to serve all children adequately has led many to embrace notions of individual choice in a marketplace and a retreat from civic engagement. For instance, as conditions for the poor under neoliberal policies continue to deteriorate, some groups, like the Black Alliance for Education Options (BAEO), have turned to market solutions like vouchers. This is an authentic response to the abandonment of many American low-income schools and neighborhoods, and needs to be addressed.

The aftermath of Hurricane Katrina is only the most dramatic case of the abandonment of millions of African Americans in our urban centers and inner ring suburbs. Being based on the lived experience of millions of people abandoned by our economic and educational system, I can hardly challenge the sense of desperation and hopelessness that leads to an "any port in a storm" view of vouchers. As a parent under such circumstances, I can imagine opting out of my local public school if given a voucher to a private school. After all, as Howard Fuller (1997) and others have pointed out, White and Black middle class parents already have these options, and many, including many political progressives, don't hesitate to exercise them. Abandoning the foundering ship of public schooling in inner-city neighborhoods seems like a survival impulse, one that has been fine-tuned through the historical vicissitudes of being African American in the United States. Furthermore as Pedroni (2007) has argued, there is evidence that African-American support of vouchers may represent, not so much a defection to the political right, as a risky strategy to wield political muscle. In fact, African-American activists in Milwaukee spent 10 years politically engaging the public schools, before deciding to shift their strategy to support of vouchers.

As Stullberg (2008) documents, the ebb and flow of integration and separatist movements within the African-American community is a historical phenomenon based on calculations of how authentic is the desire of White America to truly live out American principals of inclusion and quality. As recently as 2008 a major controversy erupted in Waller County, Texas over segregated cemeteries. If interracial burying is controversial today in Texas, then African Americans can be excused for being cynical about the provision of quality public schools for their children.

Even as we have deconstructed race biologically, it continues to be engrained in the American psyche. Immigrant groups in the United States of all shades have strategically defined themselves as not Black in an attempt to avoid the stigma of race in the U.S. context. Even many Black Latinos, West Indians, and Africans have been careful to distinguish themselves from African Americans. As the competition state further discourages solidarity and promotes the maximization of one's individual advantage, the idea of human solidarity or a common good becomes a more distant utopia. It is understandable that some will give up political struggle as futile and opt for individual solutions. Voucher and charter schools, as long as they are means tested, nonprofit, and of high quality, can be accommodated within a vibrant public sector. However, any wholesale elimination of a public space in which political activity can take place may foreclose the very notion of collective struggle in the future.

Once we have destroyed those public spaces where citizenship instead of consumerism dwells, what will we replace them with? What is, after all, a theory of democracy that would replace a public sphere? The private sector is just that: private. On private property we lose many of our rights of citizenship. Private institutions are under no obligation to open their books to the public, no matter how much the private sector preaches transparency. It is ironic that a private sector that wants schools to be more tightly regulated is itself becoming more deregulated. As markets become the new discipline for the public sector, not only do they distort the essence of what schooling is about, they become a poor substitute for the kinds of transparency that a sovereign people should demand from institutions that belong to them.

While public schools in low-income communities desperately need reform, they also represent a public space that belongs to the community. Many children's parents and grandparents went to local public schools, and there is often a strong sense of belonging, in spite of overcrowded classrooms and teachers and administrators who too often are out of touch with local communities. As large high schools in New York City are broken up into small schools with new names, many communities have insisted that the campus retain the name that it is known by locally even if the schools within have new names.

There is no evidence that schools in low-income communities will learn to be more responsive through punitive reforms like high stakes testing and threats of closure, much less by being run by a private corporations. In fact, they could become worse. Like public transportation in many American cities, which is underfunded and only used by the poor, our public school system could become a series of even more poorly funded institutions to warehouse surplus populations.

As I will argue in more detail in the next chapter, schools in low-income communities improve as local communities gain resources through more equitable social policies and through the development of local community leaders who can hold their schools accountable. As Parker and Margonis (1996) have documented, school choice policies are a poor antidote to policies of racial containment that have left inner cities without jobs and social infrastructure. Trading in a public space for a privatized one or one that imposes a system of testing that classifies most low-income schools and children as failures, is a trade-off that many educators and community leaders are not willing to accept.

Some social commentators argue that we are experiencing a period of "antipolitics" in which our society is fast becoming depoliticized (Plank & Boyd, 1994). As many communitarians and researchers of civic engagement have pointed out, when people lack opportunities to participate in civic life, the result is political atrophy. According to Boggs (2000), a depoliticized public has five broad features in common:

> An unmistakable retreat from the political realm; a decline in the trappings of citizenship and with it the values of democratic participation; a narrowing of public discourse and the erosion of independent centers of thinking; a lessened capacity to achieve social change by means of statecraft or social governance; and the eventual absence of a societal understanding of what is uniquely common and public, what constitutes a possible general interest amidst the fierce interplay of competing private and local claims. (p. 22)

Defending public schools and insisting on retaining distinctions between the public and private has much higher stakes than many realize. The marketization and privatization of the public sphere is not a harmless reform that toys with incentive structures and retools notions of accountability; it represents a new and dangerous concentration of power and is a radical departure from the founding ideals of our nation.

Conclusion

Advocating for authentic school reform will require rethinking superficially appealing, but ultimately inauthentic approaches to reform. These include attempts to socially engineer schools through externally imposed high-stakes accountability systems, as well as approaches that attempt to commodify schooling by replacing political citizenship with individual choice within real or quasi markets. Table 2.1 provides a list of the various characteristics of authenticity that this chapter has discussed.

First, the notion of *congruence* is often used in leadership preparation to refer to the extent to which a leader's theories of action guiding their espoused theories and theories-in-use are congruent (Argyris & Schon, 1974). While this addresses the internal consistency of a leader's beliefs and practices, leaders also have to achieve congruence between their fundamental beliefs and those they are expected to project in order to legitimate the school to its institutional environment. In such instances advocacy leaders have to carefully gauge what level of political risk-taking they are comfortable with. Congruence at the individual level becomes more unlikely as a society strays further from its cherished ideals of democracy and equity.

Second, Dewey's writings on experience and education, Gonzalez, Moll, and Amanti's (2005) research on community funds of knowledge, and accounts of community organizing, all promote the notion that education should be *experience/community-based*. The idea that education should engage students through connection to their lived experiences is central to the notion of authentic teaching, leading, and assessment. Third, society systematically excludes on the basis of income, race, gender, sexual orientation, disability, and other characteristics. Because schools tend to both reflect society and influence it, authentic schools are those that insist on *inclusive* practices throughout the schools (Frattura & Capper, 2007; Ryan, 2006).

Fourth, all social practices within society are *nested* within other social practices. The closing of a hospital, the recruitment of a low-income student by a military recruiter, a child who reads four grades below grade level, are never merely local phenomena. To view them as such is to engage in inauthentic practice. This is a key flaw of NCLB because it wants us to believe that we can raise all students to the same educational level without addressing the very social policies that create such an "unlevel playing field." Such events are located within concentric circles of segregated communities, regressive tax codes, illegal wars, lack of universal health care, and global capital flows. While policies of inclusion within schools can help to mitigate these events and model another reality, authentic leadership is leadership that includes advocacy for changing those policies that produce them.

Fifth, it matters whether we trade in our identities as citizens for identities as consumers. It matters, first because in a marketplace those with more capital will always fare better. But it also matters because we *construct authentic social selves* within our institutions and as we engage with our neighbors over what kinds of institutions we want for ourselves and our children; without this civic engagement, we become increasingly commodified as each of us makes our individual choices, leading to greater social stratification and segregation. And finally, inauthentic and unrealistic policies encourage multiple forms of fabrication and dishonesty that threatens the integrity of educators.

While most agree that American society has become more corporate-dominated, more market-oriented, and more privatized, there is little analysis of these trends among scholars of education and even less work that links these trends to current policies and practices. The following chapter provides some history of how corporate power has grown over the years, and how it has increased its influence on American education.

3

The New Economy of Schooling

For every complex problem there is a simple solution—and it is wrong.

H. L. Menken

In 2003, New York Mayor Michael Bloomberg, a wealthy businessman, moved the Department of Education from Brooklyn to Tweed Hall in Manhattan, where his new Chancellor, Joel Klein, also a noneducator, created all the trappings of the new business model. Rather than bureaucrats in cubicles and offices in the old Board of Education at 110 Livingston Street (which Bloomberg referred to as "the Kremlin"), Tweed Hall had adopted a transparent look with entrepreneurial young noneducators sitting around conference tables in large domed halls. This performance of openness and accessibility lacks authenticity if you consider the school system was gutted of community participation and budget oversight. Diane Ravitch, whose main ire against Bloomberg and Klein was their choice of a balanced literacy program instead of a phonics program, takes them to task for their antidemocratic approach to reform. According to Ravitch (2005),

> In the reorganization, the central Board of Education was replaced by a powerless panel that serves at the pleasure of the mayor. Without an independent lay board, the Department of Education is free to allocate its budget without public oversight or transparency. Previously, no-bid contracts were rare, seldom amounting to more than $1 million per year, and were reviewed in public meetings. In the past two years, the Department of Education has awarded over 100 no-bid contracts for over $100 million with no public review. (p. 15)

Even the "powerless panel" snubbed the mayor and chancellor by boycotting their lobbying trip to Albany, accompanying the union instead (Herszenhorn, 2006).

Typical among the new 20- and 30-something MBAs and entrepreneurs Klein brought to Tweed was Jeremy Lack, 27, a Cornell and Oxford-educated son of a state senator, who headed up the department that handled enrollment. Before coming to Tweed, Mr. Lack and several other Klein hires worked with McKinsey, a high profile management-consulting firm. In classic business lingo, he acknowledged his lack, and that of many of his colleagues at Tweed, of any experience in education,

> "One of the things we are not is a content expert. Our skill set would be to talk to many different people, aggregate many different thoughts, do some sort of cost-benefit analysis, tee up for decision-making. It's part of the crucial process of how a decision is made." (quoted in Herszenhorn, 2004, p. 25)

While it would be a cheap shot to pick out a unique example of business babble, the above quote is by no means unique. I have attended many New York Department of Education events and the language of business has all but eclipsed any talk of education. At a panel I attended recently, a young superintendent with no educational experience appeared to be doing a *Saturday Night Live* valley girl impression. "Like, I am so psyched by this new book I just bought—I can't tell you how awesome it is. It's called *Execution* and it takes you through how to execute projects, how to become a doer not just a thinker. We have too many thinkers who can't do anything." Such a "can do" attitude, what in New York is better known as chutzpah, is also handsomely paid, as most of these young MBAs make salaries unheard of in education circles.

While it may be fun to parody the young noneducators who are turning the New York City school district into a marketplace, there is no denying that the frenzied activity at Tweed Hall has been a serious attempt to corporatize, marketize, and privatize a system that was infamous for its bureaucratic lethargy. Many applaud the notion that the system needs new blood and more school-level flexibility and autonomy. Although most became badly distorted over time, the New York City reform incorporated some potentially progressive practices, including small high schools, a balanced literacy program, school inspections, leadership and inquiry teams, parent coordinators, and report cards that include data that measure student improvement.

I begin this chapter with a brief and somewhat satirical description of the New York City reform because, while not the first, it is perhaps the most extreme attempt to corporatize, privatize, and marketize a school system in the United States (Scott & DiMartino, in press). Bloomberg and Klein, in true "third way" form, have taken a series of conservative and progressive reforms and merged them into a hybrid, neoliberal reform. First, the progressive side; Klein appointed as his vice chancellor, Michelle Cahill, a former community organizer. He also implemented a reading series inspired by Lucy Caulkins, a Columbia Teachers College professor, who promoted a balanced literacy approach.[1] Small schools have been created in large high school buildings throughout the system.

On the neoliberal side, Klein has brashly aped the private sector, by creating a special Market page on the DOE website. Appropriating the progressive discourse of "empowerment," the marketization of the system has become almost complete.

Empowerment schools will have access to a new "market" comprised of buyers (Empowerment schools) and sellers (vendors both internal and external to the Department of Education). (New York City Department of Education, 2007, p. 1)

A new Department of Education Market Maker office helps match schools with vendors. While the notion that schools purchase things like textbooks and services from vendors is not new, Klein has fetishized and expanded the notion of choice, markets, and competition.

But, Klein is not the first noneducator to run a district like a business. UCLA business professor William Ouchi (2004) has described three districts in which he believes a business model has proven successful. Ouchi has advised several education leaders, including Richard Riordan, both when he was mayor of Los Angeles, and later as Secretary of Education under Governor Arnold Schwarzenegger. In an article in *The School Administrator*, a publication widely read by superintendents, he recommends seven keys to success for district leadership:

> Every principal is an entrepreneur.
> Every school controls its own budget.
> Everyone is accountable for student performance and for budget.
> Everyone delegates authority to those below.
> There is a burning focus on student achievement.
> Every school is a community of learners.
> Families have real choices among a variety of unique schools. (p. 21)

These seven keys have become a kind of mantra for district leaders adopting a business model. Foundation money provided by businessmen like Eli Broad has financed professional development retreats where for years superintendents have been drilled on these principles.

Remarkably, one of the three school districts touted by Ouchi was Houston, Texas. Rod Paige, the Secretary of Education brought to Washington by George W. Bush, was the former superintendent of the Houston Independent School district from 1994 to 2001. The district had been promoted as a jewel in the crown of the "Texas miracle" (the assumption that test scores in Texas improved due to a high-stakes standardized testing program) in school reform circles. In 2002 it won a $1 million prize as best urban school district in the country from the Broad Foundation. During the 2000 to 2001 school year, Houston schools reported that only 1.5% of its students dropped out. While any savvy administrator would have been skeptical, this data, combined with the conservative Broad Foundation's award, attracted much positive media attention. The success of Page's former district was put forth by some as proof that the Texas Accountability system was an excellent model for the nation.

Then on July 11, 2003, a front page *New York Times* article reported that "the results of a state audit found that more than half of the 5,500 students who left their schools in the 2000–2001 school year should have been declared dropouts but were not" (Schemo, 2003, p. A1). The audit recommended lowering the ranking of 14 of the 16 audited schools from the best to the worst.

Another exemplary district that Ouchi selected was Seattle, Washington, which had appointed U.S. Army General John Sanford as superintendent, followed by investment banker Joseph Olchefske, who had been Sanford's chief financial officer. Howard and Preisman (2007) analyze fiscal and testing data from the district at the end of their terms and conclude that their performance was lackluster, leaving the district deep in debt and producing test scores lower than the rest of the state.

While business influence in education is hardly new, dating back to the mid-19th century (Callahan, 1962; Welch, 1998) the current effort to privatize public schools is unique. While still not widespread, Howard and Preisman (2007) document entire school districts that have been turned over to for-profit corporations.

While the education sector has perhaps held the line to a greater extent than some other social sectors, we have much to learn from privatization in areas like public health and national security. For instance, unknown to most Americans, the current administration has contracted out virtually every function they can, including a massive mercenary force in Iraq (Singer, 2003). In 2001 Donald Rumsfeld, as the new defense secretary under George W. Bush, addressed the former corporate CEOs from Enron, Northrop Grumman, Aerospace Corporation, and General Dynamic, who he had appointed his top deputies at the department of defense. In a pre-9/11 talk to them he issued a declaration of war,

> The topic today is an adversary that poses a threat, a serious threat, to the security of the United States. This adversary is one of the world's last bastions of central planning. It governs by dictating five-year plans. From a single capital, it attempts to impose its demands across time zones, continents, oceans, and beyond. With brutal consistency, it stifles free thought and crushes new ideas. It disrupts the defense of the United States and places the lives of men and women in uniform at risk…. Perhaps this adversary sounds like the former Soviet Union, but that enemy is gone: our foes are more subtle and implacable today. You may think I'm describing one of the last decrepit dictators of the world. But their day, too, is almost past, and they cannot match the strength and size of this adversary. The adversary's closer to home. It's the Pentagon bureaucracy. (quoted in Scahill, 2007, p. xiv)

This adversary that is worse than the Soviet Union and brutal dictators is none other than American social institutions that have not yet received the alleged benefits of privatization.[2]

Contracting public services to the private sector—a cornerstone of Bloomberg and Klein's education reforms—goes well beyond contracts for a mercenary army such as Blackwater (Scahill, 2007). As a front-page article in the *New York Times*, stated, "Without a public debate or formal policy decision, contractors have become a virtual fourth branch of government " (Shane & Nixon, 2007, p. 1). In an age of obsessive accountability in the public sector, these contractors are largely unaccountable to the public.

Issues of fraud and waste make headlines, but their unaccountability has other implications. (1) There is a lack of competiveness for contracts. In 2007, only 48% were competitive contracts, down from 79% in 2001. (2) Although, government regulations forbid inherently government work from being contracted out, there is a dramatic increase in outsourcing of secretive and delicate jobs in intelligence gathering and budget preparation. (3) The system does not reward contractors who do the best work, but rather those most aggressive at lobbying Washington. "The top twenty service contractors have spent nearly $300 million since 2000 on lobbying and have donated $23 million to political campaigns" (Shane & Nixon, 2007, p. 26). (4) Because contracted companies do not have to open their books, there is less public scrutiny. Corporations, unlike government agencies, are not subject to the Freedom of Information Act.

My cautions about rampant privatization of the federal government may seem overly alarmist. After all, the federal government plays a relatively small role in education. Furthermore, the intermediary organizations partnering with schools in New York City are largely nonprofits, and as Minow (2002) compellingly argues, there are legitimate areas in which the private sector can bring greater dynamism to the public sector. Nevertheless, there is plenty of evidence that the corporate sector has its eye on potential profits to be made in the education sector. According to Education Industry Association's website,

> Education is rapidly becoming a $1 trillion industry; representing 10% of America's GNP and second in size only to the health care industry. Federal and State expenditures on education exceed $750 billion. Education companies, with over $80 billion in annual revenues, already constitute a large sector in the education arena. (p. 1)

This pressure for profits, along with references by Bloomberg to the New York City Board of Education as the Kremlin, bears an eerie resemblance to Rumsfeld's speech equating the Pentagon to the Soviet Union. As Lakoff (2008) points out, the political right masterfully uses language to promote their ideological goals. By associating the public sector with the Kremlin and the Soviet Union, they play on old cold war rhetoric that discursively positions their opponents as socialists. Limiting school partnerships to nonprofits in New York City accustoms the public to privatization, while also making it less likely they would oppose reforms than if for-profits were included. Joel Klein's right hand man, Christopher Cerf, is former president of Edison Schools, a for-profit corporation that manages schools, which suggests a future role for the for-profit sector in school management once the ideological terrain has been prepared.

Bloomberg and Klein have to tread lightly in introducing for-profit partnerships into the New York City schools as a result of recent community resistance (Fruchter & Scott, in press); however, this is apparently not the case in Chicago. As part of Chicago's Renaissance 2010, Mayor Daley is creating 100 new small schools in which for-profit EMOs will have major participation and will operate outside the union contract (Ayers & Klonsky, 2006).

This "hollowing out" of the government through massive contracting to the private sector is generally viewed positively by neoliberals in both political parties. In an op-ed essay Stanger and Omnivore (2007) expressed the mainstream view,

> Some are tempted to turn back the clock and reassert traditional government authority, denouncing private-sector greed and the "coalition of the billing." But that would be a terrible mistake, for outsourcing is in part a rational response to the new possibilities of the information age. The challenge will be to manage creative forms of collaboration between government and the private sector in ways that serve the public interest. (p. A25)

Who could disagree with a vision of the public and private sectors collaborating to serve the common good? The problem is that there is ample evidence that there seems to be little will within the government or the private sector to place the public interest before profits through appropriate forms of regulation and accountability. Such a position is also ahistorical. Corporate power has increased exponentially over the past 200 years, swallowing up more and more of the space once occupied by the public commonweal.

Corporatization, Marketization, and Privatization

In this chapter, I will attempt to bring some historical and conceptual clarity to the recent blurring of the public and private sectors by describing three areas of influence that have impacted education in the last three decades. In some cases these areas of influence represent relatively new phenomena, and in others they are an intensification of social phenomena that have been around for over a century. The three overlapping influences that are having a powerful impact on education are: (1) *corporatization* or a greater role for business, particularly the corporate sector, not only in education but in society at large; (2) *marketization* or a tendency to view individual choice in a marketplace as a more efficient and effective way to allocate resources and values in society, as well as a more effective form of accountability for public institutions; (3) *privatization* or the transfer of public institutions into private hands.

There are other related tendencies that could be included here, such as *commercialization*, which opens schools up to commercial exploitation (Feuerstein, 2001; Molnar, 2005), *militarization*, or the growth of military recruitment and an increasing presence of Junior Reserve Officers Training Corps (JROTC) in schools (Anderson, in press; Bartlett & Lutz, 1998) and *criminalization,* which makes schools part of the pipeline to prison with an increased presence of police officers in schools (Dunbar & Villarruel, 2002). The last two are related to an increased emphasis on the maintenance of a new "security state" (Saltman & Gabbard, 2003) linked to a growing privatization of prisons and the armed forces. While these areas merit in-depth discussion and are closely related to the others, the scope and focus of this book will not allow it. It is important, however, to stress that criminalization and militarization are occurring primarily in schools with low-income students and students of color. This means that the new competition and security state is heavily racialized and class-based.

While corporatization, marketization, and privatization overlap considerably, I will discuss them separately because each has different implications for schools and school leaders. My basic premise is that any time we transfer ideas and perspectives from one sector to another we must look carefully at whether the fit is appropriate and carefully analyze the motivations behind such a transfer. Not only are many attempting to argue that what is good for business is also good for education, but there are some who suggest that democratic public institutions are obsolete and need to be replaced by more market-oriented, private ones (Chubb & Moe, 1990; Friedman, 1962). Some blurring between sectors is inevitable and may be quite benign (Minow, 2005). But I will argue throughout this book that the only way to create an authentic public sphere is through political and social processes that treat human beings as a community of shared interests and responsibilities, not atomized individuals seeking the maximization of their own and their family's good at the expense of others.

Gelberg (1997) argues that the tendency of education to ape business can be traced back to the administrative progressives of the early 20th century, and some scholars trace it back much further (Welch, 1998). Cuban (2004) believes that this long history of business influence on public institutions has created in policymakers and the American public a deeply held belief that business and markets are the solutions to "failing" public institutions.

> The application of business-crafted solutions to public schools (better managers, getting the incentives right, choice, market competition, accountability) has become so thoroughly embedded in policymakers' thinking about improving schools, particularly in urban districts, that these policies are taken for granted and often seen as "common sense" rather than as having been borrowed from the corporate closet. (Cuban, 2004, p. 13)

While the interest of the business community in education waned somewhat in the postwar years, its presence during the last two decades of the 20th century and the first decade of the 21st, has been powerful, though, not always speaking in a unified voice. The worldwide protests regarding the World Trade Organization (WTO), popular corporate exposés like Michael Moore's *Roger and Me,* the Enron debacle, the subprime mortgage crisis, and a long list of other corporate scandals have made a large dent in the commonsense notion that many Americans hold of the benign corporation whose interests reflect our own.

Nevertheless, it would be a mistake to move to the other extreme and vilify corporations because they play an important role in American society and are not inherently good or bad. The question is largely one of sovereignty. Are Americans a sovereign people under a representative government or do corporations and their interests excessively control our social policies and our lives? This growing attention to corporate control has opened up a relatively hidden history of the growth of corporate influence worldwide. The following section will review this history and its implications for the public sector and public schooling in particular.

A Brief History of the American Corporation

Few Americans are aware that the King of England chartered the first corporations in America. The notion widely held today that corporations are private enterprises would have appeared nonsensical to any American up to the end of the 19th century. Corporations under the British monarchy were formed to promote the interests of the monarchy and they were held on a short leash. Many of the original American colonies, such as The Massachusetts Bay Company were in fact British corporations chartered to stake claims in the new world. After the American Revolution, corporations were chartered by the American states in the interests of their citizenry, which at the time was limited to White, propertied males.

At least legally then, corporations were public institutions created by special charters of incorporation granted by state legislatures to serve the common good. Much like today's charter schools, if corporations failed to meet the goals established in their charter, it could be revoked. While many corporations chartered to build such things as canals or colleges created wealth for individuals, the primary function of the corporation was to serve the public interest. People through their legislature retained sovereignty over corporations and legislatures dictated rules for "issuing stock, for shareholder voting, for obtaining corporate information, for paying dividends and keeping records. They limited capitalization, debts, landholdings, and sometimes profits" (Grossman & Adams, 1995, cited in Derber, 1998, p. 124).

However, popular sovereignty and legislative control over corporations began to unravel during the late 19th century. The 14th Amendment, created to protect the rights of freed slaves, was used as a legal tool to provide corporations with the legal rights of a person. Much like today, conservative judges during the Gilded Age of the early 20th century were cynically allied with powerful corporate friends. These judges and corporate leaders colluded to turn public control over corporations into a violation of the 14th Amendment, which holds that no state "shall deprive any person of life, liberty, or property, without due process of law." Thus, the courts of the Gilded Age broke with the state-grant theory of public accountability over corporations and supported instead a conception of corporations as a voluntary contract among private persons. In this way, a public institution, created and controlled by a sovereign people became a private institution or enterprise whose existence was independent of the state *and largely immune from public accountability*. In recent years courts have used the First Amendment to the Constitution to equate massive corporate contributions to political campaigns as an expression of free speech, thus supporting the notion that a corporation is the equivalent of a human being under the law.

What is perhaps even more remarkable is that this history of the shift of corporations from publicly accountable, chartered enterprises to private enterprises is virtually unknown among the general public in the United States. Such accounts do not appear in high school history texts, nor are they taught in colleges of education, in spite of the current attempts to privatize schools.

Why should we care whether a corporation is state controlled or not? This question goes to the heart of the debate about public school privatization. What are public institutions and what makes them different from private ones? Increasingly, corporations are taking over many public functions and impacting, if not actually making, public policy. Corporations affect political outcomes with their campaign contributions and lobbyists. "More than 500 corporations maintain political offices in Washington and, along with trade associations, employ thousands of lobbyists who often end up writing the bills that affect their industries" (Derber, 1998, p. 24). Many see the growing economic influence of corporations and their control of major media as a threat to American democracy.

How Public Schools Subsidize Corporations

While many school administrators and teachers think that corporations generously help to subsidize public education, the truth is quite the opposite. Corporations are constantly in search of tax breaks that take public money away from education. Because they are mobile, they can pit communities, states, and even countries against each other by requiring tax concessions and other favorable legislative changes. Then, having wrested concessions, increasing the local population's taxes, and saving millions, corporations can turn around and make "philanthropic" contributions that build positive public relations for the company. Although many local politicians are aware that they are essentially being blackmailed, they often feel they have to play the game or lose jobs. In reality, many of these companies only stay for the period of their tax breaks, and most transfer or import higher-paid workers from outside the community (Shuman, 1998).

An extensive study of five states by the National Education Association (NEA Research Working Paper, 2003) demonstrates how tax abatements for corporations divert resources from public schools and questions whether these tax subsidies promote balanced economic development. In addition, the study suggests that "today's development subsidies may be enriching corporations at the cost of the education of tomorrow's work force" (p. 1).

Unfortunately the extent to which the public subsidizes corporations is greater than tax breaks, since public schools subsidize the training of future workers. One might ask whose responsibility it is to prepare workers for employment. Corporations have a right to expect public schools to produce well-educated citizens with literacy and numeracy skills. Beyond that, who bears the cost of more specific, vocationally oriented education? This debate has raged since the late 19th century. Welch (1998) describes how U.S. business turned to the public schools to subsidize its training of workers through vocational education.

> US business interests, having consistently failed to invest in the training of apprentices, became increasingly alarmed at the paucity of skilled person-nel that was available to serve the needs of an industrializing economy. Given this lack, two strategies suggested themselves: either to import foreign labor (particularly from Germany, whose technical and industrial education was universally admired) or to train the future workers in the US. However, the industrialists did not wish to adopt the financial burden of training US youth themselves. Thus, the tactic adopted was to press the state to adopt the burden. (Welch, 1998, p. 8)

Thus, the burden of training workers for industry was shifted from corpora-tions to the public schools through vocational education programs. The irony of this turn of events is that at the same time that manufacturers succeeded in unloading this financial burden onto the taxpayer, they have over the years criticized schools for not preparing workers to the specifications of industry (Callahan, 1962).

The idea that corporations are private entities with the rights of persons and that the public schools should subsidize the training of corporate workers are notions that are now taken for granted by most Americans and therefore be-yond critique. Having established this level of hegemony in American society, corporations are now moving on to demand more concessions. Some of these will be discussed in the following sections.

The Corporate Impact on Cities, Districts, and Schools

While we have already discussed how corporations play cities off each other for tax concessions, corporations impact education in other ways. Corporate CEOs sit on school boards, national task forces, and are on boards of foundations that fund task forces, conferences, research grants, think tanks, and commissioned reports that reflect their economic and political worldview (Mickelson, 1999). Organizations, such as the Business Roundtable and local chambers of commerce directly promote the interests of business and are highly influential, presenting proposals for school reform in many state legislatures. Thus, corporate influence is pervasive, coming from multiple sources, levels, and media.

Though I will discuss this in more detail in the section on privatization, it is important to add that corporations also sell their services to public schools, reaping significant profits. These include educational management organizations (EMOs), cafeteria, custodial, maintenance, security, and busing services. They also sell products that range from paper to computers to sports equipment and media productions like Channel One. The increased prevalence of outsourcing of services, costly test and textbook purchases, metal detectors and video surveillance equipment, and special contracts with soda and sneaker companies constitutes a lucrative and often overlooked dimension of privatization (Burch, 2005).

Mickelson (1999) provides a case study of the impact of a single corporation (IBM) on a community (Charlotte, North Carolina). Her case study demonstrates how IBM worked to create policy changes in Charlotte that would help provide high quality, racially segregated schools for their incoming professional and executive families. The Charlotte community approved an $82 million bond initiative to fund a state-of-the-art, four-school magnet cluster named Education Village. Meanwhile, IBM executives, working directly with the Charlotte school superintendent, John Murphy, received verbal permission to set aside one-third of the seats for their employees. Mickelson documents the significant influence IBM was given because of a $2 million contribution it promised to the new magnet cluster. Ultimately the school board, under pressure from the community, successfully challenged the deal, which enraged the IBM executives. A local business leader wrote in an editorial published in the *Charlotte Observer*:

> These companies [which donate money to schools] do not need to have their motives questioned. They do not need to be hassled. They do not need to be set straight by public officials. They need to be persuaded to offer even more support. Like me, people in other businesses are watching the Education Village situation unfold. If our school board can't understand the grant's purpose, won't honor agreements and can't act graciously, other companies will think twice before extending new offers of support. (quoted in Mickelson, 1999, p. 10)

The corporatization of Charlotte involved an intensification of social class and racial segregation in a community that had previously been viewed as a national model of desegregation. Corporations sought not only to provide an elite public education for incoming professional workers and executives, but also an educational environment that was racially segregated.

Shipps (1997) documents corporate influence in Chicago (see also Lipman, 2004). In 1988 Chicago experimented with a democratic community-based reform that gave greater control over schools to local community boards. She documents the battle between business interests and community-based advocacy organizations and the resultant corporate reforms of 1995. According to Shipps,

> The view of the two reforms that emerges when the business role is understood focuses less on the growth of parent power and democratic revitalization than on the replacement of centralized professional control with decentralized business management. (p. 3)

The 1995 legislation "gave sweeping new powers to a school district management team whose titles read more like those of a Fortune 500 corporation than an urban public school system (Shipps, 1997, p. 1). The superintendent's cabinet, all appointed by the mayor of Chicago, had names like *chief executive officer* (superintendent), *chief financial officer, chief operations officer.*

> Together they have authority to determine which schools require intervention; to dismiss, lay off, or reassign any and all personnel in them; and to dissolve elected Local School Councils (LSCs). They are also empowered to cut costs, privatize work usually performed by employees, and abrogate many collective bargaining agreements. (Shipps, 1997, p. 1)

In many ways the corporate-led reforms in Chicago were more sweeping than in Charlotte because they resulted in profound structural changes that made the school district operate more on the principles of a private business than of a school district. That relatively few people see this as a problem is an indication of how successful the corporate community has been at promoting their worldview.

The Corporate Influence on Educational Administration and Teaching

As I discussed previously, much of the new language that entered the lexicon of educational administration came from an army of workshop leaders and professors that taught the principals of total quality management (TQM), which became popular in the 1980s and 1990s. In reality, TQM had already been critiqued within the corporate world, when educators picked it up. Terms like *continuous improvement, teaming, customer, quality,* and *excellence* became in this period part of administrators' vocabulary. TQM principles were even promoted in classrooms through the Baldridge business-inspired approach to instruction.

TQM devolved decision making to workers, promoting teaming and site-based decision making. However, as Harley (1999) and many others have pointed out, "while strategic decisions continue to rest with management, there is a devolution of responsibility for tactics to the core workers" (p. 316). This essentially becomes a new and more sophisticated motivation theory in which workers—or teachers—have the illusion of control over their workplace, while real control is consolidated at higher levels of the system.

The other aspect of TQM that has infused education is the notion of statistical control and the elimination of variance. In most businesses it makes sense to want to produce products that eliminate variance. A quality product is one that does not vary, such as a McDonald's hamburger or an air filter for an automobile. Any variation is viewed as a defect and the use of statistical control helps to eliminate variation. This notion, lifted from business and applied wholesale to education, became a strong ideological support for expanding standardized testing regimes that exert "statistical quality control" over student achievement. The only problem is that the core technologies of business and education are fundamentally different. Successful student achievement depends on valuing and addressing variation in students, and the essence of education is helping each student find her or his own individual and unique self-actualization.

This new *managerial* school leader is modeled after the CEO, and represents a return to a time when school leaders were viewed more as school managers than as instructional leaders. This new managerial model includes a focus on instruction, but frames leaders less as supervisors and mentors of teachers, than as accountants who manage test score data, linking resources to results. As schools compete for students, as public sector professionals are encouraged to be more entrepreneurial, as schools outsource services, and as departments of education and school districts become populated by MBAs, the new model of the state becomes the corporate enterprise.

As I have tried to indicate in this section, corporate influence in education, while not new, is stronger today than at any time in our history. Corporations have given us much that is good. Business as a social enterprise is a cherished foundation of our economy and society. No economist today would argue that a country could prosper without a vibrant private sector. However, humans are more than consumers, and our schools were never meant to merely serve the needs of business. Corporations have a place in our society, but sovereignty belongs to the public. Without a government and public spaces independent of corporate control, the notion of a sovereign "public" in public schooling is called into question.

Marketization: Transferring Market Principles into the Public Sphere

A transfer of business and market ideology from the private sector to the public sector accompanied the ascendancy of corporations in American society during the 20th century. This process is often referred to as "marketization." Transferring market principles to the public sphere means a shift in language and values that replaces a concern with the common good with values of competition and self-interest.

In the postwar years, a group of University of Chicago economists promoted a view of human nature as *homo economicus,* based on assumptions of individuality, rationality, and self-interest. Milton Friedman, Gary Becker, and George Stigler had prepared the intellectual groundwork for what Peters (2001) calls the imperialistic form of free market economics in which neoclassical economics was deemed to provide a unified approach to the study of human behavior. This approach was to be extended into areas that are traditionally the preserve and prerogative of political science, sociology, and the other social science disciplines (p. 15). Think tanks funded by private foundations are a key vehicle for the dissemination of the new neoliberal market gospel and neoconservative views on values, choice, and standards. The Heritage Foundation, the Hudson Institute, the Manhattan Institute, and the American Enterprise Institute are the most important bases of neoliberal and neoconservative analysts such as Denis Doyle, Chester Finn Jr., Diane Ravitch, and Bruno Manno who, among others, use these foundations as a platform to disseminate ideas and influence public opinion. Doyle is a member of the advisory board of *The Education Industry Report*, Finn was an Edison consultant, and all of them have combined public positions in Republican administrations with strong pro-school choice activism.

These groups see the logic of the market as appropriate for all aspects of society and the solution to all problems. As a form of accountability, this logic is viewed as complementing current testing regimes. Using private schools as a model, they argue in true Darwinian fashion that opening up schools to consumer choice will force schools to improve or "go out of business." Unfortunately this "free market" system is highly idealized and some claim, does not exist in the real world of business (Kuttner, 2007). Some research is suggesting that it doesn't work in education either (Cuban, 2004; Gewirtz, 2002; Howard & Preisman, 2007).

The market is also seen as a replacement for politics and democracy. Chubb and Moe (1990) in *Politics, Markets, and America's Schools* argue that:

> The most basic cause of ineffective performance among the nation's public schools is their subordination to public authority.... The school's most fundamental problems are rooted in the institutions of democratic control by which they are governed. (p. 267)

According to advocates of marketization, the downside of participation in the form of school boards or school-level shared governance is their inherent ineffectiveness, making choice in a quasi-market preferable to voice in a politicized environment. However, it is important to understand the differences between participation as consumerism and participation as citizenship. In a marketized environment, the role of citizens is limited to that of passive consumer of "products" provided by others. If they don't like the product, there is no need to become involved in changing it; they can merely—in theory, at least—select another one. They become passive spectators of a political spectacle in which they rarely participate directly. In this way school reform based on market principles is profoundly antipolitical and leads to the atrophy of skills and dispositions for political participation (Boggs, 2000). Frank (2000) calls this conflation of democracy with market principles "market populism."

From Deadheads to Nobel-laureate economists, from paleoconservatives to New Democrats, American leaders in the nineties came to believe that markets were a popular system, a far more democratic form of organization than (democratically elected) governments. This is the central premise of what I will call "market populism": that in addition to being mediums of exchange, markets were mediums of consent. Markets were a friend of the little guy; markets brought down the pompous and the snooty; markets gave us what we wanted; markets looked out for our interests. (p. xiv)

Marketization has more recently been promoted as a solution to the plight of poor urban parents who want to escape mediocre neighborhood schools. For example, some have pointed out the hypocrisy of White middle class parents who critique voucher plans for poor parents while using their resources to obtain choices for their own children (Fuller, 1997). Brantlinger, Majd-Jabbari, and Guskin (1996), in interviews with White, middle class mothers, demonstrate how politically liberal discourses were often used as a "cover" for the protection of self-interest when it came to their own children's schools. Why not give poor and working class parents, disproportionately from communities of color, the same choices that middle and upper class parents have?

Parker and Margonis (1996) counter that market-based plans underestimate the complexity of the decision-making processes engaged in by urban minority parents, as well as their access to transportation, information, and the cultural and social capital required to finesse the system. More importantly, they document the patterns of urban racial and socioeconomic containment practices (housing, occupational, and school segregation as well as housing and employment discrimination) and their devastating impact on persons of color in economically depressed urban areas. They argue that market driven responses to these conditions are not a break with past racist policies, but are in fact consistent with the lack of national commitment to urban issues. Viewed through the Reagan-Bush conservative political era of dismantling federal aid to the cities, they view school choice as a simplistic solution that ignores the structural constraints that poor urban residents face. This is another case of the political spectacle's displacement of targets, focusing on "choice" while ignoring the larger and more costly infrastructural neglect of poor neighborhoods. In this way, the political spectacle steers the public's attention away from neglect in more costly social sectors and toward so-called failing public schools where a constant call for more educational "reform" can replace real social investment.

Not all parents in urban, low-income communities of color see privatization as the answer to bad schools. Scott and Fruchter (in press) have documented the response of low-income communities of color to an attempt to bring private management of public schools to New York City. In 2001, then Mayor Rudolph Giuliani and Chancellor Harold Levy invited Edison, the for-profit educational management organization to take over five low-performing middle schools in New York City. In response, the Association of Community Organizations for

Reform Now (ACORN) and a coalition calling itself People's Coalition to Take Back Our Schools began organizing to oppose the plan, charging that parents were shut out of the process. These groups were led by and largely made up of African-American and Latino/a parents. In spite of mayoral support and a promotional campaign by Edison, the parents of the five schools all voted against letting Edison take over their schools.

The point here is not to defend the inequitable public school system we have, nor to eschew choice in all cases, but rather to promote a view of public schools in a strong and healthy public sector that is being undermined by neoliberal economic policies. There is nothing wrong per se with providing choices for children and parents, just as there is nothing wrong with exchanging goods in a marketplace. However, as Deborah Meier (1995) argues, "...we must shape the concept of choice into a consciously equitable instrument for restructuring public education so that over time all parents can have the kinds of choices the favored few now have, but in ways that serve rather than undercut public goals" (p. 99). Current school reform, while claiming to improve the education of all children, too often appears to undercut those very goals.

Perhaps more importantly, school is where we learn the skills of democratic citizenship, skills that are different from those of being a consumer and maximizing individual choices. The antipolitics position that Chubb and Moe take has a certain appeal. In a sense, it is easier to do away with the "unpleasantness" of school boards and having to debate issues. Communities have been torn apart by educational debates that find people lining up on opposing sides. Chubb and Moe argue that if people don't like the school they're in; they can simply pick another one. You don't like your PC computer? Get a Mac! But this has nothing to do with democracy. I again turn to Deborah Meier (2002) for an eloquent defense of political democracy:

> All the habits of mind and work that go into democratic institutional life must be practiced in our schools until they truly become habits—so deeply a part of us that in times of stress we fall back on them rather than abandon them in search of a great leader or father figure, or retreat into the private isolation of our private interests, the unfettered marketplace where one need not worry about the repercussions of one's individual decisions. (p. 177)

The Growing Privatization of Education

Privatization in American education is not new. In fact, private schools predate public schools and vendors have sold textbooks to schools at least since the McGuffey Reader. Minow (2002) asserts, "It is not unusual for the boundaries between public and private to blur. The lines themselves are historical inventions. Nor is it unprecedented for governments to work closely with non-profit and religious groups" (p. 22). What is new is the increasing pace of privatization and the extent to which it has expanded beyond its traditional boundaries. Minow (2002) is also concerned that "shifts do seem to be occurring especially around collective commitments to provide for the basic human needs for food, shelter, education, medical care, and justice" (p. 22).

Levin (2001), in setting out a research agenda for privatization, suggests that the following areas are key to understanding where major shifts are occurring in privatization in the area of education: (1) how education is financed; (2) whether schools are sponsored by the private or public sector; (3) who operates schools; (4) who benefits from schools; and (5) for-profit providers. In nearly all cases the balance is rapidly shifting from the public to the private, and within the private sector the balance is increasingly shifting to the for-profit sector as opposed to the nonprofit sector. Moreover, it is important to clarify the increasingly blurred distinction between the for-profit and nonprofit private sector.

Nonprofit enterprises engaged in delivering social services increasingly collaborate with and mimic for-profit business. To be a nonprofit organization does not mean never making a profit; it means that any profit cannot be paid out to a residual claimant, like a shareholder. In fact, as we have all learned from the dot. com debacle of the 1990s, for-profit organizations sometimes do not make a profit, but rather speculate on the willingness of stockholders to invest in them.

Educational Testing Service (ETS) is usually regarded as a nonprofit, but that may be about to change. ETS president Kurt Landgraf is a former DuPont executive brought in to diversify ETS. He is busy developing for-profit subsidiaries to bolster the nonprofit sector of the company. Landgraf believes that as long as the nonprofit arm of the company is fulfilling its mission, the for-profit arm, even if it becomes 50% of ETS's business, is defensible (Merritt, 2004). This raises serious questions about whether the boundaries between the nonprofit and for-profit sectors have blurred to such an extent that they have become almost indistinguishable. But most importantly, whether nonprofit or for-profit, private organizations escape the public scrutiny and accountability required of public organizations.

NCLB has been a boon to the nonprofit and for-profit sectors. The provisions of NCLB that provide money to private tutorial services has turned small tutoring companies like Sylvan and Kaplan into corporate giants. But NCLB has boosted profits in other sectors as well. Using data from the American Association of Publishers, Clark (2004) provides data on the impact of NCLB on the profits of the testing-related educational publishing business and the textbook industry in general.

Sales of printed materials related to standardized tests nearly tripled from 1992 to last year [2003], jumping from $211 million to $592 million, according to the American Association of Publishers. Three corporate giants dominate both testing and textbooks: CTB-McGraw Hill, Harcourt (owned by London-based Reed Elsevier), and Houghton Mifflin, which together control about 80% of the market. The total market in textbooks and related educational materials is over $7 billion.

Literature on privatization makes a distinction between "hard services," like contracting out bus, cafeteria, custodial services, and textbook purchases from "soft services" like counseling, teaching, professional development, student assessment, and so on. Hard services are those that are easy to calculate and assess (i.e., buses arrived on time or they didn't). Soft services are more multifaceted and their assessment is more ambiguous. Hard services have been privatized to some extent for some time and this trend continues to increase (Burch, 2005), but the privatization of soft services is new. This traditional distinction has been thoroughly breached Boyles (2000) says: "'Soft services' are treated as 'hard' services in order to reduce costs and subsume due process and academic freedom under market logics" (p. 119).

Drawing on Whitfield's (2001) study of the privatization process in Britain, Ball (2007) describes three stages through which the creative destruction of the public sector is accomplished. While this is not a coordinated, linear process, it has the following internal logic. The public sector is *destabilized* through constant ridicule to undermine its credibility. This is accompanied by *disinvestment* from and shifting resources within the public sector. As public institutions like schools and universities become more financially strapped, they need to seek funding from the private sector, in many cases from new philanthropic organizations with privatizing agendas. Ball quotes a deputy head teacher, "You can't run on your ordinary budget, everyone knows that, so you have to get involved in various initiatives and cater for that, the initiative's priorities, and bend your curriculum and your priorities in order to get hold of that bit of money" (p. 23). In addition, public–private partnerships help to breach and rework key boundaries between the public and private. Finally, a process of *commodification* "reworks forms of service, social relations and public processes into forms that are measurable and thus contractible or marketable…" (Ball, 2007, p. 24). In this way new markets are created that attract private providers and thus create whole new arenas of commercial activity for "social entrepreneurs."

This process of creative distruction can be seen in many of the changes at The New York City Department of Education where moneys have been shifted from the public to the private sector by essentially dismantling the school district and replacing it with a services mall.

> …Schools will receive an average of $100,000 in newly unrestricted funds and $150,000 in new, discretionary funds made possible by streamlining the central and regional DOE bureaucracy and redirecting financial resources back to the schools…. The DOE is creating a lean, new, customer service-focused support system to help empowerment school principals. Part of this support system will be a "market maker" function, which will help principals (buyers) and regional DOE staff (sellers) connect in

a new Empowerment School marketplace. (New York City Department of Education Web site)

While money is portrayed as flowing from the bureaucracy to schools, most of it will flow from the public sector to the private sector. The market maker department opens up a market for the for-profit sector that did not previously exist. According to the Department of Education, principals can now contract with for-profit providers for a long list of services that includes such things as attendance improvement, college counseling services, professional development for teachers and principals, and safety-related professional development prevention and intervention packages.

On the Department of Education website, business and market language is boldly asserted with no sense that this might seem controversial to many. While an argument might be made for the privatization of the public sector, this massive transformation of public service delivery is taking place without any democratic process that includes any citizen input. Through mayoral control, and a chancellor with a single-minded privatization (and antiunion) agenda, massive and irreversible transformations have occurred with little to no public input.

Conclusion

Trends toward greater corporatization, marketization, and privatization are often subsumed under the rubric: globalization. George Soros (2002), one of the world's most successful capitalists, provides a critique of globalization's adherence to market fundamentalism, "which holds that the allocation of resources is best left to the market mechanism, and any interference with that mechanism reduces the efficiency of the economy" (p. 4). This means that capital should not be taxed or regulated in any way. According to Soros (2002),

> Globalization is indeed a desirable development in many ways. Private enterprise is better at wealth creation than the state. Moreover, states have a tendency to abuse their power; globalization offers a degree of individual freedom that no individual state could ensure. Free competition on a global scale has liberated inventive and entrepreneurial talents and accelerated technological innovations.
>
> But globalization also has a negative side. First, many people, particularly in less-developed countries, have been hurt by globalization without being supported by a social safety net; many others have been marginalized by global markets. Second, globalization has caused a misallocation of resources between private goods and public goods. Markets are good at creating wealth but are not designed to take care of other social needs. The heedless pursuit of profit can hurt the environment and conflict with other social values. Third, global markets are crisis prone. People living in the developed countries may not be fully aware of the devastation wrought

by financial crises because they tend to hit the developing economies much harder. (pp. 4–5)

Furthermore, though corporations don't generally start wars, many corporations profit handsomely from war and are increasingly profiting from war and other disasters, such as the devastation of hurricane Katrina. Klein (2007) documents a historical connection between disaster and capitalism, using as a primary example the link between the development of neoliberalism at the University of Chicago and the military coup in Chile that opened up the country to neoliberal economic experimentation.

Based on 2007 estimates from the Congressional Budget Office, the cost of the war in Iraq to the American taxpayer was $450,525,500,000: that's billions, not millions. The National Priorities Project (2007) calculates that with this same amount of money, we could have provided nearly 22 million students with four-year scholarships at public universities, or provided health insurance coverage to nearly 270 million children for one year, or hired nearly 8 million additional public school teachers for one year.

With corporations, markets, and business ideology increasingly calling the shots in education, why isn't there more resistance from educational leaders? While there is a significant amount of protest that I will discuss in more detail in the final chapter, the next chapter will suggest that we have insufficiently understood the role of educational leaders in schools and school districts. I will argue that the role expectation of educational leaders, much like that of journalists and academics, is one that views them as legitimators of the dominant social ideology, not challengers.

4
Disciplining Leaders
Mediating the New Economy[1]

With each job description I read, I felt a tightening of what I must call my soul. I found myself growing false to myself, acting to myself, convincing myself of my rightness for whatever was being described. And this is where I suppose life ends for most people, who stiffen in the attitudes they adopt to make themselves suitable for jobs and lives that other people have laid out for them.

V.S. Naipaul, *A Bend in the River,* **pp. 144–145**

As is the case with many teachers, I was surprised to find myself doing things in the classroom that I never thought I would do, things that went against my ideals or my emerging professional judgment. As new teachers learn to cope with issues of discipline, classroom management, and the avoidance of controversy, survival becomes an overriding consideration. Cherished values and instructional ideologies often fly out the window in a utilitarian search for "what works" within the constraints of one's job. As months and years pass and survival recedes as the main goal of teaching, many teachers are able to return to their cherished values and develop as reflective professionals. For others, their early coping mechanisms morph into their teaching practices, resulting, at best, in strongly disciplined, but pedagogically and relationally impoverished classrooms.

Something similar happens with many administrators. As I moved from teaching to administration, I remember resisting the trappings of hierarchy. When I was promoted to bilingual coordinator, I at first refused to leave the large collective teachers' office with its noisy collegiality to take an office down the hall. My colleagues were oddly disapproving of my reticence. How could I become an administrator and remain one of them? In talking to other administrators over the years, the issue of whether you can be friends with teachers or not was always a conundrum that some solved better than others.

Later as principal, I found my finger constantly in the air, measuring the way the wind was blowing politically. I had to somehow represent and interpret students to teachers and teachers to students, teachers to central office and central office to teachers, teachers to parents and parents to teachers. Publicly everyone wanted policies to be consistently implemented, but privately sought exceptions for their kids or themselves. Were authentic values and relationships possible in such a politicized world? While I knew compromise came with the territory, how compromised could one be and still view one's work as advocacy for children?

In the mid-1980s, I left school administration to do a doctorate and ultimately a dissertation. Central to my thinking throughout was the issue of how we tend to be socialized away from our authentic values toward politically expedient ones, as well as, how, like William H. Whyte's (1956) *Organization Man*, we are social-ized to protect, at all cost, the image and legitimacy of our school. This usually included the unequal social arrangements that schooling helps to legitimate. I explored literature on professional socialization. I carefully read Howard Becker's *Boys in White*, a classic study of how medical interns become doctors. I began my dissertation study, prepared to interview principals and superintendents about their experiences with professional socialization. Unlike medical interns, who were learning mostly specific technical skills and entering a largely skills-based profession, the work of school administrators, while certainly containing some technical knowledge and skill, seemed to be more about managing relationships and institutional legitimacy.

The principals I interviewed talked endlessly about being caught in the middle. One district's principals' meeting I observed summed it up. The principals had collectively decided teachers in the district should elaborately code lesson plans to state standards for an outside evaluation. Teachers were angry and grumbled that the elaborate coding system was busywork, taking time away from planning and teaching. The district ultimately received a positive evaluation, but the report mentioned that the elaborate coding was overdone and was, they felt, too time consuming for teachers. The principals were divided over whether to show the report to teachers. Some felt it was a vindication of teachers' heated objections to coding and would leave them with egg on their face. Others felt they had been overzealous in their insistence on the coding scheme, and that the teachers had a right to the information, even it did make them look bad.

But it was the tone of being caught in the middle and having to "manage" information as it flowed up and down the hierarchy that stood out. While holding onto some aspects of role theory, I largely gave up the professional socialization literature and instead stumbled onto Meyer and Rowan's (1977) early article on institutional theory.

According to Meyer and Rowan (1977), organizations exist within a larger institutional environment within which they struggle for legitimacy. In order to be viewed as legitimate they develop "legitimation rituals," such as report cards, promotion from grade to grade, and graduation ceremonies. It is these rituals, they argue, rather than what actually happens instructionally in classrooms, that create legitimacy. Instruction then was viewed as "loosely coupled" from the institutional environment and therefore protected from scrutiny. More recently, theorists of the "new institutionalism" see pervasive accountability systems based on high stakes testing as leading to a shift to more tightly coupled and narrowly controlled instructional practices in schools (Rowan, 2006b).

I realized that much of this legitimation work fell to principals and superintendents. They were charged with legitimating their school to multiple publics as well as legitimating decisions and policies among diverse groups within the school and community. They were not only managers of schedules, testing, discipline, buses, and budgets, discursively, they were also—and perhaps primarily—managers of meaning (Anderson, 1990, 1991), and this management of meaning often occurred as part of managing schedules, discipline, assessment, buses, and budgets.

The Ideological Work of Educational Leaders

This idea that school leaders are members of middle management who must interpret different constituencies to each other, may seem similar to the research on school micropolitics that I discussed in chapter 2. Micropolitics focused on the behind-the-scenes, daily struggles over different interests of individual teachers, students, parents, unions, and school boards (Blase & Anderson, 1995). Micropolitics research is aimed at understanding how power operates at the informal organizational level, and how this less visible level of struggle influences organizational outcomes in important ways. It tends to draw on traditional "pluralist" notions of politics and power as exercised in public arenas and typically involving a clash among individuals and interest groups (Dahl, 1961).

Newer views of power and politics employ theories that stress the various ways people's interests are shaped ideologically. Following Gramsci (Forgacs, 2000), many contemporary theorists argue that the exercise of power includes the social construction of our very "interests" and "needs." Thus, many instances of discrimination and inequality in schools are not challenged because they are taken for granted or viewed as "just the way things are." Their existence comes to be viewed as common sense and thus beyond question. This break with previous behaviorist and pluralist notions of power has shifted attention to more unobtrusive and cognitive modes of social control.

These more cognitive notions of power have helped to explain the outcomes of conflict and political struggle (or the lack thereof) in a postindustrial, information age in which the manipulation of public opinion has become a fine art that—as discussed in chapter 2—is achieved through political spectacle (Edelman, 1988; Lukes, 2005). Conflict management may involve helping people negotiate immediate conflicts of interest, but it also seems to involve the management of meaning and the legitimacy of the organization—what is increasingly referred to as "impression management." This means that leaders are essentially mediators, who mediate among people, among institutions, and among ideas. They are entrusted with managing the legitimacy of the school and of the social arrangements surrounding the school, including, for instance, racial and socio-economic segregation.

This new view of power, discourse, and ideology means that the micropolitics of schools involves a wider set of tactics and strategies than those described by traditional micropolitical literature. Thompson (2008), for instance discusses the continuum of resistance and compliance among principals, which includes such tactics as simulation (as in simulating consent while resisting), emulation (taking actions to meet expectations), accommodation (e.g., complying in order to buy freedom from further surveillance), and creative forms of mediation (of structures and policies). Views of school leaders as actively engaged in decisions around compliance and resistance imply a level of agency and strategic maneuver that most micropolitics and certainly most functionalist approaches to leadership fail to capture. Because mediation is such a central role that leaders enact, I will develop this idea further below.

In my dissertation research I observed three dimensions of mediation. In the following quote from an article I published from my dissertation, I outlined my theoretical argument, which was developed in the late 1980s, but I believe is still largely valid today:

> The ways administrators' mediation role leads to the legitimation of the particular meaning system they are charged to manage is extremely complex. In this section, three dimensions of mediation will be discussed: a) mediation of conflict at the point of open contention, b) mediation as day-to-day meaning management among organizational stakeholders, and c) mediation as the cognitive task of resolving (or perhaps dissolving) contradictions within the structure of one's own ideology. (Anderson, 1990, pp. 46–47)

In this model, the first, most obvious, dimension was mediation of conflict at the point of open contention; a principal mediates a fight between two students or meets with a student, parent and teacher about alleged student misbehavior. Principals spend many hours in such meetings, and the best ones are aware that this work is both practical and symbolic. On the surface, they are mediating conflict, but in doing so, they are also accomplishing the management of meaning, which is the second definition of mediation. In the way they go about accomplishing all of their everyday practices, such as mediating conflict, supervising teachers, or facilitating meetings, they are also engaging in symbolic leadership. Harry Wolcott (1973) in his classic ethnography, *The Man in the Principal's Office*, described the mundane everyday routines that elementary school principal Ed Bell oversees. Walcott makes the point that it appears that nothing is happening on a typical day, or at least nothing of import; but social reality is always being constructed, deconstructed, and legitimated through everyday interactions that on the surface may appear to be mundane. It is through how these mundane, ritualistic interactions are approached that the status quo is either reinforced or problematized by leaders.

In this type of symbolic mediation, administrators head off possible censure from within and without the school. Through their mediatory role, they are expected to maintain social cohesion and the stability of the organization and its nonproblematic status as a legitimate social institution. This mediation occurs vertically within the hierarchy as principals interpret central office to teachers and students and interpret teachers and students needs to central office. It also occurs horizontally between school professionals and the school community, although this mediation is viewed as a buffering or public relations role and therefore tends to be more unidirectional. It is precisely this shift from viewing one's role as buffering the school from the community or as public relations expert to a bidirectional relationship with the school community that advocacy leaders struggle to achieve. Creative mediation allows advocacy principals to engage strategically in various forms of compliance and resistance while calculating the potential threat to the school's perceived legitimacy.

In my study, I documented the ways in which suburban principals were expected to project the normalcy of the provision of a resource-rich education to a relatively elite (and largely White) population, while urban principals were charged with legitimating the normalcy of providing a resource-poor education to the children of poor and largely non-White children. To aggressively delegitimate these social arrangements was to invite censure from local suburban school boards or urban educational bureaucracies. Through this ideological work, administrators help to maintain or "reproduce" the institutionalized meanings that are incorporated in the structures, policies, and practices of the organization. Theorists of organizational change have argued that this process of meaning management can be used either to maintain the status quo or to change it. However, the impetus to change an equilibrium so carefully maintained requires tremendous risk and courage as well as deep ideological changes at the level of meaning, which brings us to the third dimension of mediation which I described in the following way (Anderson, 1990):

> The third dimension of administrator mediation is cognitive and involves mediating contradictions within ideology. Because administrators often mediate among organizational publics and internal organizational levels with contradictory goals, a mediatory role is not without its psychic costs. In order to project the almost commonsense plausibility of organizational life, the administrator must develop a coherent ideology, which requires the production of mediatory myths that can dissolve organizational and social contradictions sufficiently for the administrator to function. (p. 48)

Abravenel (1983) borrowing from Seliger (1976) described organizational ideology as a set of fundamental ideas and operative consequences that are linked together into a dominant belief system that often produces contradictions but serves to define and maintain the organization. According to Abravenel,

> Ideology operates in two dimensions; it maintains allegiance to a purity of moral principals (the fundamental) and to practical and immediate considerations (the operative). Like the Church, ideology must be faithful both to its central beliefs and to its immediate concerns about survival. (pp. 280–281)

Because contradictions and inconsistencies between these two dimensions of ideology are inevitable, administrators need legitimating mechanisms to mediate between dimensions and restore coherence to the overall ideology that sustains the organization. The need for congruence between moral principals and practical considerations reflects the fact that, because organizational members must make directives and take purposive action, they cannot rely on an ambiguous belief system. If administrators are to mediate the two levels successfully within the organization, they must mediate, on an ongoing basis, the two levels within themselves (Anderson, 1990).

In many low-income urban schools that serve mainly students of color, this third form of mediation often requires that leaders hold on to cherished notions of meritocracy and individual upward mobility in the face of daily evidence to the contrary. This approach is not unlike Argyris and Schon's (1974) theories of an action model that involves seeking congruence between a leader's espoused theories and theories-in-use. Both involve surfacing largely out-of-awareness assumptions. However, while Argyris and Schon see this process as potentially leading to organizational learning, Abravenal (1983) cautions that these contradictions are resolved though mediatory myths that allow leaders to act, but may work against organizational learning and a perceived need for advocacy.

This three-tiered mediation model describes a process that occurs at the personal and organizational level, but is nested within and helps to sustain a larger system of legitimation at the institutional and political economy level. Meyer (2006) uses institutional theory's emphasis on legitimation to argue that American public schools are in crisis in part because the older mediatory myths of the "common school" have run their course. Public schools were at the forefront of American progressivism and the postwar years represented the promise of an inclusive welfare state that aimed at a war on poverty and a great society. These mediatory myths that sustained the legitimacy of public schools came under attack form the political left, right, and center. The left argued that schools were agents of social reproduction that favored the privileged classes, the right saw them as agents of big government that abridged their religious and political freedoms, and the center critiqued them for being too bureaucratic, inefficient, and unbusinesslike. This assault on public schools left them vulnerable on all sides, and since the late 1970s there has been a struggle between those who wish to bolster older legitimating myths and those who wish to forge new ones.

Through reports like *A Nation at Risk*, human capital theory was effectively promoted as the new legitimating myth that raised the profile of schooling as a key investment in a competitive economy, while at the same time noting "the rising tide of mediocrity" of our public schools. This delegitimitation of public schools became part of a larger mediatory myth about the inefficiency and mediocrity of the public sector in general. At the level of educational administration and public management, public sector discourses are being replaced by private sector, business language. We have become increasingly aware that shifts in management discourses have accompanied ideological shifts with important implications at the level of political economy.

In the following section, I provide a discourse analysis of the national standards for certification in educational leadership and the exam that has been designed to enforce them. Discourses such as standards and exams are increasingly shaping administrative discourses and practices. My concern with the exam is that it seeks to "discipline" administrators through legitimating a particular way of thinking about their role. As aspiring administrators, they are struggling to form a coherent ideology, to link moral principals with the exigencies of everyday constraints. As they take the exam, they must make choices among fundamental beliefs and operative consequences, and rehearse discourses that represent "safe" response to the test questions. In a sense, the exam is teaching them to employ those authorized discourses that maintain the status quo over those that advocate for low-income children and families.

The Certification Exam as a Disciplinary Practice

No one should be surprised that after years of testing teachers and students, school leaders are now the targets of the testing industry and outcomes based reform. Educational Testing Service (ETS) has developed an examination based on The Interstate School Leaders Licensure Consortium's (ISLLC) national standards for school administrators (see appendix A for a list of the standards). This test and other similar ones are now required in most states for administrator certification. Since this new test will to a large extent drive the preparation of future educational leaders, it makes sense that we should take a close look at it. Before that, however, let's take a brief look at the new national standards that the test is meant to enforce.

ISLLC has developed six standards, each with a list of knowledge areas, dispositions, and performances. The good news is that they have, at least rhetorically, given instructional leadership a central position in the standards. For example, "a vision of learning" is central to the standards and constitutes the central concern of standard 1. The first disposition listed under standard 2 is: "The administrator believes in, values, and is committed to student learning as the fundamental purpose of schooling." To many veterans of educational administration it means a welcome shift away from administration as management to administration as instructional leadership.

Those most involved in developing the standards defend this move, arguing that "the actor we worked hard to position on center stage—learning and teaching yoked to student performance—would get displaced quickly if we populated the stage with all the relevant players who could make legitimate claims to space" (Murphy, Jost, & Shipman, 2000, p. 23). While recentering instructional leadership is a positive development, the standards are silent about what kind of teaching and learning should take place and how instructional leadership is conceptualized. Nowhere in the standards is there any mention of how teaching and learning might be "yoked" to such things as equity, communities, diversity, citizenship, our increasingly stratified labor force, or the "hidden" curriculum. Unless the standards take a position on these issues, others fill in these silences in the standards. So the bad news is that while the standards themselves are fairly predictable and benign, I will argue here, that those who have developed the exam and those who have scored it have interpreted them very narrowly. The evidence I will use to make my case is the set of sample questions and answers provided by the ETS exam bulletin, which ETS claims are representative of the exam itself.

Standardizing Instructional Leaders

The idea of an examination contradicts one of the premises of the Consortium that designed the standards which acknowledges that "effective leaders often espouse different patterns of beliefs and act differently from the norm in the profession" (p. 5). It is one thing to identify standards that represent the norm of the profession while encouraging discussion and debate and quite another to attempt to socialize all prospective leaders as the examination attempts to do. The glibness and the depoliticized and decontextualized nature of the exemplary test booklet answers, speak to an administrative discourse in which complexity, conflict, and critical reflection are banished.

Thankfully the test that was designed to enforce the ISLLC standards is not of the multiple-choice type, but rather provides the examinee with case studies with scoring rubrics. The test bulletin provides sample cases along with some exemplary responses, and each exam question has a series of rubrics that represent correct answers. For instance, on one test item, the test-taker is asked to read a brief vignette and then "evaluate the principal's action from the point of view of teaching and learning" (p. 36). There are five "correct" answers, and to get full points, the test-taker must mention two of the five correct answers. In one example a high school student is failing all of his classes and wants to drop his physics class, which is not required for graduation. The respondents who received full points cited at least two of the "correct" rubrics, but they also included some other things in their answer that could be viewed as problematic, even from the perspective of the standards themselves.

For example, one of the respondents who got a perfect score suggested that: "The parent might also want to hire a tutor in any area that is giving the student specific trouble." Even though standard 6 emphasizes "the importance of diversity and equity in a democratic society" (p. 20), apparently the inability to understand that most poor parents cannot afford to hire a tutor is not viewed as problematic. Schools that take issues of poverty seriously provide after-school and Saturday tutoring for students. The ability of middle and upper class parents to use their own resources to hire extra help for their children is one of several reasons that student achievement in school correlates so highly with social class. But this respondent lost no points for this basic insensitivity to social class differences and the responsibility of the school to provide extra help. This same respondent also wrote: "I would also want the counselor to work with the student on his mental attitude." Nowhere in the answer is there any suggestion that school failure is an interactive social construction, suggesting that the school professionals may need to reflect on their own mental attitude and the structures they need to have in place to facilitate students' success. No points, however, were subtracted for locating the problem only in the child by psychologizing what might be a broader problem that may need to be partly owned by the school as well. This tendency to psychologize and individualize problems, leaving the school professionals and broader social injustices blameless, is a theme across all sample exercises. The safest answers are decontextualized and depoliticized, leaving the individual student and family to blame.

Leadership as Public Relations

A specific example of how the standards attempt to standardize and narrow conceptions of instructional leadership is the way that the relationship between schools, communities, and student achievement is posed. Most exemplary instructional leaders would agree that good instruction, particularly in low-income schools builds on the funds of knowledge, learning styles, and concerns that students bring from their communities and that the active participation of parents in all aspects of school life is desirable. The standards exhibit a tendency to use a rhetoric of participation and collaboration while operating out of a set of assumptions grounded in a public relations model. This contradiction becomes more evident in the exam itself, which unapologetically seems to promote a public relations approach to community involvement that fails to link parents and communities to student achievement.

One sample exercise provides the respondent with a school fact sheet and a data set that gives district demographic information and the previous principal's school improvement plan. The respondent must make a series of decisions, including determining the "strategies you would implement to elicit the community's support of the school improvement plan" (Educational Testing Service, 1999, p. 38). The exam question's wording already suggests a preference for a public relations model over a democratic participation model. The school leader has already made certain decisions about the school improvement plan, and the issue now is to procure the "community's support." Thus, the exam itself, through the ways the questions are phrased, reinforces and elicits a particular type of answer.

The test bulletin provides two sample exemplary answers, both of which received full points. Both answers promote a public relations approach. Respondent 2 articulates an explicit, unambiguous public relations approach to community relations.

> The broad based issues the school must resolve are in the areas of communication and public relations,... There is a need for *communication and p.r....* Whenever there is a letter writing campaign, this issue as a *public relations* concern must be addressed...or *a domino effect will likely occur.*" [A single letter from a parent concerned about the school's use of cooperative learning was included in the sample exercise.].... The public at large also *needs to be educated.* Although the PTA is *an effective arm of the school*, there needs to be budgetary line items allotted to parent training. (emphases mine)

Another respondent, who emphasizes the importance of promoting community participation in decision making and suggests implications for instructional leadership, received only two of the three available points. This respondent articulates an explicit, unambiguously democratic participation approach. Moreover, unlike respondent 2, who never explicitly links the issues to instruction, this respondent makes instructional issues central:

> What specific changes have to be made based on research, staff, parent and community input?... Meet with PTA, Educational Council, Board members, community representatives. Gather input. Discuss concerns/ what is cooperative learning?... Involve all members of community in planning. Special effort made to elicit help from parents/people in new housing project.... Report card committee can work on alternative assessment and how to report to parents.

This respondent is more focused on the democratic participation of the community and on instruction; other parts of the response indicate an inquiry approach to problem solving, an understanding that multiple models of cooperative learning exist, and a strong commitment to cultural diversity and ongoing evaluation. Unfortunately, the exam provides no rubrics to cover these areas. For instance, one rubric indicates that the respondent should "address the implications of a growing, more diverse community and student population and declining test scores." Will any implications do? The respondent who lost points went to great lengths to respond to the changing cultural diversity, and, unlike the first two respondents, did not use code words to do so:

> Given the change in the complexion, socioeconomic, and presumed racial and ethnic makeup of the district, there is a need to address the differences

and multicultural aspect of the school.... Stress differences in background, initiate cultural fairs, "Proud to Be Me," Affirmations Week, lunch with Principal, and peer leadership and mediation groups at all grade levels.... Utilize cultural diversity issues and needs to look at alternative methods of instruction and project-based as well as alternative assessment along with differing learning styles and approaches.

Meanwhile, the respondents who received full points largely glossed over issues of class and race and their impact on instruction, seeing the new population as largely an inconvenience with the potential to create conflict. Respondent 1 comments:

The different socioeconomic groups will need to be *assimilated* into the school population. The school climate/culture may need to change and adapt *in order to prevent possible conflict between groups*. (emphasis mine)

Respondents 1 and 2 appear to operate out of a deficit theory, seeing diversity as a problem of assimilation and conflict avoidance. Because technically they do discuss the implications of a changing community, they have addressed the rubric and therefore get full points.

This suggests an inherent problem with rubrics. They represent a crude attempt to turn complex narrative answers into a point system, to quantify qualitative data. The respondents who address the greatest number of rubrics receive the highest grade even if their work is generally mediocre and even if they include problematic ideas that contradict the standards themselves.

The Right Stuff: Be Glib, but Be "Convincing"

If the Educational Testing Service exam drives the curriculum of administrator preparation programs, such programs will increasingly find themselves in the business of providing future administrators with "safe" discourses that will not offend pluralist interest groups. Respondents are rewarded for keeping issues at a superficial level. Although time constraints operate in any exam situation, glibness seems to be a characteristic of the answers that receive full points. In nearly every case, respondent 3 addressed issues in greater depth and complexity than the two respondents who received full points because they addressed more of the rubrics, even though they often answered with sound bites. But more important, according to the test scorers, respondent 3's answers were not as "convincing" as the others.

What makes an answer "convincing"? Are responses more convincing when they are written in depoliticized, decontextualized language? Are they less convincing if they are thoughtful and raise more questions than they answer? Are they less convincing if they suggest that the respondent views schools and school improvement as complex and messy endeavors that require debate and reflection rather than "strategies you would implement to elicit the community's support of the school improvement plan," as the exam asks?

None of the responses in the booklet indicates that a respondent has read any professional literature or knows much about either instruction or leadership. No respondent alludes to, much less cites an education researcher or author. Respondents occasionally refer to specific instructional programs such as Reading Recovery or general approaches such as cooperative learning, but responses do not indicate that important conceptual debates exist about instructional methods, approaches to school governance, or the role of schools in society. Responses do not suggest that any of these future educational leaders read anything beyond technical manuals and highly condensed administrative textbooks. One respondent lost points because the scorer felt that "throughout, responses are weakened by suggestions for solutions that are *outside the principal's control*" (emphasis mine) (Educational Testing Service, 1999, p. 48). This notion that principals should see themselves as mere technocrats without a larger vision of change is reinforced by the role expectations embedded in the exam and the scorers' evaluations. The exam seems to fuel the notion that well-educated, critical school leaders with a commitment to rigorous and equitable instruction should be replaced by glib CEOs with brief, narrow, but "convincing" answers to every problem.

The ISLLC Standards reflect mainstream thinking in educational leadership. They move instructional leadership to center stage, emphasize parent involvement, advocate the educability of all children, promote professional growth, and call for safer schools. These are all laudable goals. However, embedded in the language of the standards lurk the old assumptions of a conservative field that has historically been less influenced by education or advocacy, than by military science ("strategic planning"), social engineering ("alignment," "operational procedures," "core technology"), industrial psychology ("human resources management"), and business ("acts entrepreneurially to support continuous improvement," "ownership," "marketing strategies").

Finally, the current obsession with adding additional layers of accountability on educators' work feeds on the crisis climate of texts like *A Nation at Risk* (National Commission on Excellence in Education, 1983) with its emphasis on preparing students for the needs of corporations, which have themselves not been held socially accountable. However, except for placing instructional leadership on center stage, a trend that preceded the development of the standards, they do not represent a fundamental shift in thought in educational leadership. The narrow view of instructional leadership that this exam appears to promote represents a missed opportunity to promote the ways leaders of outstanding, low-income schools provide effective, critical, and culturally responsive instruction. To what extent an examination of any kind is an appropriate incentive for creating such leaders is a discussion we apparently will not be invited to participate in. The testing genie is out of the bottle and getting it back in will not be easy.

The School Leadership Standards and Exam as Discourse-Practices

In the larger scheme of things, these certification exams may not seem like a big problem. Most students instinctively know that answering test questions has little to do with real life and that the test game involves figuring out what the test designers intended as the correct response, not one's own authentic response. This is particularly true of open-ended questions that are scored by rubrics. These lessons in inauthenticity are part of the hidden—and increasingly, explicit—curriculum of every classroom in America. Furthermore, it is unlikely many students will fail because the exam itself is a legitimation ritual designed to bolster educational administration's claim to professional legitimacy. In order to understand its true importance in the larger scheme of things, we need to take a brief detour through some concepts developed by Michel Foucault, who spent his entire life studying social institutions and the ways in which power circulates within and around them.

The concept of *discourse* is central to Foucault's (1977) work, but he uses the term broadly to include more than oral and textual linguistic practices (Fairclough, 1992). To Foucault discursive practices are the link between knowledge and power. Social practices, like educational administration or teaching are viewed by Foucault as forms of knowledge. "Because they are knowledge constituted, not just in texts, but in definite institutional and organizational practices, they are 'discursive practices': knowledge reproduced through practices made possible by the framing assumptions of that knowledge" (Clegg, 1989, p. 54). Because discourses shape practices and practices produce discourses, some authors use the term *discourse-practice* to denote this circular dynamic (Cherryholmes, 1988).

Discourse-practices determine what counts as true or important in a particular place and time. For example, administrative interns want to become good school administrators. Becoming a good school administrator currently means that one must acquire skills so as to maintain an orderly and disciplined school, motivate teachers, manage conflict, improve test scores, promote a vision, and engage effectively in public relations with the school community. Good school administrators seek to master "appropriate" discourse-practices of administration. The importance of these skills at any particular time and place is the result of a battle over competing discourses or what Foucault calls a *politics of truth* resulting in a *regime of truth* (Foucault, 1979).

This battle among discourses is seldom carried out in the open and most often is not part of the consciousness of those who are shaped by it. According to Cherryholmes (1988), "educators adapt as a matter of everyday professional life to contractual organizational demands, to demands of professional discourse, to expectations of professional peers, and to informal as well as formal job expectations" (p. 35). Administrative preparation programs seldom interrupt this socialization and help to reproduce discourse-practices through what is assessed (and not assessed) in assessments that screen applicants into and out of programs, through what is taught (and not taught) in courses, and what is learned (and not learned) in internships with veteran administrators. This reinforcement through discourse continues throughout an administrator's career.

Peter Gronn, in a 1983 study entitled "Talk as the Work: The Accomplishment of School Administration" pointed out that between two-thirds and three-quarters of the total working time of a principal or superintendent is spent talking. It is likely that much of the remaining time they are dealing with various written texts in some form. Thus, leaders are constantly immersed in discourse. Their daily exchanges with colleagues and subordinates, the meetings they attend, their professional development workshops and conferences, the professional journals and books they read, the memos, directives, and e-mails they send and receive, all shape who they are as a leader and the ways they manage and legitimate a particular social arrangement.

In an information age, we increasingly live in a semiotic world of texts and images. Language is increasingly used not simply to communicate, but also forms part of a larger arena in which struggles over meaning and power take place. For instance, the language of business creeps into education talk and texts without anyone really noticing. Equity language, like "No Child Left Behind" is used to promote conservative policies. Expressions such as *homeland security,* and others like it, initially have an Orwellian feel to many, but seep into our everyday language through their constant use in the media, and soon they seem normal. New expressions like *ownership society* are floated by government officials to prepare new ideological terrain. The multilayered complexity of everyday discourses requires a form of analysis that can explore the relationships between everyday discursive practices and the larger world of shifting power relations in society.

Historically, the growth of Taylorism during the last half of the 19th century led to the need for the production of new discourses and the inculcation of new identities of workers under the new factory system. Likewise, we are today living through a historical shift that is often presented as a natural process of "globalization," but is in fact a power struggle over discourses and the shape that social practices—like teaching and leading—will ultimately take. There is nothing natural about these historical shifts; they are not historical shifts in the way that continental drift is a historical shift, though they are often presented that way in history texts. They are instead the result of social struggle and the ability of certain groups to define discourses and impose social practices. Fairclough (2005) sees these historical processes as "a matter of people coming to 'own' discourses, to position themselves inside them, to act and think and talk and see themselves in terms of new discourses" (p. 25). Discursive shifts accompany historical shifts such as those from craft to wage labor in the 19th century or the current shift from welfare state to competition or neoliberal state. One way critical discourse analysts think about studying this phenomenon is to study the ways in which the *social practices* discursively mediate between *social structures* at the macrolevel and *social events* at the microlevel.

Fairclough (2003) views complex modern societies as the networking together of social practices across different domains such as education, health, policy, the economy, the family, and the law. Thus, the domain of education is composed of social practices such as teaching, administration, and counseling. These social practices are immersed in and interconnected by discourse in the form of texts, defined broadly as written texts, spoken interactions, and the multmedia texts of television and the Internet. According to Fairclough, the transformation of what he calls *new capitalism* can be seen as transformations in the networking of social practices and discourses.

This networking of texts is what linguists call *intertextuality* and refers to the ways that a text borrows from previous texts—verbal or written. According to Fairclough (1992), "The concept of intertextuality sees texts historically as transforming the past—existing conventions and prior texts—into the present" (p. 85). Bakhtin argues that all texts and utterances are shaped by prior texts that they are responding to and by subsequent texts that they anticipate. According to Bakhtin (cited in Fairclough, 1992) "our speech...is filled with others' words, varying degrees of otherness and varying degrees of 'our-own-ness'" (p. 102).

Therefore, it is not surprising that the ISLLC standards incorporate previous texts that have influenced the field of educational administration over the years: texts from business, the military, and public administration. There are also in the ISLLC standards text (see appendix A) moments of potential departure from prior texts, but these discourses of diversity, community, and equity are generally captured within the logic of prior texts. For example, contested concepts like "community" are not well defined, leaving to the reader the task of seeking coherence. However, leaders are encouraged in the standards to have knowledge and understanding of "community relations and marketing strategies and processes." This public relations paradigm predominates as opposed to, for instance, a paradigm of community organizing. Whatever the examination question is for standard 4, citing a community organizer like Saul Alinsky or Martin Luther King would clearly not correspond to the rubrics that merit points.

My interest in using discourse analysis is to better understand how the everyday social events that occur in schools are influenced by the subtle ideologies embedded in texts. The importance of educational leaders like principals and superintendents in this process is their location as mediators. They occupy pivotal discursive spaces though which policies and practices flow. The texts I analyzed above—the national standards and a certification exam—are a single node within a much larger network of texts, both written and oral, that influence the social practice of school administration (and teaching), including texts used in coursework they take, school district memos and documents, policy texts such as *A Nation at Risk*, best-selling books on leadership, professional journals, the district website, and other WebPages, Internet communications, and newspapers and magazines. Texts as social interaction include workshops, conferences, meetings, and daily interactions with teachers, other administrators, parents, and students, both in person and over the Internet. This constant discursive interaction over time results in shifts in administrator discourse, which result in shifts in practice.

While I have described this as a top-down linear process, the relationship between social structure and human agency is always dynamic and interactive. Principals are not exactly "trapped" within discourses and roles. There is always some level of dissonance. Though less common, discursive shifts can also push upward from the grassroots and discourses can be taken up in unpredictable ways. However, much recent research suggests that new policy discourses linked to business models and market-based ideologies are intentionally and strategically promoted though privately funded think tanks and other media. More research is needed to track these shifts in administrator and teacher discourse over time and to identify more specifically how ideology is promoted through the discursive strategies of oral and written text, and what forms of resistance administrations engage in.

At a macrolevel, it may seem farfetched to link something as simple as a professional examination to the forces of neoliberal globalization. And yet many scholars argue that "explaining this process requires analysis of institutions, not at a broad societal level, but at the level of component practices and discourses" (McQuarrie, 2007, p. 37). These standards and the exam that enforces them are just one of the texts that form the ideological air that educators breathe since the shift in our political economy from welfare state to competition state.

Leadership and Policy Texts as Ideology

One of the most important recent genres of texts that promote ideology is commissioned reports. Full of pomp and circumstance, and linking education exclusively to human capital theory, commissioned reports are released frequently. There was a time when commissioned reports were only issued by government agencies in times of real or perceived crisis. Now commissions proliferate at the drop of a hat and are distributed in more sophisticated ways than ever before. These commissions and the, largely neoliberal, think tanks that often sponsor them have become effective at saturating the media with their ideologies (Haas, 2007).

Self-help literature and management theory have recently merged to create a new genre of leadership books. These books bolster administrators' self-esteem while providing a set of individualistic and depoliticized slogans they can use to motivate themselves and others. Over the past three decades, books like Tom Peters and Rob Waterman's (1982), *In Search of Excellence: Lessons from America's Best-Run Companies*; Stephen Covey's (1989), *The 7 Habits of Highly Effective People;* and Spencer Johnson's (1998), *Who Moved My Cheese?* became best-sellers and were used widely in management workshops and assigned as readings in education administration classes. This new genre draws on a previous genre of "success rhetoric" from Dale Carnegie's (1936) *How to Win Friends and Influence People* through Norman Vincent Peale's (1956), *The Power of Positive Thinking* (Ramage, 2005). These self-help manuals of an older generation have merged with a new genre of narratives about the virtues of the bottom line and the heroic leaders who run lean and mean corporations. Every major airport has an entire wall of books—print and audio—dedicated to these business and management gurus.

But these books are about more than merely propping up anxious and insecure leaders, they are also about legitimating corporate ideology. Institutional theory linked to Foucault's notion of discourse-practices are two theories that provide insights into the ways that corporate culture has gained greater legitimacy, pushing school leaders to want to look more like CEOs. Frank (2000) describes this process,

> The management theory of the nineties was consistently more about the nature of the corporation than about improving its processes or products. The real object of the "revolutionary" management theory of recent years was not efficiency or excellence or even empowerment, but a far more abstract goal: the political and social *legitimacy* of the corporation. By the nineties, the problems of efficiency and production had long since been solved: the wars against the working class had largely been won; even the state had been harried back into its laissez-faire cage. But how could things be kept that way? How was the corporation to prove itself a worthy ruler, a power that the people would happily obey, a sovereign for whose betterment we would toil and maybe even die? These, not the mundane questions of shop-floor efficiency, were the burning issues of the business revolution. (p. 178)

What Frank (2000) does not address is that the next step for corporate culture was to colonize noncorporate sectors of society. As we have seen, this ascendancy of business in American culture is not new; it occurred in the 1920s. However, neoliberal economic theories today lend markets even greater intellectual legitimacy than they had when Keynesian economics was dominant. Moreover, since the 1920s, countervailing forces, both international and domestic, held corporations somewhat in check. Today, with no cold war pressure to treat workers well, and with no union pressures, depoliticized, free-market corporate discourses are triumphant and enter the education field through multiple discourse-practices. Many of these have already crossed over from ideology into common sense, and unless another countervailing force appears, we should anticipate that the already ambiguous line between the public and private spheres will continue to blur, transforming traditional notions of political democracy.

5

Toward an Authentic Distribution of Leadership[1]

All systems set up to enact democracy are subject to corrupt manipulations, and that is why the public commitment to democratic involvement is so vital. Genuine, robust democracy must be brought to life through democratic individuality, democratic community, and democratic society.

Cornell West, 2005, p. 203

In the last decades of the 20th century and the first decade of the 21st, a pervasive discourse of participation, empowerment, and distributed leadership entered professional and lay discussions of education in the United States. We have seen a variety of restructuring initiatives using democratic sounding language that include school choice, distributed leadership, empowerment, administrative decentralization, local autonomy, parent involvement, shared governance councils, and leadership teams. These discourses of inclusion can still be found in current reform documents in spite of the fact that educators and parents were largely excluded from the halls of power in which No Child Left Behind (NCLB) was negotiated. The apparent incompatibility of these decentralizing discourses of inclusion with a current centralizing reform agenda that mandates high-stakes testing, reconstitution of schools, mayoral control, and the deprofessionalization of teaching is confusing to many.

Most of these discourses of inclusion, participation, and distribution are not really intended as democratic reforms, although neither are they antidemocratic. Instead, most are attempts to increase institutional capacity and productivity through work redesigns that involve team-based management and decision making. Such reforms are much needed, and should be supported in principle. Most schools today have some form of leadership team, data team, or some other form of learning community, and when authentic, they create norms of collegiality, share expertise, and can provide a greater voice for teachers at the school level.

However, when drawn form business models like the "quality circles" of total quality management (TQM), these discourses tend to promote "autonomy" at the local level and heavy-handed accountability measures from above. These new systems combine tight and loose coupling, usually involving outcomes-based pressure from above and limited autonomy and inclusion locally, and are aimed at "shaking up" and bringing dynamism to the system in order to raise production—however that is defined. While promoted as new and cutting edge, it is an old fashioned mechanical model of social engineering, composed of bureaucratic "sticks" and human relations "carrots," mixed with a new element of market choice and administrative deregulation at the local level. In fact when most proponents of NCLB talk about its combination of top-down and bottom-up pressures, the bottom-up or decentralized pressures are seldom viewed as broad inclusion in school decision making and civic engagement. Rather, the bottom-up pressure is the threat that consumer-oriented, school choice reforms will provide the option of parents exiting low-performing schools, usually for charter schools. Thus there are two types of parent participation at play; one that is consumer-oriented, viewing the market as a source of school accountability, and the other that is citizen-oriented, viewing parents and community members as providing local school accountability through political participation.

Because discourses of participation tap into feelings that run deep in the American psyche, they can easily become rhetorical strategies to promote various interests. Textbook images of U.S. democracy portray town meetings, voting booths, and the public square as well as organized struggles in support of women's suffrage, labor, and civil rights. Meanwhile, viewed as an antidote to entrenched bureaucracy, hierarchy, and excessive specialization, discourses of participation appear to have strong support among superintendents, principals, teachers, and the general public, regardless of their political ideologies.

The discourse of participation has become hegemonic not only in the United States but around the world as reforms in highly centralized educational systems from South America to Asia contain large doses of administrative decentralization, and parent, teacher, and community participation (Beare & Boyd, 1993; Gorostiaga & Paulston, 2004).[2] After all, so the argument goes, isn't it self-evident that student achievement is stifled by excessive bureaucratic regulation, intransigent teachers' unions, and out-of-touch reformers imposing ideas from their positions at the top of a rigid hierarchy? Isn't it obvious that those "closest to the action" and those with a stake in the enterprise should have a strong voice in decisions and be accountable for them? The discourse of participation and the reforms that are promoted under its umbrella, have for many taken on the force of common sense. What is often missed is that under the discourses of autonomy and participation, a tighter iron cage is often created for school professionals and school communities, leading to fewer, not more, authentic structures for participation.

School reformers often use these discourses of participation and democracy strategically, as part of a larger scheme to restructure school systems using business models and rational choice theories. Reformers have become experts at using hybrid discourses that combine elements of democracy with reengineering or conservative policies with democratic or even civil rights discourses. In this chapter, I will attempt to sort out which of these discourses have the potential for creating authentic democracy; which discourses are legitimately put in place to distribute cognition (knowledge and expertise) to build capacity; and which are hybrid discourses that employ a democratic discourse to sell a top-down reform. Although the boundaries among the three are never crystal clear, advocacy leadership can only thrive in organizational and community contexts in which authentic participation is elicited and in which there is a real possibility to devolve power to those left out of the reform conversation (Herr & Anderson, 2008).

Participatory Reforms: Authentic or Strategic?

Although not new, discourses of participation, parent involvement, and civic engagement entered contemporary education discourse from several developments. Some of these developments were legacies of community empowerment and civic engagement movements like the 1968, Oceanside–Brownsville conflicts over community control in New York City and others were more school-based attempts to empower school professionals, often at the expense of community empowerment. In 1973, in an attempt to give low-income parents greater influence on how Title I funds were spent, Public Law 93-380 required school districts to implement Title I Parent Advisory councils (TOPACS). Fege (2006) summarizes attempts to provide poor parents with greater participation in their children's education through a 1978 amendment to the law that,

1. Required parents to be involved in governance, establishment of programs, and provided with information about Title I progress and on the progress of their children;…
2. [M]andated the inclusion of parents of students who were eligible for Title I services and could not participate previously because of funding shortages;
3. Allowed the advisory councils to veto school districts' plans for the use of federal funds;
4. Required the local school district to work with the advisory councils in planning, implementation, and evaluation of programs; and
5. Provided training for council members. (p. 576)

In 1981, in part because of pushback from school and district administrators, Congress and the Reagan administration reduced involvement to a consultancy role, made TOPACs optional, and removed district requirements to fund them. Nevertheless, these Title I requirements put the idea of site-based decision making on the agenda in many states and school districts.

At about the same time, a research-based view of school leadership was also vying for legitimacy. The *effective schools* research of the late 1970s and early 1980s was based on studies of schools that were effective with low-income students of color (Edmonds, 1979). While this research identified parent involvement as a correlate of effective schools, also identified was the notion of strong principal leadership. Teachers who were interviewed evoked the lone, heroic principal who came in to turn their school around. Based on this research, a generation of principals was trained in this strong leadership model. While much of this research was quite diverse and nuanced, in the conservative climate of the Reagan administration, it tended to be boiled down to between five and seven rather narrow correlates organized around a "back to basics" theme.

Shortly thereafter, literature from business management gained increasing popularity. Inspired by business guru W. Edwards Deming, total quality management (TQM) was the fad of the day, and terms like *continuous improvement, statistical control of product quality, quality circles*, and *data-based decision making* gained popularity. Thus, sometime during the 1980s, the heroic principal was replaced by a principal that was expected to facilitate site-based, shared governance—at least in theory. By the late 1980s school districts were again requiring school-based councils, but unlike the Title I TOPACs, provisions for the inclusion of low-income parents were often absent.

There was, then, a confluence of the promotion of site-based councils by Title I and the popularity of Deming's business theories of worker participation in decision making. In this way, hybrid discourses were often formed by drawing similar ideas from very different intellectual and ideological traditions. But in most instances, institutional theory may be a better explanation for these discourses than conspiracy theory. The adoption of school-based councils often occurred less as a conspiracy to stave off authentic and broad participation by implementing inauthentic and narrow forms of participation, than as an attempt to adopt popular and thus, legitimacy producing, practices in schools and districts.

By the 1990s, there were signs that these shared governance approaches to educational management were running into problems. For example, several case studies suggested that shared governance structures may not result in significant participation in decisions (Malen & Ogawa, 1988), often resulted in contrived collegiality (Hargreaves, 1994), could reinforce rather than interrupt privilege (Lipman, 1997), and were even likely to create a tighter iron cage of control for participants (Anderson & Grinberg, 1998; Barker, 1993). There was also evidence that they were costly to service, often wasted members' time, delayed important decisions, and led to inefficiency and lower productivity (Beare & Boyd, 1993). Moreover, teachers in many schools were increasingly complaining that participation was often bogus, took time from their interactions with students, and intensified an already heavy workload leading in many cases to teacher burnout (Campbell & Neill, 1994; Chapman & Boyd, 1986; Gitlin & Margonis, 1995).

In industry, workers were becoming increasingly aware that while they were being "empowered" on the shop floor through participation in selected work-related decisions, their unions were being busted, their companies downsized, their jobs moved overseas, and their salaries and benefits slashed (Brecher & Costello; Smith, 2000). Many participants were reporting a sense of disempowerment rather than empowerment from so-called participatory reforms and, in the case of education, were increasingly calling for more authentic ways to participate in the governance of their schools.

School practitioners were less and less willing to give time to participation schemes they saw as inauthentic. Some of the problem was attributed to ineffective implementation; primarily by principals who were conflicted about giving up power when they were the ones accountable for decisions. But another part of the problem was an approach to participation that was inherently ambiguous. School professionals wanted symbolic participation from parents and the community. Parents and the community were led to believe the school wanted authentic participation.

Meanwhile a growing coalition of poor and minority parents and communities, home schoolers, and the religious right were giving up on achieving more authentic forms of participation in decisions that affected their children, and some were turning instead to a growing school choice and voucher movement that would allow them to choose their own schools. By the late 1980s two radical—but ideologically very different—attempts at shifting power to parents were underway; one was the school choice movement, and the other was the devolution of decision making to community councils in Chicago. Referring to this 1988 participatory reform movement in Chicago—perhaps the most radical attempt at broad-based participation in school governance—Katz (1995) presented a view of America's public schools as teetering on the verge of disaster: "Chicago school reform stands as the major alternative to the assimilation of schooling to a market model. If it fails, the advocates of choice across public and private schools will inherit the field" (p. 130). Declared a failure by 1995, Chicago reform shifted from community control to mayoral control, an increasingly popular school reform strategy.[2] Today we are at a crossroads. While choice policies and privatization have made powerful inroads, they have not won the day. Our public schools, while less democratic and more under the influence private corporations and noneducators, are still largely intact.

In the following sections, I will explore the ways in which the current discourse of participation has absorbed, and been absorbed by other discourses that promote a variety of goals, values, and interests, some of which may actually be nondemocratic in practice. First, I will argue that the current discourse of participation is part of a historical concern by school administrators with public relations and—particularly in periods when schools are viewed as in crisis—the creation of greater institutional legitimacy. Second, I will explore how participation can turn into a more sophisticated technology of control and the ways structures set up for greater participation often become sites for collusion among dominant groups. And finally, I will discuss how movements promoting parental school choice in an educational marketplace are framed by a discourse of providing greater parental "participation." Advocacy leaders in low-income schools will need to have a keen instinct for inauthentic participatory reforms and fearlessness about encouraging civic engagement even when keeping the community at bay may appear simpler.

My intent in providing this analysis is not to perpetuate a growing cynicism about our prospects of creating more participatory, just, and equal schooling. In fact, my central argument is that current limited approaches to participation should not be dismissed as mere instruments of domination and cooptation. They should instead be seen as contested sites of both discourse and practice that contain transformative possibilities if we know how to "read" them. But these transformative leaders cannot be the heroic, adversarial leaders described in chapter 2. Advocacy-oriented leadership cannot happen in the absence of broad participation, but the participation has to be authentic. In an effort to sort out these issues and move toward more authentic forms of participation, a conceptual framework guided by five fundamental questions that orient participation efforts will be provided.

Democratic Theory, Civil Society, and Participation

A discussion of authentic participation requires a working theory of democracy and civil society. Most educational proposals for greater participation, if they emerge from a concern with democracy at all, view democracy as either premised on "liberal" or "representative" models or confuse democracy with choice within free-market capitalism. In these instances participation is achieved mostly at a distance, through voting for representatives, or locally, through free and informed consumer choice.

Currently, terms like *participatory* or *strong* democracy, based on more deliberative models (Barber, 1984; Gutmann & Thompson, 2004) and "radical democracy," based on a politics of social equality, identity politics, and new media (Fraser, 1997; Dahlberg & Siapera, 2007) point us toward forms of direct, local democracy that more adequately address issues of an increasingly pluralistic society. Drawing on Dewey's notion of democratic community, participatory democrats argue that the future of democracy depends on the existence of local social spaces in which human actors can learn and exercise the skills of dialogue and debate necessary for the development of a democratic citizenry.

However, there is considerable debate about what such a space might look like. In recent years, there is growing attention to the idea of a civil society in decline (Bellah et al., 1985; Putnam, 2000). Others point to shifts in civil society from traditional spaces where people came together, to newer ones, such as the Internet (Dahlberg & Siapera, 2007), and a growing attention to community and youth organizing or service learning (Ginwright, Noguera, & Cammarota, 2006).

In third world countries that experienced exploitation from a corrupt or nondemocratic state, civil society has represented a viable third space in which to organize opposition and build greater democracy. However, in the United States, where liberal democracy existed alongside a welfare state, promoting civil society is more complex. For instance, some see voluntarism and public–private partnerships as part of a growing civil society movement. Others see such innovations as part of a conservative movement that wants to replace "big government" with "a thousand points of light" or a privatized and marketized social space.

For example the dilemma for nonprofit organizations that partner with small public high schools in New York City is that by becoming so closely aligned with the Department of Education, they lose their political autonomy and with it their critical voice. Thus, while some see civil society as a space within which to bring about change, others see it as largely at the service of corporate funders and government bureaucrats. This is why the defense of public schooling as a public space of state provision is so important. The defense of public schools is less a defense of the status quo than it is a defense of the public space that schools represent.

Preconditions for Democratic Participation

To speak of authentic participation is to ask who participates, in what areas, and under what conditions. In this sense, it is authentic if it includes a wide circle of stakeholders and creates relatively safe, structured spaces for multiple voices to be heard. These measures address the issue of participation as an exercise of citizenship and the constitution of democratic subjects, but by themselves they fail to address the ultimate ends of participation.

Most argue that, as with any school reform, the ultimate ends of participation should be greater organizational effectiveness leading to increased student achievement (Borman, Hewes, Overman, & Brown, 2003). I will argue that the ultimate ends of participation should be the constitution of a democratic citizenry and redistributive justice for disenfranchised groups. This will require giving all children high levels of achievement and a well-rounded education, but higher test scores and greater organizational effectiveness in the absence of greater opportunities is inauthentic reform. My view, while acknowledging the value and importance of other associated outcomes of participation, retains a view of participatory reform as linked to broader democratic concerns, not merely student achievement.

Limiting the discourse of participation to local school-site effectiveness and productivity is to ignore the ways in which the reality of local school settings is implicated in larger structures of inequality and social policies that hold it in place (Anyon, 2005). Within this context, to open up local participation to poor, inner-city residents of neighborhoods gutted of resources through White and middle class flight to suburbs, redlining practices by banks, and other policies of racial containment can be viewed as cynical at best. In such cases we promote a micropolitics of inclusion alongside a broader politics of exclusion.

As Casanova (1996) reminds us, local forms of participation are not inherently progressive, as local control became the rallying cry for White privilege in segregated Southern U.S. schools. Therefore, the notion of authentic participation that I develop here should result in both *the strengthening of habits of direct democratic participation and the achievement of greater learning outcomes and social justice for all participants.* In this sense, authentic participation requires attention to the local micropolitics of participation as well as the broader policy decisions that undercut the redistributive ends of participation. Authenticity, then, is concerned with both an authentic process and an authentic product.

Advocacy leadership requires a *critical* theory of participation, one that identifies and defends those versions that ultimately aim toward membership in a more just and equitable society. However, advocacy leaders will need to hone their authenticity barometer, and this can only be done through an understanding of the many subtle ways that power flows through practices that appear to be authentic on the surface, but can in fact be inauthentic.

Participation as a Legitimation Ritual

In the previous chapter, I argued that school leaders are at the nexus of multiple constituencies and, as organizational sense-makers they mediate the management of organizational meaning. If they are true to role, they do this in a way that makes their school look legitimate to its institutional environment. In this way, they become part of a larger political spectacle as described in chapter 2 (Edelman, 1988). By emphasizing this political dimension of leadership, I want to highlight the need to more carefully scrutinize neutral policy discourses that fail to explore the ways that policies and practices are implicated in symbolic actions that serve to legitimate a particular set of social relations. If the main goal of school reform were to create excellent and equitable schools that educated all children well, then one could expect that we would have achieved some semblance of success decades ago.

If we could defeat Hitler, help to economically rescue Europe with the Marshall Plan, successfully explore outer space, and fight a $3 trillion war for reasons still unclear to most Americans, then clearly we could make the kind of investment in economic and human resources needed to provide a quality education to all of our children. Given how intertwined education is with other social institutions, it would also mean that real resources and power in society would have to be distributed more equitably, and yet, since the late 1970s, just the opposite has occurred (Anyon, 2005).

If school reform is largely a political spectacle, then one might ask why this spectacle is needed. What is it that school reform is meant to accomplish? One possibility, following Meyer and Rowan (1977) is that school reform is a legitimation ritual that staves off a larger legitimation crisis in American society. As our society becomes less and less equal, a discourse of school reform, particularly one with equity and "social justice" goals, becomes an effective legitimation discourse. Slogans like "Leave no child behind," "Success for all," and "No excuses," particularly when performed by African-American bureaucrats in the service of the Bush administration, are effective distractions from the real threat to

American democracy that the widening gulf between the economic haves and have-nots has created.

At the school and district level, it wasn't that long ago that parent and community participation in schools was understood almost exclusively within the paradigm of public relations. For educational administrators a public relations model involved mostly one-way communication; that is, keeping the community informed through PTA meetings, newsletters, and annual reports to the local school board, a body which then served mainly to legitimate the superintendent's decisions (Kerr, 1964).

While more recent discourses (and in most cases, educational practices as well) of participation have moved beyond a narrow public relations approach, some would argue that current mechanisms of participation continue to be viewed by school leaders more for public relations and legitimation purposes than for authentic democratic participation. Whereas, in the 1960s, legitimacy was achieved when school professionals appeared to be in control and wield the latest tenets of scientific management, in recent years participatory structures appear to better respond to the climate of distrust of large, nonresponsive public bureaucracies.

Many critical theorists see a larger legitimation crisis arising from contradictions between capital accumulation and social inequality,

> The state has to promote capital accumulation, which, in a capitalist structure, always generates inequalities. At the same time, the state has to promote and sustain the legitimacy of the overall political and economic system. (Torres, 1996, p. 272)

While this legitimation crisis within capitalism is not new (Habermas, 1975), as levels of social inequality in the United States grow and become more visible, reforms are needed that define the problem not as one of resource redistribution, but rather as a need for greater system efficiency and production of human capital.

At the institutional level, the increasing bureaucratization of public life has been linked to large-scale state service agencies associated with the post-World War II growth of the welfare state. Ironically, these welfare state bureaucracies were created as an attempt to stave off a severe legitimation crisis within capitalism during the Depression of the 1930s. These large public institutions, including schools, have come under increasing attack from both the left and the right for their hierarchical design and excessive bureaucratic rigidity (Chubb & Moe, 1990; Ferguson, 1984). Thus global movements that call for decentralization, privatization, institutional autonomy, and participatory, site-based management are responding to a crisis of legitimation at the level of the state as well as a perceived crisis in the effectiveness and efficiency of public institutions.

Weiler (1990) argues that in the midst of a legitimation crisis, the state (and its various governance units) gains added legitimacy or "political utility" by appearing to be sensitive and responsive to democratic expression and local needs. This is, however, a risky process for any centralized system since, if decentralization represents an authentic devolution of decision-making power, the center will experience some loss of power. This is why some school districts have pulled back from school restructuring councils in which communities have successfully exerted sufficient control to challenge central office decisions.

According to Weiler (1990),

> A major challenge for the modern state lies in reconciling these two conflicting objectives: retaining as much centralized control over the system as is possible without a severe loss in legitimacy, while at least appearing to be committed to decentralization and thus reaping the benefits in legitimization to be derived from that appearance. The frequent wavering between centralized and decentralized modes of behavior—or, to be more exact, between decentralization rhetoric and centralization behavior—may well have to do with this difficult task of walking the fine line between the conflicting imperatives of control and legitimacy. (p. 422)

Weiler further argues that in highly contested arenas such as educational policy, decentralization allows sources of conflict to be diffused throughout the system and provides additional layers of insulation between the state—or in the specific case of participatory, site-based management, the school district—and the rest of the system.[3] Such a strategy is particularly helpful in the current era of cutbacks and "downsizing." When school districts have to cut back their budgets, they can diffuse conflict to the local school sites by allowing individual schools to decide where to cut. Under the guise of participation, the central office both gains democratic legitimacy and diffuses criticism for massive cutbacks. In this way, the selective devolution of decision-making power can be an effective way not only to gain legitimacy, but also to manage conflict.[4]

At the organizational level, legitimation may be achieved through the use of participatory mechanisms. During the 1980 and 1990s that mechanism was site-based management (SBM), a reform that was promoted as creating greater participation for teachers and parents. While some schools still have mechanisms for community involvement in decision making, SBM is largely being replaced by more current notions of "distributed leadership," "leadership teams," and "school learning communities" (SLCs), which are largely limited to distributing leadership among school professionals.

While a return to limiting school decision making to school professionals limits inclusion, researchers have documented the ways that participation can be subverted even when diverse groups are brought to the table (Henry, 1996; Malen, 1994; Malen & Ogawa, 1988; Sergiovanni, 1999) Malen and Ogawa (1988) studied shared governance arrangements in schools in Salt Lake City that were set up with near ideal conditions. All relevant stakeholders were included and given broad jurisdiction, policy-making authority, parity protections, and training provisions. Existing literature suggests that such conditions should enable teachers and parents to wield significant influence on significant issues. However Malen and Ogawa (1988) found the following:

> First, although the site councils are authorized policymakers, they function as ancillary advisors and pro forma endorsers. Second, teachers and parents are granted parity, but principals and professionals controlled the partnerships. Third, although teachers and parents have access to decision-making arenas, their inclusion has maintained, not altered, the decision-making relationships typically and traditionally found in schools. (p. 256)

According to the authors' findings, this lack of parent and teacher influence was the result of the following arrangements: Principals ultimately controlled knowledge and resources in the school, defended administrative "turf," and viewed the councils as "channels for dispensing information, moderating criticisms, and garnering support, not as arenas for redefining roles, sharing power, and making policy" (Malen & Ogawa, 1988, p. 259). Teachers did not challenge administrative authority because they feared social and professional sanction, or else, as was the case for many issues, they shared a common professional perspective with administration. Parents tended to lack "insider" information and familiarity and were unclear on the parameters of their power. They also shared many characteristics, and thus interests, with the teachers and principals (i.e., middle class, Caucasian, and well-educated). Furthermore, council agendas were generally controlled by principals (even though the councils were chaired by parents) and confined to safe issues. Institutional norms of propriety and civility kept principals, teachers, and parents on traditional "turf" and cast disagreements as personal affronts, thus restricting discussion, suppressing conflict, and confining discussions to noncontroversial matters. Finally because district oversight of site council regulations and procedures was minimal, they were often disregarded. Thus, the micropolitics of participation are such that even when participation is carefully orchestrated, most often power and influence remain in the same hands.

This led the researchers to ask what political utility these councils may have had. There is considerable evidence that principals found the councils useful as a way to present themselves as democratic while essentially retaining decision-making power in their office. As the notion of democratic participation is increasingly linked to choice in an educational marketplace, this need for legitimation through the spectacle of participation may be diminishing. As Rowan (2006b) points out, gaining legitimacy in the current institutional environment increasingly requires behaving more like a CEO than a democratic leader.

Participation as a Disciplinary Practice and Technology of Control

While the previous section described the ways that participatory reforms can provide institutional legitimacy, in this section I will discuss the ways that participatory reforms can result in giving up control in order paradoxically to gain greater acceptance of regulatory control from above. In other words, increasing professional or democratic control too often appears to have the effect of increasing self-regulation rather than empowerment.

To the extent that greater professional control of schools increases teachers' sense of efficacy, it can be a positive development. As I have argued elsewhere, professional disempowerment and deskilling have characterized teaching throughout its history, and teachers are right to demand more control over their work and their workplace. However, as Hargreaves (1994) points out, to understand the move to greater participation in educational institutions, it is also necessary to see it as influenced by theories of employee motivation promoted by the human relations movement dating back to the early part of the 20th century (Mayo, 1933).

The human relations movement created a much-needed concern in organizations with human motivation and increased attention to group process (but see Carey, 1995, for an account of how the human relations movement emerged as a response to labor-management conflict and a reinvigorated union movement in the 1930s). However, these concerns were absorbed into an institutional logic that viewed attention to the social and human needs of organizational members as an instrumental value that not only increased members' motivation toward increased productivity, but also became a set of "disciplinary practices" that normalized individual and group behavior (Foucault, 1977). As with the human relations approaches, the discourse of participation tends to be absorbed into a managerial bias and institutional logic in which it advances the apparently neutral and supposedly agreed upon purposes of the organization. The discourse of participation in schools is tightly connected to the human relations notion of "building ownership" in which organizational members "buy into" goals that are often determined elsewhere, are the product of a leader's "vision," or are buried in the rhetoric of mission statement generalities. In most management and leadership models, participation is not used to create or challenge goals, but to incorporate members into existing ones.

Although he takes his examples from industry rather than professional organizations, Barker (1993) has developed a theory of concertive control that is useful in understanding how self-regulation works in organizations. He argues that in postbureaucratic institutions control is increasingly exercised by shifting "the locus of control from management to the workers themselves, who collaborate to develop the means of their own control" (Barker, 1993, p. 411). Barker calls this "concertive control" which, he claims, results in the negotiation of a new set of consensual core values among organizational members. Unlike bureaucratic control, which invests control in supervisors who enforce bureaucratic rules, concertive control through self-managing teams or councils hands over the creation and supervision of rules and norms to organizational members. While this may seem like a positive development—and under certain conditions may be so—it also increases the intensity of control while it hides its sources. Barker describes a kind of *Lord of the Flies* environment in which peer pressure, surveillance, and even humiliation become daily events. According to Barker,

> Concertive control is much more subtle than a supervisor telling a group of workers what to do. In a concertive system…the workers create a value-based system of control and then invest themselves in it through their strong identification with the system. (Barker, 1993, p. 434)

This strong identification makes the enforcement of rules among themselves appear a natural process and they willingly submit to their own, often harsh control system.

The potential exercise of power by superordinates through concertive control has important implications for participatory decision making. Once we view management teams, shared governance councils, parent involvement models, or distributed leadership as potential disciplinary practices which represent efforts to normalize and control individual and collective action, we must reexamine the increasingly subtle ways in which power is exercised in more horizontal, "network" organizations (Anderson & Grinberg, 1998; Sennett, 1998). Participation becomes a potential disciplinary practice that embodies forms of nonovert control in which control no longer appears to come from outside the organizational members' sphere of activities. According to Barker (1993), "the relative success of participatory approaches hinges not on reducing control but on achieving a system of control that is more effective than that of other systems" (p. 433).

Participation as concertive control tends to increase self-identification with goals and result in increased levels of surveillance, stress, and work intensification; it also tends to thwart the devolution of power to those with less power. However, as we have seen, even well-intended attempts at participatory management tend to reproduce rather than challenge institutional power relations (Malen, 1994; Malen & Ogawa, 1988). How this, sometimes unintended outcome occurs is the subject of the next section.

Participation as Collusion

While ostensibly participation in decision making is intended to provide more opportunities for disenfranchised groups to have a greater voice in organizational life, in fact, too often the opposite occurs. Participation becomes a form of collusion in the sense that it reinforces the power of groups with similar interests. In fact, many advocates of liberal democracy claim that participatory democracy actually fosters inequality. According to J. R. Lukas (quoted in Bachrach & Botwinick, 1992), "Any system that calls for more than minimal participation will favor the active over the apathetic and the rich over the poor.… Participation is inegalitarian" (p. 23). In education, inegalitarian outcomes of participation occur, in part, because of the numerous ways that participation is limited and co-opted, often in spite of good intentions. However, as we will discuss below, even when participation is reasonably egalitarian, it has seldom seriously challenged power relations (Lipman, 1997; Malen & Ogawa, 1988).

While we tend to see administrators, teachers, counselors, parents, communities, and, less often, students as principal players in school participation, the common use of these as discrete and essential categories is misleading. For instance, school administrators, teachers, and counselors tend to share a common professional culture and often collude against lay outsiders, generally dominating shared decision-making councils (Henry, 1996; Johnson & Pajares, 1996). Even distributed leadership models that are largely limited to teacher participation tend to reinforce professional control over lay concerns. Zimet (1973), in his case study of the 1969 education decentralization law in New York City provides an illustration:

> There is an underlying difference in philosophy between the efforts of the professional staff and those of the United Bronx Parents. The efforts of the professional staff are directed toward inducing the community to improve its understanding of the school system and to adjust to it. United Bronx Parents, on the other hand, places its emphasis on the failure of the system, and demands that the system understand and adjust to the needs of the community. Until this basic conflict is resolved, progress in the direction of integrating school and community is likely to continue to be slow. (p. 141)

Henry (1996) points out that school administrators are often torn between empowering the school professionals or the parents, but tend to come down on the side of school professionals since "it is the faculty that she must work with on a day-to-day basis and to whom she is most directly responsible in the organization of the school" (p. 56).

In special education, Mehan (1993) and Ware (1994) discuss case study research that demonstrates how parent participation in individualized education program (IEP) meetings is devalued through the ways that power is embedded in a hierarchy of knowledge that places "expert" professional knowledge, replete with test scores, technical language, and institutional authority, at the top. In this way, participatory spaces meant to foster dialogue, end up producing a professional monologue that results in a parody of collaboration (Ware, 1994).

This returns us to an old debate about the respective roles of professionals vs. community (Driscoll, 1998). Henry (1996) suggests that professionalism need not be rejected as a value, but rather redefined so that "to be a professional educator would include the ability to relate to and team with a variety of people and organizations—such as parents, citizens, and social agencies" (p. 63). Such abilities represent an important dimension of becoming an advocacy leader.

While this failure even of authentic participatory management can seem discouraging, there is a growing body of research that suggests that there are new ways that leaders can link to low-income communities to leverage more power for their students. Shirley (1997) has documented the struggles of the Industrial Areas Foundation (IAF), a community-organizing group in Texas and the Alliance Schools that resulted from their struggle. Research for Action, a Philadelphia-based group has documented the successes of the Cross City Campaign of community organizers (Gold, Simon, & Brown, 2002). Mediratta, Lewis, and Fruchter (2002) have documented links between community organizing and public schools in New York. Beyond community organizing, Shutz (2006) suggests other ways of linking schools to communities, including the creation of school–community dialogue or study circles; community development agencies; nonprofit, local education funds; and youth organizing.

While parent participation through community organizing can be a powerful form of democracy in low-income neighborhoods, parent participation can also be a form of collusion when it empowers middle and upper income parents who know how to capture quasi-democratic spaces and use them to advocate for their children's interests within the system. As my narrative in chapter 2 about my daughter's tracked elementary school illustrated, those who have the time, interest, and cultural capital to participate in schools tend to be middle class parents whose class socialization is similar to that of school personnel. In such cases one often has middle class administrators, teachers, and parents making decisions that favor middle class children, as occurred in my daughter's school (Brantlinger, Majd-Jabbari, & Guskin, 1996). Schools, like classrooms, have what Delpit (1995) calls cultures of power in which the norms and values of a White middle class culture are reinforced.

Collusion can also occur at even broader levels as community participation stands in for distributive justice. For the privileged, community participation may be viewed as an intervention to legitimate current social arrangements since it can serve to defuse political conflict, restore trust in the political system, and conserve the essentials of the status quo (Popkewitz, 1979; Weiler, 1990). For example, discussing the work of Altshuler (1979) on race, Popkewitz (1979) argued that since Whites really have no stake in who governs inner cities and reservations, participatory reforms are favored over reforms that would require distributive justice for racial minorities.

> The critical issue, according to Altshuler, is to persuade the disenfranchised that the system is fair. Perhaps its most important positive potential, from the standpoint of citywide elected officials, would be to divert as much of the force of community dissatisfaction from them to neighborhood leaders. From the perspective of those in power, community participation can be a social control technique used to maintain stability without conceding resources to the discontented. (p. 209)

On the other hand, many advocates of poor and disenfranchised groups claim that participation in any form holds out the possibility of greater accountability from educational institutions that have tended to at best ignore them and at worst pathologize them. Scott (1990) reminds us that even progressive discourses that are meant to be merely symbolic can become resources for the disenfranchised. Once schools claim to make community participation one of their cherished ideals, communities can take them at their word and demand authentic forms of participation, even where these might not have been intended. In the final chapter, this idea of *policy appropriation* as a strategy for moving toward a post-reform agenda will be discussed in more detail.

Toward Authentic Participation

By suggesting in previous sections that the discourse of participation has been absorbed into educational institutions in ways that are often manipulative and nondemocratic, I am not arguing that this co-optation of participatory discourse for nondemocratic ends is always done with Machiavellian intentions. In many cases, attempts at increased participation are sincere, but poorly conceived and implemented or caught up in a larger institutional and societal logic that is antithetical to norms of participation. Shifting our notions of participation may require not only understanding the contradictions, inauthenticities, and ideological agendas of the current discourse of participation, but also creating new discourses that address broader democratic issues of social justice, but are also "doable," in the sense that they address current barriers to participation at both micro- and macrolevels.

In the remaining sections of this chapter, I will propose a conceptual frame that might aid in determining the degree of authenticity of participatory practices. In Table 5.1, I present a series of interrelated questions through which to interrogate the authenticity of current approaches to participation and the problems documented in previous sections. This framework consists of five central questions: (1) Participation toward what end? (2) Who participates? (3) What are relevant spheres of participation? (4) What conditions and processes

Table 5.1 A framework for moving toward authentic participation

Micropolitical considerations:	
Authenticity as...	**Key question**
Broad inclusion	Who participates?
Relevant participation	Participation in which spheres?
Authentic local conditions and processes	What conditions and processes should be present locally?
Macropolitical considerations:	
Coherence between means and ends of participation	Participation toward what end?
Focus on broader structural inequities.	What conditions and processes should be present at broader institutional and societal levels?

must be present locally to make participation authentic? (i.e., the micropolitics of participation); (5) what conditions and processes must be present at broader institutional and societal levels to make participation authentic (i.e., the macropolitics of participation)? Since considerable literature exists that discusses issues like who participates, in what spheres, and toward what ends, I will discuss in greater detail the more neglected areas of the micro- and macropolitics of participation.

Participation Toward What End? Authenticity and Ends-in-View

As I have argued in the above sections, the discourse of participation has been used to promote a variety of—often contradictory—social policies. It has also been used as a cover term for institutional arrangements and management techniques that, while purporting to advance democracy and change, too often tend to support an inequitable status quo or provide cover for changes at other levels of the system. A genealogy of participation would show that its origins are diverse, drawing on such disparate traditions as U.S. pluralist democracy (Dahl, 1961); participatory business management and quality circles aimed at raising productivity (Deming, 1993); claims of distributive justice through rational choice in the marketplace (Chubb & Moe, 1990); multicultural education aimed at raising formerly silenced voices (Weiss & Fine, 2005); community control movements (Perlstein, Sadovnik, & Semel, 2004); traditions of community organizing and empowerment of the marginalized (Freire, 1970). In these latter, more grassroots traditions, issues of social equality, political struggle, and consciousness raising are emphasized over those of majority vote, employee motivation, administrative decentralization, and increased productivity. All of these diverse traditions are evoked by the discourse of participation, providing it with a subliminal appeal to individuals across the political and ideological spectrum.·

Given this multiplicity of goals, the determination of the success or failure of participatory reforms requires first answering the question: Participation toward what end? For example, if our end-in-view is increased productivity or capacity then our approach to the implementation of participatory reforms may be different from a situation where equity concerns are dominant. Or if increased student achievement scores on standardized tests are the ultimate goal, then Wohlstetter, Smyer, and Mohrman (1994) suggest that participative structures should exclude parents and community members because their inclusion lowers teachers' sense of efficacy. Thus, one aspect of authenticity is a more explicit linking of means to ends. Misunderstandings occur when participants are expecting outcomes related to equity and democracy, when, in fact, productivity concerns are paramount. In some cases, the same solution can be proposed with different ends in view. From the right, parent vouchers are promoted using a productivity argument (Chubb & Moe, 1990), while from the left, they are promoted using an equity argument (Fuller, 1997; Gintis, 1994). However, in either case, authenticity depends on the explicitness of the ends in view and the extent to which a discourse of democratic participation is used merely for legitimation purposes.

At more microlevels, authenticity as ends-in-view takes the form of achieving a match between management's espoused theories and their theories-in-use (Argyris & Schon, 1974). In other words, do those who are in positions of power in organizations behave in ways that are consistent with their espoused policies? Teachers report that leader authenticity is obtained when principals "practice what they preach." Authentic principals treat teachers with respect and act on their own values and beliefs rather than in compliance with bureaucratic roles (Blase & Kirby, 1992).

Who Participates?

As I discussed in the previous section, the question of who participates will partly depend on the ends-in-view. For example, if a major goal of participation is to build the skills of a democratic citizenry in the tradition of participatory democracy (Barber, 1984), then students, parents, community members, and teachers would logically be included. Chubb and Moe (1990) argue that too much democracy creates bureaucratic and ineffective organizations, and they would want only parents with children in schools to participate and only through the marketplace. Wohlstetter et al. (1994), as previously noted, would limit participation to teachers. Most current research on distributed leadership seems to take a similar position as this research tends to not view students, parents, and community organizations as within their sphere of distribution.

While limiting participation might be argued from positions that claim different ends-in-view (e.g., parent choice, capacity-building), according to the proposed framework in Table 5.1, they would also have to address the conditions and processes that need to be present at micro- and macropolitical levels for participation to be authentic. For example, Parker and Margonis (1996) see the policies that turn participation over to the marketplace as part of a much longer history of neglect and racial containment of American inner cities. Likewise, researchers who argue that limiting participation to teachers leads to capacity-building or increases student achievement, may neglect evidence that culturally relevant teaching requires the participation of parents and community members and the "funds of knowledge" that community-mediated instruction provides (Gonzalez, Moll, & Amanti, 2005; Ladson-Billings, 1995). Exclusion of any stakeholder from participation must be carefully argued within the context of the other orienting questions of the proposed framework.

What Are Relevant Spheres of Participation?

Presenting empirical data on teacher participation, Bacharach, Bamberger, Conley, and Bauer (1990) argued that school reformers needed to progress beyond the "monolithic myth" of teacher participation in decision making and determine which specific decision domains teachers wished to participate in. While there is still some disagreement on specifics, most researchers in the area of teacher participation agree that core areas of participation which are both central to the core technology of the school as well as core areas of interest for teachers are the areas of budget, personnel, and curriculum (Reitzug & Capper, 1996). Although most of a school's budget goes to teacher salaries, there are often considerable discretionary funds for site-based budgetary decisions. Besides budget, teachers also want input into personnel issues, particularly hiring, an area in which principals and teachers currently have greater participation. On the other hand, decision making that impacts curriculum and instruction has been largely taken out of the hands of teachers and principals in many urban districts. Teachers for the most part do not want to have to divert time and energy into decision-making domains that they view as nonrelevant or frivolous.

For parents, and particularly low-income parents, authentic participation would have to move beyond volunteering to (1) governance and decision making; (2) organizing for equity and quality; (3) curriculum and its implementation in the classroom; and (4) home educational support (Parent Involvement, 1993). Much current literature also questions whether parent and community participation can be effective without understanding how particular parents or communities view their schools and how they define involvement. Many forms of parental involvement are often not recognized as "participation" by schools. According to Hoover-Dempsey and Sandler (1997) these forms of participation include home-based involvement such as "reviewing the child's work and monitoring child progress, helping with home-work, discussing school events or course issues with the child, providing enrichment activities pertinent to school success, and talking by phone with the teacher" (p. 6). School-based activities also include such activities as "driving on a field trip, staffing a concession booth at school games, coming to school for scheduled conferences or informal conversations, volunteering at school, and serving on a parent-teacher advisory board" (p. 6).

Student participation and community participation beyond those parents with children in the school is largely absent from mainstream literature on shared or distributed leadership. In urban settings, school choice policies have changed how we think about "communities," which has served to make forms of community organizing to influence schools more complex. For middle and high school students, participation increasingly goes beyond serving on student councils or mostly symbolic attendance at school-based councils. Nor are students typically learning the skills of civic engagement in classrooms. However, there has been an important growth of programs from service learning to student organizing that are generally located outside the school through after-school programs and nonprofit organizations (Ginwright et al., 2006).

What Conditions and Processes Need to Be Present Locally for Participation to Be Authentic?

There is a wealth of literature that argues for structures of participation in schools that guarantee not only the inclusion of diverse stakeholders, but also conditions that allow those stakeholders, once they are at the table, to have a significant impact on decision making. There is general agreement that authentic participatory structures should provide participants with broad jurisdiction, policy-making authority (i.e., not limited to an advisory function), equal representation of relevant stakeholders, and training provisions. In this regard, authenticity can be thought of as the extent to which participatory structures are fully and successfully implemented.

Nevertheless, as Malen and Ogawa (1988) found in their Salt Lake City study, full and successful implementation is not a guarantee of authentic participation. They found that while formal implementation was successful, more subtle factors at informal levels, such as fear of social and professional sanction, tended to thwart authentic participation:

> Fear of sanction was evident in general comments, such as "people feel threatened, in recurrent concerns about being labeled as a "troublemaker," coming across as "unpleasant" and "argumentative, feeling vulnerable, getting ignored."…Vindictiveness occurs through innuendo, behind the back remarks that ruin your reputation and your chances for advancement. (p. 261)

A similar process occurs with parents as they come up against the professional (and middle class) culture of the school. This raises for parents and their children, particularly those from low socioeconomic backgrounds and racial and cultural minority groups, the question of whether authentic participation—whether at the classroom or school level—can occur when they are expected to participate in a culture of power in which the exchange value of their cultural capital is perceived as low.

Some would argue that while their parents are denied access to school decision making, poor and minority children are also denied access to literacy and other skills in the classroom through instructional and organizational arrangements that disadvantage them (Delpit, 1994; Oakes, 1985). Lipman (1997) found that participatory school restructuring cannot transform the educational experiences of marginalized students unless educators' beliefs and assumptions as well as relations of power in schools and communities are challenged.

> Without multiple voices, without authorization and support to re-examine critically the very core of beliefs and practices related to disempowered students, without a public agenda which challenged the culture and power of dominant interests, teachers had few tools to begin to critically examine

prevailing ideologies and political and structural arrangements. Thus, race and class divisions, exclusion, silencing, and lack of engagement across differences were seemingly unmitigated by new opportunities for collaboration. (p. 32)

In this sense, participation is viewed not only as individuals and groups participating in decision making but also as creating the conditions for deep conversation about obstacles to student achievement. Advocacy leaders are leaders who have the will, courage, and relational skills to create these conditions.

Warren (1996) adds other barriers to authentic participation:

> …a lack of democratic experiences, the absence of structured public spaces within which individuals might learn to be comfortable with political dialogue, a political system that makes it very unlikely that dialogue could have any significance, and a co-optation of public dialogue by mass media. (Warren, 1996, p. 244)

Furthermore, he argues that forms of participation that involve deliberation about important and controversial issues are unattractive to most people, who prefer conflict avoidance to the discomfort of political discussion. According to Warren (1996),

> Most social interactions we can take for granted—not because they do not involve risks, but because the risks are contained; they are covered by a myriad of intricate forms of shared social knowledge, such as the rules governing reciprocity when one gives and receives gifts. Politics emerges when these forms of shared knowledgeability fray and become contestable, so that the risks of social interactions are no longer predictable; it develops at those moments in which the "automatic" regulations of social interaction become problematic and must somehow be restored, adjusted, or established under pressure of needs for collective decision and action. (p. 245)

From a micropolitical perspective, I would like to suggest that many well intended participatory restructuring and reform efforts in education fail, because they undermine institutional spaces within which a relatively clear set of rules, norms, and identities regulate social interactions, creating what Warren calls "arenas of social groundlessness," without a plan for the collaborative reconstruction of a new social ground.

In a sense, defining politics as a departure from taken-for-granted norms of social relations is rather narrow since it misses the ways the taken-for-granted norms, rules, and identities that constitute a secure social ground are themselves political. Nevertheless, it helps to explain why, when spaces are opened up for deliberation through institutional restructuring, the emotional and often material risks of participation are perceived as extremely high. Because restructuring that opens up spaces for participation, does represent the potential for redistribution of power, many are tempted, however cautiously, to participate.

The response of participants to these spaces will vary depending on how they calculate the level of risk and the degree of authenticity of the process. This may help to explain why school restructuring councils generally are forums for the polite rubber-stamping of administrative decisions when the old social grounds are still operative (Malen & Ogawa, 1988). It also explains why they can become extremely contentious and unproductive forums for discussion when an old social ground is destroyed. Thus, restructuring cannot proceed with the old social grounds, yet it cannot eliminate social grounding altogether. It must open up spaces while instilling the confidence that democratic deliberation will generate new social grounds where old ones have crumbled or been torn away. These problems suggest that the role of conflict in participatory approaches to institutional change may be undertheorized (Knight Abowitz, 1997). Too often our work in these areas betrays a prescriptive managerial bias concerned with the management of conflict, culture, diversity, and anything else that could potentially lead to authentic change, but which might upset the current balance of power in the institution.

In spite of the many barriers, I would argue that the attempt to create authentic spaces in educational institutions is worth pursuing and achievable if we rethink the roles of "leaders" and "followers" in the creation of authentic participation. This interdependence between advocacy leaders, who have the commitment and skill to open up democratic spaces, and courageous and critical followers, who can appropriate these spaces to defend diverse interests, challenges currently popular leadership theories. Bachrach and Botwinick (1992) critique positions that see the problems and solutions lying primarily with either transformative leaders on the one hand or an empowered citizenry on the other:

> We consequently disagree with Benjamin Barber (1975), who contends "that a paucity of values that might sustain leadership" is not due to "a failure of leadership but a failure of followership, a failure of popular will from which leadership might draw strength" (pp. 51–54). And we disagree with the opposite position, which places the responsibility upon leadership. James MacGregor Burns (1978) holds that the so-called failure of followership can be overcome by the "transforming leader," who "taps the needs and raises the aspirations and helps shape the values—and hence mobilizes the potential—of followers." (p. 42)

Thus, the potential of participation is most fully realized when the commitments and energies of democratic leaders are directed in concert with courageous followers toward the elimination of the institutional and psychological barriers to authentic forms of democratic participation. In such a way, as old social ground shifts, creating the potential for either conflict avoidance or the politicization of everything, new social ground that reestablishes and facilitates norms of dialogue and participation can be sought.

Based on a national study of social change organizations (SCO), Ospina and Foldy (2005) suggest that SCOs are a neglected source from which to enhance our understanding of leadership. SCOs are generally located within a growing civil society sector of advocacy organizations within both the public and non-profit sectors. They include "community-based and alternative organizations and groups connected to social movements, as well as networks of organizations engaged in civic reform" (p. 6). For these grassroots organizations, leadership is directly focused on goals of advocacy and social change. The democratic goals of these organizations lead, according to Bryson and Crosby (1992), to problems of sharing power within the organization as well as through interorganizational coordination. They suggest that this creates the need for a form of public leadership that is essentially different from leaders pursuing more restricted organizational goals.

As school and district leaders begin to view themselves as advocates for children and communities, models of leadership developed from SCOs might be more instructive than those developed from corporate organizations. The leadership framework that Ospina and Foldy (2005) developed,

> poses that the consistent use of a set of leadership drivers, anchored in a set of assumptions and core values of social justice, helps members of these organizations engage in **practices and activities** that **build collective power,** which is then **leveraged** to produce **long-term outcomes** for social change. Together, the drivers, assumptions and core values act as an integrated philosophy or worldview that becomes a powerful source of meaning to help frame and to ground the practices, activities and tools used to engage in action and accomplish the work effectively. (bold in original; p. 12)

Central to SCOs, is the emphasis on shared assumptions and core values focused on social justice and the ongoing dialogue required to reach sufficient consensus to act together, but it is largely neglected in schools because it is too often viewed as producing conflict. Like other organizations, SCOs struggle with conflict, but there is an acknowledgment that underlying assumptions and core values are central to the organization's very existence. Schools that serve low-income children and children of color are often operating on a set of underlying assumptions that hold unjust practices in place. Johnson (2002) calls this stage of school change "killing the myth and building dissatisfaction" and calls for deep dialogue about teachers' assumptions regarding their students and commitment to social justice before proceeding with school change.

But it is also in the realm of practices and activities that lead to the building of collective power that school leaders might benefit. The model calls for a series of ongoing practices that include: cultivating collaborative capacity, using collective identity narratives to build solidarity, engaging in dialogue across dif-ference, organizing, public policy advocacy, community building/development, direct service provision, grassroots leadership development, developing inter-organizational capacity, and network building. While these activities are not all foreign to school leaders, they are far from central to the leadership models that they are exposed to. Furthermore, when they are used in schools, they are often used to consolidate power within a school rather than leverage power toward educational and social change.

What Conditions and Processes Must Be Present beyond Schools to Make Participation Authentic?

Many of the links of participation to broader issues of social justice, legitimation, and control have been developed above and there is no point in repeating those arguments here. It is important, however, to make the case that while a deeper understanding of the micropolitics of participation is a necessary move toward more authentic forms of participation, we must also not assume that educational institutions and systems will tolerate authentic spaces once they are created (Anderson & Herr, 2008; Miller, 1990). Habits of authentic participation that give voice to subordinate groups have a ripple effect that affects power relations in other settings such as district offices, state legislatures, community organiza-tions, and corporate offices. To the extent that authentic participation enhances institutional legitimacy without exacting too many costs, it will be tolerated. To the extent that authentic participation threatens structured power relations at the institutional, community, or societal levels it should expect to trigger a backlash by those who may see their privileges threatened.

We are beginning to better understand the ways organizational politics are a mixture of micro- and macroforces. Recent advances in institutional theory and institutional ethnography have provided explanations of how external interests get organized into the internal politics of schools and school districts (Andre-Bechely, 2005; Rowan, 2006a). Added to this is an understanding that when differences of class, race, and education overlap with geographic location, there may be little shared experience and few opportunities for dialogue to take place. In such situations, increasingly the norm in the United States, participation may accomplish little more than the reinforcement of existing social arrangements (Lasch, 1995).

Conclusion

It is a challenge to create authentic forms of participation within a top-down reform driven by high-stakes testing. Authentic participation cannot be part of a work redesign scheme nor can it be socially engineered. The barriers to authentic participation we have described above are real and we should not gloss over the fact that to speak of opening up authentic participatory spaces within institutional and social contexts that are antithetical to their creation would be foolhardy and place people at risk. Because schools and universities are implicated in broader social power relations that are economic, gendered, and racial, there will always be some risk involved in eliciting authentic participation by teachers, parents, community members, and students.

On the other hand, the costs of inauthenticity are high indeed. George Herbert Mead (1967) stressed the psychological nature of inauthenticity as a form of dissociation that attacks our very sense of selfhood. Hardt (1993) states that "the question of an authentic life emerges from American social thought as a confirmation of reigning democratic principals and the expression of mutual interests and shared communities of values through which individuals would discover the self and be reinforced in their understanding of an authentic existence" (p. 55).

As organizational life and intensified individualism dominate the average American, and as the United States becomes increasingly divided by class and race, the constitution of an authentic self through participation in a democratic community may become increasingly rare. As market-oriented principles threaten to replace those of democratic participation, it is crucial that we better understand not only how authentic forms of participation can constitute more authentic private selves and public citizens, but also how they can lead to the creation of a more just society.

6

Toward a Post-Reform Agenda

When one is through parsing NCLB, with all its erroneous assumptions and failure to provide resources, all one is left with is an aching emptiness.

Thomas Sobol, former New York State Education Commissioner quoted in Levine, 2007, p. 32)

While there are many reasons to propose an agenda that might replace NCLB, Thomas Sobol's reference to "erroneous assumptions" captures the essence of why this reform paradigm cannot be tinkered with in its details, but must be replaced rather than reformed. The "aching emptiness" comes upon realizing that the well-meaning equity rhetoric is betrayed not only by its narrow, social engineering assumptions, but also its failure to link school reform with the kinds of social reforms required to make efforts to achieve greater social equality authentic.

Some might logically ask what I mean by a post-reform agenda. After all, schooling in the United States has gone through many reform cycles, particularly during the 20th century. Am I just anticipating the next cycle or wave of school reform? By *post-reform*, I am referring to the reform period that followed the 1983 publication of *A Nation at Risk Report* and has culminated in current NCLB requirements (National Commission on Excellence in Education, 1983). This reform period has gone beyond the usual tinkering with schooling to become what many have called a school reform industry. While the reform has been pervasive, it is encountering serious resistance from many quarters. As this reform cycle begins to lose legitimacy, a new paradigm shift may be possible, one that breaks with the past and moves away from viewing education policy as a form of social engineering from above.

But unless a shift in our policy paradigm is accompanied by a political ideological shift, things will change little for low-income communities and their schools. Although the ideological shift was a gradual one, the 1980s ushered in a political, economic, and cultural shift from a welfare state to a new competition and security state. School reform debates too often are divorced from these larger ideological battles, and even when they engage in social critique, they tend to fail to move from critique to proactive proposals. Those of us who critique the current policy paradigm and economic model, have to be ready with workable ideas for a post-reform agenda. Many of these new ideas are already in the process of being worked out in multiple forums. Some are new ideas or ones that have been "lying around" but not picked up; others are emerging out of alternative settings; others are the product of political engagement in communities and other social movements.

In this chapter, I will briefly discuss the kind of ideological shift that is needed in our view of the state and the economy, and the kind of paradigm shift that is needed in the ways we think about the relationship between policy and practice. I will then discuss some of the advocacy strategies that will be needed to make these shifts in both policy and practice. And finally, I will attempt to provide some idea of what this post-reform agenda might look like in terms of new forms of accountability, leadership, and pedagogy. This is a pivotal historical moment in which models of leadership, education and social policies will be reframed for the decades ahead. These changes will either be led by the current mix of corporate/political leaders and new philanthropists or it will be led by a broader advocacy community of educators and organized citizens.

The State of the Welfare State

A post-reform agenda will require a deep understanding of the current shift in the role of the state with regard to public education. In 1983, when *A Nation at Risk* was published, Ronald Reagan's radical neoconservative and neoliberal agenda (called Reaganomics at the time) for education was to abolish the Department of Education and promote vouchers and tuition tax credits. These two goals advanced his agenda of rolling back government and marketizing the public sector. While *A Nation at Risk* did not call for vouchers or for abolishing the Department of Education, it did set the stage for a crisis discourse that continues to surround public schools. While Reagan failed to marketize education and abolish the Department of Education, the Reagan "revolution" massively altered our tax system, increasing the size and wealth of American elites and contributing to the massive economic inequalities we observe today. Ironically, the Department of Education ultimately became a tool to leverage federal control over education.

While processes of marketization and privatization described in chapter 3 are proceeding apace through other avenues, they have been slowed considerably by reluctance on the part of Democrats and some within the business community to completely marketize and privatize the system. While the welfare state has been badly damaged, its fate and that of public education still hangs in the balance, and will depend on future policy struggles. Given this political and ideological context, post-1983 school reforms cannot be understood if we see them merely as an attempt to improve schools. They are intimately linked to a broader neoliberal project of radical social transformation.

Post-1983 reforms have gone through several iterations. No Child Left Behind (NCLB) is the culmination of several previous reforms including early standards and outcomes-based reforms, the 1989 education summit, Goals 2000, and ongoing attempts to promote school choice and vouchers. In spite of NCLB's equity provisions and increased federal leverage in education, elements of this neoliberal transformation have largely appropriated school reform as a vehicle for the right's political agenda. It has succeeded in moving attention away from broad welfare state provisions as a way to promote equal opportunity toward schooling as the sole institution responsible for providing opportunity. Defending the state becomes increasingly difficult as it is stripped of its social welfare functions in favor of corporate welfare and militarism, including, most recently, a $3 trillion war (Steiglitz, 2007). Repairing the damage of three decades of a neoliberal model and restoring the state to its function of providing a social infrastructure and regulating capital will require winning both an ideological struggle and applying political pressure. In this larger context, it seems clear that NCLB is not part of that advocacy agenda, and may, in fact, work against it.

Welfare state researchers are divided on how resilient the welfare state is. Some see it as surviving in a different—even improved—form, while others see it as being largely dismantled (Gilbert, 2002; Lewis & Surrender, 2004). While definitions of the welfare state vary, most see a quality education as a basic right of every citizen. Although public schooling was until recently viewed as less vulnerable to antiwelfare state rhetoric than such programs as Medicaid and Social Security, school reform advocates have gone a long way to undermine confidence in public schools, attacking them as a welfare state "public monopoly" that needs to be marketized and privatized.

While few would argue that the old welfare state didn't need reforming, we are currently witnessing a struggle over what kind of state will replace it. Neoliberalism promotes a competition and security state whose role is limited to protecting private property and providing national security, while expanding an unfettered private sector to compete more effectively in world markets (Friedman, 1962). While Friedman's economic theories have gone from lunatic fringe to mainstream in a few decades, its pure form has proven elusive, although it remains a discursive resource and a social goal in some powerful sectors. Harvey (2005) documents how the theory and reality of neoliberalism are two quite different things since the state has actually expanded under both Democratic and Republican neoliberal administrations, particularly the military budget.

From Welfare State to "Third Way" Politics

In the 1980s, "third way," "new democrats" associated with Bill Clinton and the formation of the Democratic Leadership Council (DLC) abandoned the welfare state for the so-called enabling state in which welfare was replaced with workfare (Gilbert, 2002). Sometimes called the Schumpeterian workfare state, it is contrasted with the Keynesian welfare state, which came under attack during the economic recession of the 1970s. In Britain, neoliberalism was implemented under the Thatcher administration, followed by a more hybrid, third way version under Tony Blair's New Labour Party.

The American version of third way politics has largely been promoted by the Democratic Leadership Council and its affiliated think tank, the Progressive Policy Institute (PPI), a nonpartisan 501(c)3 research and educational organization. A report by the Open Society Institute characterizes PPI as aiming

> ...to achieve a new synthesis of liberalism and conservatism for today's electorate. PPI's vision generally blends a traditional liberal politics (universal health care) with more market-oriented solutions and individual choice (Medicare choice, charter schools, a limited role for unions), then adds to the mix a strong dose of the moralism usually claimed by conservatives (welfare reform, v-chips, school uniforms), and a sprinkling of thinking about civil society (Americorps, community policing). It holds traditional liberal constituencies such as unions and African Americans at arm's length, while actively courting corporate leaders and the white middle class. (Kallick, 2002, p. 4)

Although a few progressive think tanks exist, the PPI is often viewed as the only ideological competition against better funded, right of center groups like the Heritage Foundation (neoconservative), the Cato Institute (Libertarian), or the American Enterprise Foundation (neoliberal). The Democratic Party has absorbed more and more of the right's platform in order to win back Reagan Democrats. Welfare state scholars point out that this shift looks different from country to country, with more traditional forms of welfare state social democracy still more intact in some Scandinavian countries, and hybrids developing in the rest of continental Europe and Britain (Lewis & Surrender, 2004).

While the discourse of a third way between the state and the market (sometimes viewed as "civil society") has gained popularity, it opens up a large analytic space that produces a broad continuum between the state and the market. The term *third way* is usually attributed to Anthony Giddens's (1994) *Beyond Left and Right*, in which he argues that "welfare" should be redefined as part of a generative politics within civil society that enables people to bring about changes in their lives rather than encouraging passivity.

The welfare state is often portrayed as a failed social experiment that stands in the way of unleashing a dynamic private sector. But, I want to suggest that the notion of social engineering from the top down, a problem with the central planning associated with the welfare state, is still alive and well, but implemented in perhaps a more sophisticated manner. In both cases, those with power, in or out of the government, assume they know best what the average citizen needs. Traditional forms of bureaucratic control are replaced by more sophisticated forms of control that steer the system from a distance. While this approach might unleash the private sector, it does not unleash the kind of democratic participation that might steer the private sector in directions that benefit citizens rather than a limited number of shareholders. The narrative in chapter 2 about LaPorte, Indiana was meant as a cautionary tale about what happens when the private sector is unleashed and unregulated.

The more straightforward neoliberalism of the Reagan administration has morphed into the third way neoliberalism of policies like the bipartisan NCLB with its negotiated mix of left and right polices. The new competition state is characterized by an eclectic pragmatism that includes mixes of top-down approaches like mayoral control and high-stakes performance measures, human relations and local autonomy, and market-based, choice policies that collectively are fraught with tensions. Table 6.1 compares Keynesian welfare state social and educational reforms with those of the new third way competition state. These are both compared with a third set of social and educational reforms that represent what a "post-reform" settlement might look like. To borrow a dialectical page from Karl Marx, it appears that the instability of the current school reform settlement might contain the inner contradictions that will lead to a new shift that represents a new paradigm. This new paradigm, while appropriating some of the workable aspects of the current reform settlement, has the potential to move a post-reform agenda further away from the neoliberal end of the continuum and back toward many of the ideals of social democracy.

Just as education has been central to American politics over the years, since 1983 it has become an ideological battle over competing visions of the nature of the state, markets, and civil society, institutional effectiveness, policy paradigms, modes of governance, macroeconomic models, and conceptions of the common good. While U.S. and British third way models are much closer to the neoliberal end of the market–state continuum, the rest of Europe has remained closer to a tradition of social democracy. Whether we ultimately drift even closer to the market end of the continuum with its vast social inequality or defend a market–state equilibrium that promotes greater social equality and democracy will become clearer in the next decade. What is also clear is that this will depend less on who is in the White House, than on the strength of advocacy movements that can place pressure on politicians.

One of the stumbling blocks educators must confront is the tendency in the United States to think about social equality almost exclusively in political terms and in terms of equality of opportunity rather than outcomes. This is a fundamental reason that so many Americans buy the idea that NCLB has a strong social equality agenda. The next section will take up the issue of broadening our conception of social equality.

Broadening Conceptions of Equality

Grubb and Lazerson (2004) point out that Americans have always emphasized *political* equality—equality before the law, voting rights, etc.—above *economic* equality to a greater extent than Europe. During much of the 20th century Americans debated whether the ideal of equality should be extended to economic equality. The fact that, for the most part, it was not, explains why the United States developed a much weaker welfare state than those of European countries. The only version of economic equality that has taken hold in the United States is the notion of equality of opportunity, or in the present vernacular, "leveling the playing field." Overlapping with the protestant ethic of individual effort, equality of opportunity has permeated schooling, particularly once schooling moved away from the civic and moral purposes of the common school movement. As schools began to be viewed as allocators of future vocations during the early part of the 20th century, equity issues turned to increasing access to education.

However, while access to schooling has increased over the years, it has not made us more equal. In early America families fostered success for their children through a family business or good marriage, but there has been a vast shift from direct family influence to schooling as a mechanism for upward social mobility. This is so for the many well-researched ways that schooling favors the economic, social, and cultural capital of middle and upper class families and disfavors that of low-income families (Bourdieu & Passeron, 1977/1990; Stanton-Salazar, 2001). It has also occurred because while we have increased access to education at all levels, each level has become more stratified. Many more students attend higher education, but whether you attend a community college, a second or third tier university, or an elite one will still determine which occupational slots are open to you. Grubb and Lazerson (2004) remind us that: "High-status parents still tend to beget high-status children, to the same extent that they did before schools were important" (p. 225).

Advocacy educators cannot fail to continue to address these issues of opportunity and to mitigate, if not eliminate, barriers within schools that are created by unequal levels of social, cultural, and political capital of their students. After all, the school is clearly within their span of control. And yet, a new paradigm would not expect schools alone to undo decades of growing social inequality and residential segregation. To charge educators to take on this task alone and then blame them when they fail is to ensure a burned out and demoralized profession.

Tyack and Cuban (1997) document how schools have in recent history been the stage upon which America's dramas have been played out, from busing to achieve racial desegregation to testing to close the achievement gap. The expectation that schooling alone will resolve America's ills has long been a favorite American belief; one Grubb and Lazerson (2004) call the Education Gospel. Though we have embraced the notion that schools *influence* society, the fact is that schools are far more likely to *reflect* society. Against the Education Gospel, they argue that a new conception of the state is needed that honors both the important role of schooling, but that acknowledges that schooling can only promote social equality if it is allied with a supportive state.

> Americans now have a nearly impotent welfare state that asks educational institutions to redress social problems that they cannot possibly solve on their own. This creates an impossible dilemma for schooling, particularly in a country with such high levels of inequality. Our country needs a different conception of public responsibility—one that we call—the Foundational

State —that would provide the preconditions or foundations for a richer, more equitable version of the Education Gospel. (p. 215)

While I will use the term *empowering state* to describe a post-reform state rather than Grubb and Lazerson's term *foundational state*, their description of a new state that provides preconditions for empowering education matches my own view. Not only will a new paradigm require a shift in our conception of the state's role in providing social equality, it will also require new ways of thinking about educational policy.

A Policy Paradigm Shift for a Post-Reform Agenda

A post-reform agenda will need to propose a new paradigm for thinking about school reform and educational policy. Part of this new policy paradigm will require broadening the scope of what counts as policy and better understanding how policy is interactive among macro-, meso-, and microlevels. We will also need a new educational discourse that can appropriate some remnants of previous policies while bringing in new ideas. Neoliberals have understood that the language we use to talk about reality is as important, if not more, than reality itself. The right has constructed and framed a new neoliberal common sense, while the left, in trying to accommodate to it rather than reframe the issues, has moved to the political right (Kumashiro, 2007; Lakoff, 2004).

Second, to think about classroom and school-level practices independent of social policies that impact kids is to plays into the hands of economic neoliberals, who want to shrink government and unleash market forces on education. How did educators buy the notion that to raise issues about a lack of resources or regressive social policies was to make excuses or to believe poor kids can't learn? This has important implications for the largely depoliticized preparation of teachers and administrators, and our subsequent failure to prepare our students for political citizenship. Increasingly, teacher preparation is being narrowed to a series of "methods" courses, with little preparation in child and youth studies (especially beyond the elementary level), let alone, policy studies. With the exception of a handful of lobbyists and some union advocacy in state legislatures, a generation of educators (in schools and universities) has largely been caught off guard by changes that have occurred over their heads in policy arenas that threaten their professionalism. So what is the policy paradigm we've bought into?

Today education is "reengineered" from the top and "recultured" from within. Here by recultured, I mean that the language and ways of thinking are "managed" to conform to the new paradigm of performance outcomes. This new paradigm is not merely applied to educational institutions. Within public sector management, it is known as the *new managerialism* or the *new public administration*. Critiques of the excesses of this rationalistic, performance-oriented approach have become more frequent (Nichols & Berliner, 2007; Radin, 2006), but it has become so

Table 6.1 Shifts in social and educational policies from welfare state to third way state

Time period	Keynesian welfare state/ social democracy (1930s to 1970s)	Third way neoliberalism (the competition state) (1970s to present)	Third way social democracy (the empowering state)
Level of reform	Social reform	Social reform	Social reform
Political–economic stance	Commitment to distributive justice	Commitment to unregulated markets and competition as creating greater prosperity	Recommitment to distributive justice as well as a politics of representation
View of individual	Individual and social welfare	Competitive individualism	Individual and social empowerment
Social welfare provision	Social welfare provision primarily through government	Increase of social welfare provision through the private sector	Social welfare provision primarily through government with some civil society participation
Corporate accountability	Corporate accountability through government regulation	Less corporate accountability through government deregulation	Corporate accountability through a mix of government regulation and incentives
Equity of taxation	Progressive income tax	Regressive income tax	Progressive income tax
Countervailing forces	Strong countervailing social forces from below (labor, civil rights movement, new social movements)	No or weak countervailing social forces from below	New countervailing forces from communities, an activist civil society and public sector unions
Policy and race	Race conscious policies	Race neutral or color-blind policies	Return to race conscious policies with adequate regulation and resources
Military spending	Smaller post-WWII military until increased spending for Vietnam War	Post 9/11 perpetual war. Massive military budget. Iraq as $3 trillion war. Security state and hypermilitarized society	Antiempire. Focus on diplomacy. Peace dividend
Level of Reform	**School Reform: Macro** (social engineering)	**School Reform: Macro** (social engineering "steering from a distance")	**School Reform: Macro** (policy ecology)
Form of government and governance	*Government* through bureaucratic control (as opposed to *governance* through steering, influencing, and partnering)	Minimal *government* (deregulation) *Governance* through steering, influencing, and partnering	*Government* provides needed regulation and hybrid *governance* that emphasizes professional and community control

Time period	Keynesian welfare state/ social democracy (1930s to 1970s)	Third way neoliberalism (the competition state) (1970s to present)	Third way social democracy (the empowering state)
Approach to accountability	Public school accountability primarily through mix of local control (school boards), professional supervision, testing and bureaucratic control	Public school accountability primarily through federal government regulation (NCLB). High stakes testing/outcomes-based, school choice	Public school accountability through greater public, reciprocal and internal accountability
Public/private relationship	Public–private sectors as separate realms with different aims and interests.	Public–private partnerships, Business model: marketization, entrepreneurialism, performance measurements, customers (replace citizens)	Some public-nonprofit collaboration (civil society)
High school reform	Comprehensive high schools and expansion of secondary education for all.	Small high schools	Small high schools
Teacher professionalism	Teacher professionalization and street-level bureaucracy	Teacher deskilling	Culturally responsive, professional teachers
Local school governance	District superintendents, school boards	Mayoral control, District superintendents as CEOs	District superintendents, school boards, community organizing
Role of unions	Prounion	Mostly antiunion	Prounion: Union reform and greater activism
Definition of equity	Equity defined as "equal educational opportunity" with emphasis on inputs	Equity defined as "closing the achievement gap" with focus on outcomes	Equity defined as equality of inputs and outcomes
Level of Reform	School Reform: Meso/Micro (social engineering at the base: Implementation	School Reform: Meso/Micro (social engineering at the base: Work Redesign)	School Reform: Meso/Micro (system and life world in balance)
Principal Role	Principal as formal leader	Principal modeled on CEO but lacking executive power (chooses vendors, more control over hiring, etc.)	Principal as advocate in alliance with community
Pedagogy	Subtractive pedagogy	Subtractive pedagogy	Additive pedagogy

(continued)

Table 6.1 Continued

Time period	Keynesian welfare state/ social democracy (1930s to 1970s)	Third way neoliberalism (the competition state) (1970s to present)	Third way social democracy (the empowering state)
School governance	Little shared governance	"Distributed leadership" limited to school professionals, largely advisory	Shared governance with community engagement
Teacher assessment	Teacher assessment through evaluation/ supervision	Teacher assessment through test scores	Teacher peer-assisted assessment
Student assessment	Student assessment mainly teacher centered	Student assessment through high-stakes testing	Student assessment through multiple data sources including testing and teacher centered evaluations
Curriculum	Curriculum based on textbook publishers	Scripted, "evidence-based" curriculum based on standards	Rich, rigorous, culturally relevant curriculum based on standards developed with teacher and community input

much a part of our common sense, that few critics believe it will change. Much as the There Is No Alternative (TINA) principle operates for global neoliberalism, discussions among even critics often begin with comments like the following: "I take it as a given that the world of high-stakes top-down accountability is here to stay" (Abernathy, 2007, p. 132).

What distinguishes this reform in education from past neo-Taylorist approaches is both the intensification of an audit culture based on high-stakes testing and the privatizing and marketizing tendencies of the new competition state. The two work hand in hand, since performance data on schools is a prerequisite for effectively marketizing the system by making it easier to compare and choose. Both are also seen as complementary accountability systems that wed the audit culture of testing with the discipline of the market. While no one is suggesting that we scrap accountability systems altogether, finding the right kind of accountability has been a challenge for several decades. Below, under "The New Accountability," I will discuss a proposal for what a post-reform accountability system might look like.

Apple (2006) suggests that shifting this paradigm may be even harder than we think. Not only are rationalistic, high-stakes testing approaches engrained in our cultural ways of thinking, there is a significant social sector that materially benefits from this arcane system.

For instance, at one California university where I taught, our Educational Administration Department had a difficult time attracting and retaining faculty because faculty could make two and three times their university salary consulting with school districts. As a result of NCLB's annual yearly progress requirements, local low-performing schools were required to hire an external evaluator. These evaluators often received as much as $30,000 per school.

While many evaluators were conscientious in their preparation of evaluations and action plans for the schools, some created businesses that contracted with multiple schools and hired out help. In general schools complained bitterly about the poor quality of the evaluations and action plans and the opportunities lost by not spending this money on needs perceived by the school. One school reported receiving an action plan with another school's name on it.

One colleague told me she charged at least $3,500 a day for her consulting services. When I commented that this seemed like a lot of money, she looked at me in disbelief, and said that business consultants made a lot more. Although I didn't respond, I wanted to ask her what the average per diem pay of a local teacher was. My point is that this convoluted accountability system has spawned a new lucrative sector within the school reform industry for entrepreneurial individuals and consultancy companies to flourish.

But Apple (2006) is referring to material interests that go beyond this lucrative reform industry. There is a significant professional class whose social, cultural, and symbolic capital and that of their children are compatible with an audit culture. This professional and managerial middle class can

> see themselves as engaging in a moral crusade—seeing themselves as being endlessly responsive to "clients" and "consumers" in such a way that they are participating in the creation of a newly reconstituted and more efficient set of institutions that will "help everyone"—and at the same time enhancing the status of their own expertise. (p. 106)

This audit culture also ensures that their children will have less competition from other students because they can more easily convert their social, cultural, and economic capital into high test scores, and thus, entrance to elite educational institutions and high paying professions. The advantages that increased standardization and more testing provide for middle class students far outweigh any equity effects of disaggregating test scores by socioeconomic status and race on minimum competency exams. Therefore, while this professional class may be politically progressive on many issues, they can easily ally themselves with many neoliberals and neoconservatives in their support of NCLB.

From Policy Engineering to Policy Ecology

Years of approaching policy as social engineering are in part a result of the mechanistic ways we have thought about policy and practice. Notions of "leveraging" change and "scaling" up are legacies of this mechanistic view of society. Nothing has been more problematic about NCLB than the massive distance between its espoused goals and the perverse incentives and unintended consequences it has created on the ground. Academic policy analysts with their statistical manipulation of policy variables are woefully unprepared to deal effectively with the current complexities of the policy environment. They adhere to the positivist and functionalist approaches they were taught in graduate school and in spite of a discourse of "mixed methods," most seem disinclined toward research methods fine-tuned to the realities of a complex policy ecology. A new policy paradigm will require an approach to policy analysis that values not only statistical studies, but also ethnographic and case study methods, discourse analysis, network analysis. More sophisticated ways of thinking about "causality" are required. Perhaps most importantly, we need policy studies that involve the "targets" of policy in the generation of research questions, design, and implementation. Participatory action research provides an approach that honors local knowledge and involves teams of researchers and participants in coming up with local policy solutions that are also transferable (as opposed to generalizable) to other similar settings (Herr & Anderson, 2005; Minkler & Wallerstein, 2003).

Statistical policy analyses from the Coleman Report (Coleman, Campbell, Hobson, & McPartland, 1966) to the present fetish with randomized assignment to experimental and control groups have probably caused as much policy mischief as solid policy recommendations. Not only has C. Wright Mills's (1961) critique of abstracted empiricism not been heeded by most sociologists and policy analysts, such methods were enshrined in the federal government of the Bush administration (National Research Council, 2002). Clearly there are some valuable statistical findings that can illuminate pieces of the educational policy puzzle. Although we may have expected as much, it is helpful to know that low-income kids fall behind middle class kids during summer vacation (Kim, 2004). Such studies can tell us where to focus our efforts, but several generations of research have pointed out that implementation fails unless we have fine-grained studies of practice contexts.

But even these generalizable and universal findings may not be all that generalizable or universal. School reform is a moving target and social and demographic realities change significantly every few years, making previous findings questionable. Furthermore, it turns out that the policy environment is much more complex than we previously thought. To understand the current policy environment, we will need a much larger repertoire of methodological options, broader approaches to policy analysis, and a better understanding of policy influences.

While policy can still be defined succinctly as the authoritative allocation of values (Easton, 1953), new frameworks have evolved over the years. In the 1980s, Kingdon (1984) provided a theory of *policy streams*, in which policy came about when windows of opportunity converged with political agendas and policy entrepreneurs. Subsequent theorists added new dimensions of complexity. Bensimon and Marshall (1997) highlight the need for policy analysts to "reveal the gender biases (as well as racial, sexual, and social class biases) inherent in commonly accepted theories, constructs, methodologies, and concepts" (p. 6). Edelman (1988) alerted us to the role of the symbolic, the media, and the political spectacle. Weaver-Hightower (2008), who suggests thinking of policy as a complex and fragile ecology, suggests that policy influences are nearly everywhere. He has found that popular discourses and texts can result in de facto policy.

> Key elements of policy ecologies might escape notice if analysts do not explore these notions of de facto policies and policies as texts and discourses. Documents that act in the capacity of policy create or uphold particular discourses or become de facto policy in the absence of mandates. Such quasi-policies are pivotal to the workings of many policy ecologies. (p. 158)

The importance of such texts as commissioned reports and popular self-help and management theory books discussed in chapter 4 is an example of de facto policy texts. Even popular culture like sit-coms, movies, and kitsch art and "the time-honored myths and stereotypes that it condenses have been woven into the political discourse and, far too frequently, into public policies (Lugg, 1999, p. 103).

Poststructural policy analysis presents an even less rational view of the policy process, describing policy as a process of bricolage. Ball (1998) argues that policy is:

> ...a matter of borrowing and copying bits and pieces of ideas from elsewhere... cannibalizing theories, research, trends, and fashions and not infrequently flailing around for anything at all that looks as though it might work. Most policies are ramshackle, compromise, hit and miss affairs, that are reworked, tinkered with, nuanced and inflected through complex processes of influence, text production, dissemination and, ultimately, recreation in contexts of practice. (p. 126)

Add to this the pressures for legitimation that institutional theorists describe and that I discussed in chapter 4. While school systems are still in some ways loosely coupled systems, neoinstitutional theorists are describing ways that reforms have tightened up system compliance. This tightening is increasingly done through testing regimes and through "'governance' conceived as deeply institutionalized cognitive schemata" (Rowan, 2006a, p. 25) that result in a kind of institutional "common sense." In chapter 4, I discussed the ways school leaders are expected to manage this institutional common sense in such a way as to make it appear nonproblematic, even when the constructed common sense works against their less privileged students.

Other policy influences exist in a growing school improvement industry that exists alongside formal governing agencies. Teacher and administrator training is diversifying across for-profit and nonprofit sectors. Outsourcing of services is increasing as districts outsource accounting, insurance, cafeteria, custodial, maintenance, and busing services. Other actors in the institutional environment include research and development firms, testing and textbook companies, tutoring services, manufacturing firms providing office supplies, furniture, heating and cooling systems, metal detectors, video surveillance equipment, special contracts with soda and candy companies, and so on (Burch, 2005; Davies, Quirke, & Aurini, 2006; Rowan, 2006b). These developments not only mean a sizable shift from public to private provision of services, but they have important policy implications.

In America's liberal democracy, policy is created through a complex process that includes a wide array of political actors, the most formal level being the three branches of government. While NCLB is best known as a result of federal legislation, its origins can be found in systems implemented at the state level, primarily the Texas Accountability System. There are also key nongovernmental actors, such as business, government and union interest groups, think tanks, the media, and increasingly, private philanthropy (Fowler, 2008). While any attempt to summarize the complex process of policy development will inevitably suffer from some reductionism, I think it is safe to assert that at both the governmental and nongovernmental level, political negotiations were carried out largely over the heads of educators and their advocates (for a more in depth account of NCLB as a policy process, see Debray, 2006).

From Policy Resistance to Policy Appropriation

Older strategies of local resistance to this policy context are no longer sufficient. Even though teachers and administrators have some control over how policies are implemented at the school and classroom level, NCLB has reduced their degrees of freedom substantially, particularly in the key areas of curriculum and instruction. Practitioners are still often theorized as "street-level bureaucrats" who are seen as distorting policy as they cope with the often-overwhelming demands of a policy as it settles into the routines of their daily practice (Lipsky, 1983). This notion of policy implementation as a filtering process in which policies are modified at each bureaucratic level all the way down to the street level is implicit in much policy analysis and an artifact of top-down, social engineering approaches. Such a model constructs practitioner "resistance" as a problem to solve, instead of a sign of a possible flaw in the policy process.

A dramatic case of teacher resistance was the widely reported refusal of Carl Chew, a 6th grade science teacher at Nathan Eckstein Middle School in the Seattle School District to administer the Washington Assessment of Student Learning to students (Blanchard, 2008). But school practitioners engage in thousands of smaller acts of resistance on a daily basis. While policy resistance allows for some agency on the part of practitioners in the policy process, the role is limited to a reactive stance, and is usually engaged in by isolated, individual teachers.

The notion of advocacy leadership I have developed contains a much more active and dynamic role for practitioners in the policy process, but for advocacy to be successful, administrators or teachers often need to take actions collectively with the support of the communities they serve and with their professional associations and unions. They will also have to do more than resist policies; they will need to engage in complex forms of policy appropriation.

Policy Appropriation There are various ways in which leaders engage in policy appropriation. One is to pick and chose those top-down policies one will implement rigorously and those one will implement in a largely symbolic manner. For instance, as the research by Malen and Ogawa, reported in the previous chapter, illustrated, most principals implemented site-based management in a largely symbolic way. Some even appropriated it in such a way as to augment their power. However, some appropriated it to create the kinds of democratic schools they had always wanted to promote. In those cases, the policy provided principals with legitimacy for engaging in real democratic reform, even in case when districts were worried about giving communities greater power.

In fact, some policy analysts view the forms of coping, resistance, and adaptation that street level bureaucrats engage in at the sociocultural level of schools as policy appropriation, and suggest that ethnographic research at this level could provide us with a more nuanced analysis of the processes of policy appropriation (de Jong, 2008; Sutton & Levinson, 2000). Given the broad policy ecology described above, de Jong (2008) argues that there are many potential spaces in which practitioners can rework policy discourses and circulate them in creative ways:

> The ideological, interpretative "spaces" that are inherent in policy processes create opportunities that can be explored by administrators and teachers in order to continue to engage in equitable practices. At the same time, these spaces intersect with other discourses and ideologies. As the core of policy implementation, actual classroom practices will be mediated by how teachers negotiate these multiple views and practices. (p. 21)

This view provides us with a tool for resisting policies in a way that is perhaps more strategic, although there may be times when outright defiance, as in the case of the Seattle teacher's refusal to administer the exam, may serve to galvanize broader resistance. As a political strategy, policy appropriation involves identifying workable elements of current policies and key dilemmas and contradictions of these policies that can be reframed or disembedded and rescued from the political right.

For instance, the disaggregation of data by race and socioeconomic status in NCLB is a legitimate approach from an equity perspective, in that it provides a way to hold schools accountable for all of their students. Nevertheless, this approach is captured by a neo-Taylorist logic that so narrows the instruction and curriculum for the students it is meant to empower that it makes it difficult for many to support. Nevertheless, the core notion of using disaggregation of more holistic data and disaggregating input as well as outcome data holds promise for a new approach to equity-oriented accountability. In this way the policy can be appropriated and disembedded from the Taylorist and neoliberal logics that promote reductionist forms of assessment and an exclusive focus on outcomes. In this reappropriation, one can argue that "opportunity to learn" inputs should be part of holding school accountable (Darling-Hammond, 2001).

A complex and extremely controversial example of policy appropriation is charter schools. Charter schools are generally viewed as part of an attempt to privatize education and to compete with public schools. Many see them also as ways for the middle class or religious groups to create enclaves of privilege or proselytizing. However, some progressive educators believe that charter schools represent more autonomous spaces within which to also provide a more creative and empowering education, especially for low-income youth.

Given the plight of low-income urban parents facing underresourced public schools, many argue that it is unreasonable not to provide these parents with some kind of option to exit the system. Moreover, if many of these underresourced urban schools are not healthy places for children, they are also not healthy for teachers and administrators. After a year of teaching in a large comprehensive high school in the 1970s, I myself sought out smaller, alternative schools to teach in, like the school I described in Harlem. This school had many of the characteristics of charter schools, and it provided an exciting place for young idealistic teachers to work, whose politics were honed in the turbulence of the 1960s antiwar and Black Power movements.

Stullberg (2008) describes her own similar experience in a charter school in Oakland, CA, and attempts to appropriate charter schools into a progressive discourse. Many forget that in the 1960s and early 1970s, progressives viewed urban public schools as hostile places for doing any kind of liberatory teaching and sought out spaces that were freer from state surveillance. Many African Americans, faced with the failure of racial integration in most urban centers, pursued independent options. Today as narrow testing regimes narrow teachers' creativity and initiative, it makes sense that they might seek out spaces that are somewhat freer from many traditional constraints.

So while charter schools may serve as escape valves for desperate parents, and in some cases provide spaces in which it is more likely that more creative and community-based education might flourish, they are not a progressive long-term policy option. First because the research on them shows that they are no more effective (nor creative) than public schools and in states where they are more deregulated and more pervasive, they tend to increase racial segregation and social stratification (Abernathy, 2005; Miron & Nelson, 2002; Scott, 2005). Risking our public schools for educational results that are essentially equal to those of public schools makes little sense. Furthermore, in low-income urban areas, unless they are truly community-controlled schools, there is the risk that young idealistic, but privileged teachers may impose a well-meaning, but ultimately colonizing education for the brief time they tend to teach in low-income neighborhoods. While the Teach for America program has attracted many bright young teachers to the profession, there is some evidence that employing these undercertified teachers results in lower student achievement (Laczko-Kerr & Berliner, 2002).

Nevertheless, as long as charter schools are well regulated against becoming a vehicle for "White flight," are nonprofit and means tested, and provide quality options for low-income communities, we should consider the possibility that they could be part of a strategy to improve public schools. There is a big difference between having a limited number of means-tested options for low-income parents, and opening up those options to those who would use such options to further enhance the privileges of their children. If, through the post-reform agenda proposed here, public schools become better resourced, attract better teachers, and become more integrated into local communities, parents will be attracted back. I am not referring here to the benefits of competition, but rather the kind of transformation of urban schools that can only happen with more resources, massive social advocacy, and a paradigm change in how we think about the role of local communities in civic engagement. Until then, parents without the resources to pay for real options, should have some exit strategy available to them.

There are huge risks, of course. Parents who opt out may have little reason to help create the social pressure on public schools needed to improve them. These schools also take even more resources and students from public schools. And yet, whether from an ethical or strategic perspective, it is unacceptable for those of us with options to insist that poor parents postpone their child's education while we transform public schools. Policies that encourage high quality, progressive charter schools and discourage for-profit and poor quality ones could appropriate a potentially neoliberal reform toward a stopgap option within a post-reform agenda.

So, while the notion of a paradigm shift preserves the idea that radical shifts need to occur in our thinking and in policy, the goal is to ultimately make the shift into a post-reform world of education not with whole cloth, but rather as a combination of new ideas and a reworking of the current patchwork of ideas and policies. Throughout the discussions in this chapter, the reader should refer to Table 6.1, in which I provide a snapshot of education under the Keynesian welfare state that existed from roughly 1930 to 1980, followed by the current third way competition state, which dates from the 1970s to the present. The third column represents a possible empowering state located closer to social democracy than to neoliberalism. Such a shift would make a post-reform paradigm in education possible, since the agenda I am proposing cannot be successful unless it is linked to policy advocacy at broader levels.

Table 6.2 Toward a post-reform agenda

Areas of reframing	
New leadership role definition	Leadership as advocacy for children and youth.
New accountability	Reciprocal accountability, public accountability, balance between external and internal accountability
New policy paradigm	Change from policy engineering to policy ecology
Additive pedagogy	Pedagogy focuses on what students bring to the classroom rather than deficits
Multilevel perspective	Advocacy needed at multiple levels: child, classroom, school, social policy, international
Authentic participation	Participation for both capacity-building and democratic deliberation
Expanded educational goals	Assess goals beyond cognitive achievement (physical, social, civic, emotional, artistic, vocational, critical thinking)
Expanded equality	Balancing political (equality before the law, voting rights, etc.) with economic equality (moving beyond mere equality of opportunity to distributive justice)
Educational and human rights	Emphasis on education as a human right rather than only human capital development
Advocacy strategies	
Policy appropriation	Includes the deconstruction of current policies and practices, but also their partial appropriation as new policy proposals
Leadership as strategic mediation	Using the leaders' mediation role to manage meaning toward advocacy
Discursive strategies	Use language strategically; hybrid discourses
Broadening what we assess as outcomes of schooling	Assessing an array of noncognitive outcomes as well as expanding the cognitive beyond paper and pencil assessments
Community and student activism	Leads to public/community forms of accountability
Double consciousness	Ability to operate on parallel levels: pragmatic and idealistic
Greater activism of unions and professional associations	Individuals cannot bring about change at the level of public policy, but collectives can

As an example of policy advocacy, as of 2007, at least 14 states had opted out of federal funds for "abstinence-only" sex education programs. This program had enraged people from the school level to the statehouse. Of course, the Bush administration's Department of Health and Human Services announced that not applying for this money would hurt the youth who would be deprived of these programs. However, the Sexuality Information and Education Council of the United States, an advocacy and education group, hopes that if enough states drop out of the program, Congress will return the funding to comprehensive sex education programs that include teaching about the use of condoms and other contraceptives. Thus, resistance at the state and municipality level to neoconservative and neoliberal federal policies is a way of pushing back on policies that educators know are not good for youth.

New Frames and Language for a New Paradigm

A major arena for policy appropriation is control of language. According to Luke (2003), "educational policies are bids to centrally regulate and govern flows of discourse, fiscal capital, and physical and human resources across the time and space boundaries of educational systems" (p. 132). While the importance of fiscal, physical, and human resources is the bread and butter of policy analysis, until recently, less attention had been paid to the role of discourse. While control of discourse may not directly determine events on the ground, discourses provide the limits of what is thinkable and doable at a particular historical moment. Those who control discourses, exercise a considerable amount of influence over social policies.

Research on how political spectacle is constructed have provided a window into the importance of policy framing, the linguistic structuring of policy, and the importance of text, whether policy texts, popular texts, or media (Edelman, 1978; Lakoff, 2004, 2008). Many progressive scholars have worked to deconstruct neoliberal discourses (Fairclough, 2003; Gee, Hull, & Lankshear, 1996), particularly as they flow through policy texts and educational practices. But, neoliberals stay a step ahead, because they are more effective at producing and legitimating discourses that support their policy initiatives. Luke suggests that those who study and make education policy need to pay closer attention to the ways in which discourses are constructed.

For instance, older discourses can sometimes be rehabilitated. Survey results reported by the Harvard School of Public Health indicate that the term *socialized medicine* is gaining widespread acceptance among the American public. Historically, this term has been vilified and used to attack health reform proposals, but the survey shows that

> Of the respondents, 67% said they understood what "socialized medicine" meant. Of those, 79% said the term means that the government makes sure everyone has health insurance. Only 32% said it means that the government tells doctors what to do. Of those who said they understand the term, 45% said that if America had socialized medicine, the health care system would be better, while 39% said it would be worse. (Brink, 2008, p. F3)

This suggests that there may be some chinks in the armor of neoliberal discourse. While the survey does not speculate on what might have led to this result, a movie such as Michael Moore's *Sicko*, with its frontal attack on our corporate run health care system, may suggest that progressive educators may need to go on the offensive.

Another boogeyman regularly evoked by neoliberals is teachers' unions and unionism in general. As Weiner (2008) points out "Neo-liberal rhetoric about educational inequality has a particular resonance for those who have suffered discrimination by unions directly, or as a result of employment policies that unions have accepted. They do not easily accept the argument that labor unions are a natural ally of struggles for equality and justice" (p 252). In chapter 1 I discussed the ways in which the California Nurses Association has become involved in changing social policies that transcend their bread and butter union issues. This is because many nurses understand that it is hard for them to do their jobs well unless public health policies that support their work are in place. Rather than alienate the public, they have gained considerable support for the growing popularity of rethinking our health care system. Many teachers and administrators feel the same way, but their unions have yet to expand their roles around social justice issues. There are notable exceptions, however, and, as Weiner documents, some U.S. unions are building international alliances to share strategies.

Another strategy that conservatives and neoliberals have used effectively is what Lakoff (2004) calls semantic framing. According to Lakoff, the central frame of the political right is what he calls strict father morality. Based on the work of Christian neoconservative James Dobson, it teaches strict discipline for children, including physical punishment and belief in a strict God who demands a world of moral authorities who should be obeyed. For both neoconservatives and neoliberals this morality is linked to free market capitalism. Competition teaches discipline and only disciplined fathers can earn money to care for and protect their families. Therefore, good, disciplined people are naturally rewarded with wealth. Giving anyone something they have not earned does them harm by making them dependent. Government spending for social welfare is bad. Creating huge fiscal deficits is good, because they "starve the beast," that is, the government, which should only be used to protect private property and engage in wars.

While this is a highly condensed summary of Lakoff's (2004) overall argument, its application to education and educational reform is instructive. Lakoff explains how this frame applies to education,

> Schools should teach conservative values. Conservatives should gain control of school boards to guarantee this. Teachers should be strict, not nurturant, in the example they set for students and in the content they teach. Education should therefore promote discipline, and undisciplined students should face punishment. Unruly students should face physical punishment (for instance, paddling), and intellectually undisciplined students should not be coddled, but should be shamed and punished by not being promoted. Uniform testing should test the level of discipline. There are right and wrong answers that they should be tested for. Testing defines fairness: Those who pass are rewarded; those not disciplined enough to pass are punished. (pp. 83–84)

While most readers may find these values problematic, they serve as a frame for much school reform policy. NCLB's requirement that schools meet standards or else suffer some form of punishment is also consistent with the strict father frame, as is the idea that "failing" schools should be publicly humiliated by having their names published in local newspapers.

Schools with large percentages of low-income students and students of color are also the most likely to suffer the punishments and humiliations imposed by the reform. When scores are disaggregated by race and class vulnerable populations are singled out for more intense surveillance through testing regimes. Problems such as racism and a lack of living wage jobs are ignored in favor of a color-blind demand for greater self-discipline. Teachers and administrators themselves are singled out as scapegoats for being insufficiently strict both in terms of failing to provide a strict test-driven education and for coddling rather than punishing students.

Neoliberals sometimes use outright deceptive discourses that present language that appeals to the public, but covers up policy details the public would be less likely to support. For instance, a 2002 initiative called the Clear Skies Initiative was promoted as antipollution legislation. However, the Sierra Club took a different position on its website: "Originally proposed in 2002, the Clear Skies initiative would weaken many parts of the Clean Air Act and would result in significantly fewer reductions of air pollutants than currently required" (Sierra Club, 2007). Some would suggest that the name No Child Left Behind is an example of a deceptive discourse, since it gives the impression that it is driven by equity concerns. However, Harvey and Lowe argue that NCLB is the continuation of a postwar shift from seeking social equality through welfare state redistributive policies to the more conservative position of making education responsible for equity. Lakoff makes the point, however, that sophisticated historical arguments are no match for effective framing of an issue. If you can promote a conservative policy with an equity discourse, then your framing has achieved its goal.

In the 1980s, during the Reagan administration in the United States, the term *Back to Basics* was coined because it projected the idea that society and schooling had been neglecting traditional values and skills. The frame evoked memories of children learning penmanship, diagramming sentences, and memorizing the names of state capitals, free of the kind of political turmoil of the 1960s and 1970s. Reagan, himself, represented the strict father, who derided "soft" progressive social policies. It has been difficult for more nurturant and authentic forms of education to gain traction in the face of this strict father frame.

Allan Luke and his colleagues in Queensland, Australia have experimented with appropriating conservative and neoliberal discourses, in order to promote more progressive reforms. Reappropriating the term *basics*, he and his colleagues have created "The New Basics" project. The New Basics project is described on the Queensland, Australia government website (Queensland Department of Education, Training and the Arts). The "New Basics" refers to what students are taught; "Rich Tasks" describes how students show what they've learned; and

"Productive Pedagogies" describes how it is taught. Under "Productive Pedagogies" are a series of rubrics for evaluating instructional effectiveness. They are Intellectual Quality, Connectedness, Background Knowledge, Supportive Classroom Environment, and Recognition of Difference. While these appear to be reasonable requirements of good teaching, they represent a paradigm shift from those required within a testing culture. For instance under "Connectedness" we find such things as knowledge integration, connectedness to the world, and problem-based curriculum. Teachers can easily appropriate these frames to provide a rigorous, culturally responsive pedagogy that is connected to the world. More importantly, as an assessment tool, such concepts provide a holistic and critical set of rubrics that might provide a basis for more authentic forms of assessment.

More importantly, in an evidence-based environment, productive pedagogies developed these classroom practices based on findings of a government-funded research project, the Queensland School Reform Longitudinal Study (Education Queensland, 2001). The study built, to some extant on a 1996 U.S. federally funded study at the Center for Restructuring and Schools (Newmann and Associates, 1996). The results of this study promoted "authentic achievement" linked to school restructuring around site-based management. While authentic site-based management suffered many of the barriers described in the previous chapter, it also tended to neglect the kinds of restructuring necessary at broader levels to achieve equity. These Australian researchers, while keeping authentic teaching and learning as their core concern are careful to also insist on centralized policies and culturally responsive pedagogies that are more likely to support equity goals (Hayes, Mills, Christie, & Lingard, 2006; Lingard, Hayes, Mills, & Christie, 2003).

What I want to highlight here is their use of policy appropriation strategies. Terms like the new *basics* and *productive* pedagogies are taken right out of the managerialist playbook, but appropriated to other ends. Terms like *critical* pedagogies or *social justice* can become handy targets for the political right, especially under conservative governments. Many have reported that under the Bush administration, word checks were done on federal grant proposals to eliminate those with certain terms that were considered ideologically suspect.

The New Accountability

Because high-stakes accountability is the centerpiece of NCLB, a counterparadigm cannot and should not throw out the concept of accountability, but it can redefine it. Nobody would argue that schools, or any public or private institution, should not be accountable. Nor is accountability a new concept; public schools were designed to have community oversight through school boards. States have always evaluated schools. Principals and district supervisors have always evaluated teachers. Kids in schools have been taking standardized tests for most of the 20th century.

What is new is the expansion and intensification of the old accountability system, the high stakes associated with it, and the elimination of more democratic approaches to accountability. NCLB has also narrowed how we might think of the federal role in improving education. Instead of providing the social infrastructure that complements schooling and allows communities and families to prosper and effectively support their children's schooling, the feds have defined their role as using Title I money to leverage greater coercive power to bully administrators, teachers, and students into improving. In this way, in spite of rhetoric to the contrary, the federal government has devolved responsibility for equal opportunity to the state and local levels where segregation and tracking continue to determine the quality of schooling students will receive (Kantor & Lowe, 2006).

While standardized tests are promoted for accountability purposes, they have been present in education for decades. Traditionally, though, they have had a placement function in the sense that testing was, and continues to be, used to place students into curriculum tracks, special education, reading groups, and ultimately undergraduate and graduate schools. While many argue that disaggregation of test scores required by NCLB by race, SES, and other criteria is a positive accountability development that promotes equity, it should be remembered that the placement function of testing is still prominent. In other words, schools may be forced to raise the scores of low-income students on minimum competency exams, but the real equity test is how many of those students will effectively complete with their middle class peers on high stakes placement exams that determine who gets into honors and AP classes and the best colleges and graduate schools. Are the skills they're being taught to pass minimum competency exams and the instructional time given over to test prep, in the students' best interest when it comes to far more sophisticated placement exams? There is no evidence that our educational system is less stratified than it was decades ago. In fact, as I have already discussed, more standardized testing tends to advantage those with greater economic, cultural, and social capital. The following personal narrative contextualizes standardized testing in the lives of working class youth, who typically are not viewed as deserving of the same opportunities as their middle class counterparts. Tests have been and continue to be a form of symbolic capital that legitimates this view and reproduces class relations.

I remember vividly the day in the 8th grade when we were herded into the gym to take a standardized test for placement into high school classes. I don't recall how I knew, but I sensed that this test would determine our occupational futures. In fact, half of us were placed in ninth grade Math I and the other half in Algebra I. In other words, half of us would be placed in a curriculum that would include those courses required for college admission, and the other half would be placed in a vocational education track that would cut off any chance of attending college. As a mediocre student, I anticipated being placed in the vocational track, but to my surprise, I ended up in Algebra I. I suspect that because I sensed the importance of this test, I didn't take it the way I usually took standardized tests, which was to more or less randomly fill in the bubbles and then spend the time poking the student in front of me or staring at the clock.

I suspect some of my working class friends did randomly fill in the bubbles, or had long ago fallen behind academically. Most of the students I hung out with socially were placed in the vocational classes. To my amazement, in Algebra I was immediately thrown into a totally different social network. I received a D– in freshman algebra, in part because I was a social isolate in the ninth grade, and not part of the groups in study hall who worked together on their homework. By the 10th grade, I had shifted my friendship groups, in part because I played sports after school. Winning a varsity letter in track and field my freshman year provided me with sudden notoriety and a new social status. In the 1960s in rural Iowa, sports were not only the domain of males, but they tended to attract town kids over farm kids and middle class over working class kids. Farm kids had to go home after school to do chores and working class townies hung out downtown, smoking, cruising, or working on their cars. Because I had been placed in the college track and went out for sports, I was able to "cross-over" socially and develop new social networks. And yet, in high school, I lived within a kind of social class borderland. My middle class friends disapproved of my working class girlfriend, who was in the secretarial track. Many of my working class friends saw me as a sellout.

My D– in algebra could be seen as evidence that I was misplaced, but the fact is that many of the vocational track students were extremely bright, but, as in my case, school didn't make us feel successful or smart. School was a daily ritual of indifference at best and humiliation at worse for those who were not seen as good students. I slowly blossomed as a student because I began to learn a new form of cultural capital and associated more with middle class students.

How well we eighth graders did on the exam was not an indication of our intelligence, but rather the academic identities we had constructed in the context of our elementary and junior high school experience. In my case, and in many rural communities, we were sorted largely by social class cultural capital, but in many urban contexts where class and race overlap, placement testing results in low track classes full of students of color with high track classes considerably lighter skinned. In fact, more common, are schools with few White or middle class students attending at all.

One last anecdote sums up the ways that tracking deprives students of the social networks they need to have access to opportunities. Being in the college track in a small Iowa high school did not mean you were seen as college-bound. It only meant that you had the minimum courses the state universities required for admission. In small rural towns, only a handful of students in those days (mid-1960s) went on to college. Many students had to stay and help with the farm or they had no money for tuition and living expenses. In small towns students could not live at home and attend college as they could in metropolitan areas.

One day during my junior year of high school, I was in the locker room after football practice. Three guys were sitting on benches filling out college applications together. Apparently their counselor had told them they needed to have these filled out for the next day. I remember saying indignantly that no one gave me a college application. One of them reached under the form he was filling out and pulled out an extra form he had been given by the counselor and handed it to me. I had been thinking about my future, and it looked pretty bleak. The Vietnam War was at full throttle and the military draft loomed large. I took the application home, filled it out and sent it in. Since my grades had improved considerably by my junior year, I was accepted into the University of Iowa. I'm quite sure today, in a more competitive environment, I would not be accepted.

My story has a happy ending in terms of my educational opportunities only because in the late 1960s someone with mediocre grades and ACT scores could still enter good four-year universities. Today, I very likely would have ended up working at the local factory (an option not available to my cousins back in LaPorte and no longer available to many youth where such jobs have fled their communities) or I might have moved to Mason City (40 miles away) to work and study part time in a community college. More likely, I would have been drafted and sent to Vietnam.

Today there are community college classes offered one or two days a week at the local library in my hometown. But while access to postsecondary education has expanded, it has become far more stratified. No longer is getting into college the issue, but rather which college you get into and what you major in. As we cut back state support for higher education, we can expect to see fewer real options for low-income students. Today, as we disaggregate test scores with the intent of ensuring low-income students and students of color get a better education, even those four-year colleges like the SUNY/CUNY system in New York or the California State system are making college access more restricted and there are fewer grants and loans available for low-income students. Once again, we can only understand school reform by looking at shifts at all levels of the system and connecting the dots. Until we seriously explore the issues of who has access to educational opportunities, raising test scores on minimum competency exams will not come close to addressing problems of access.

Internal, Reciprocal, and Public Accountability

Whereas testing and assessment has generally had a placement function in U.S. education, in the 1990s there was a movement to link testing to standards. Some felt that the lack of standards that were aligned to curriculum and assessment, made test scores meaningless. This ushered in a discourse of standards, accountability, and performance assessment. In theory, this approach to accountability made sense, and early on, standards were developed with considerable teacher input. In many state capitals battles over standards were heated, but there was a sense that school professionals were the ones to turn to for creating curriculum standards. Some felt that the standards that teachers generated were too radical in terms of history or too literature-based in terms of reading instruction.

A generation of assessment experts, tired of hearing that there were no alternatives to standardized paper and pencil exams, developed more authentic approaches to assessment, but these were expensive and some were more difficult to turn into scores that could be easily compared. An "opportunity to learn" standards that focused on providing the necessary supports for success to all students were developed, but largely ignored. From being a major source of input into a standards movement early on, teachers later were framed as the problem. They were too "progressive" and their methods were not showing results on standardized tests. The "reading wars" was a major battlefield on which standards morphed into standardization.

Meanwhile, there is much evidence that the accountability system itself is robbing schools of the professionalism and capacity that would be needed to improve instruction for low-income students and students of color. Nichols and Berliner (2007) suggest some of the reasons for this: Performance standards that are impossible for schools to meet; high-stakes decisions based on a single test score; the traumatizing effects this creates for students and teachers; the unfair impact these tests have on special education and English language learning students; the implicit equation of testing with teaching; reducing the aims of schooling to a narrow view of achievement; the imposition of scripted lessons for teachers to deliver; demands that large expenditures of public funds be spent with private, for-profit corporations; the undermining of local and state authority for the operation of public schools; and the lack of attention to the out-of-school conditions that affect what happens in schools, such as poverty, segregation, lack of access to health care, and so forth.

Rather than building professional capacity and learning communities in schools, current high stakes testing works against authentic conversations about students. Nichols and Berliner (2007) suggest the following thought experiment:

> Imagine a test with consequences for students and teachers but without the involvement of McGraw-Hill, Riverside, Pearson, or other standardized test makers. Think instead of local teachers meeting and working on understanding the subject-matter standards, sharing designs and teaching tips for classroom teaching of the standards, sharing course syllabi, and making decisions about test selections, Most important, think of the teachers designing some common, locally produced tests, for the identical courses that are taught throughout the region. In this little thought experiment, imagine also that teachers are paid for these activities, for picking the cut scores to determine student proficiency, and for scoring the tests. The last activity, scoring the test, is very important. If open-ended questions, essays, writing samples, and other forms of extended response items are used—and most teachers want to use such items—then having

teachers scoring them in groups is a great way to stimulate discussion of curriculum content, and student capabilities. (p. 193)

More authentic forms of accountability empower teachers professionally in the sense that they receive more helpful data for improving instruction, but it also can stimulate different conversations among teachers, ones that are less focused on gaming the system and more focused on getting to know their students in academic and social terms. A natural extension of this type of capacity-building accountability is Peer Assistance and Review (PAR) or teachers evaluating each other with union and administrative input. Goldstein (2003) describes how PAR works:

> With PAR, designated "consulting teachers" provide support to new teachers and struggling veteran teachers (collectively called "participating teachers"), and also conduct the summative personnel evaluations of the teachers they support. The consulting teachers report to an oversight panel composed of teachers and administrators from across the district, co-chaired by the teacher union president and a high-ranking district office administrator. The panel holds hearings several times a year, at which consulting teachers provide reports about participating teacher progress and ultimately make recommendations about the continued employment of each participating teacher. (p. 14)

Goldstein acknowledges that combining support with evaluation is tricky and that veteran teachers often resist being evaluated by, often younger, peers. But the model is a step in the direction of providing teachers with greater control over professional decisions and brings the union into the process as well.

A post-reform agenda will have to press for more authentic forms of assessment, and the resources to pay for them. Also, our fetish with testing for accountability has also likely increased its legitimacy as a placement instrument, reinforcing social stratification and benefiting the children of the middle class, in spite of disaggregation strategies aimed at equity. In the following sections, I will focus on two other areas in which the accountability discourse can be appropriated toward more progressive ends: reciprocal accountability and public accountability.

Reciprocal Accountability Elmore (2002) has written about what he calls reciprocal accountability, which, in the context of professional development, he defines in this way:

> Accountability must be a reciprocal process. For every increment of performance I demand from you, I have an equal responsibility to provide you with the capacity to meet that expectation. Likewise, for every investment you make in my skill and knowledge, I have a reciprocal responsibility to demonstrate some new increment in performance. (p. 5)

While Elmore fails to play out the larger implications of this concept, Thomas Rogers (2008), the president of the New York State Council of School Super-intendents, uses the notion of reciprocal accountability in a broader sense. He argues that each level (federal, state, district, school) should be held accountable for things it can influence. So, for instance, the federal government should be accountable for such things as percent of gross domestic product spent on edu-cation, spending on research and development, percent of children in poverty, percent without health insurance, and percent with poor nutrition. Furthermore, he suggests comparing these percentages with countries that are members of the Organisation for Economic Co-Operation and Development (OECD) and have far better outcomes in these areas than the United States, and I might add, also have more robust welfare states.

Rogers (2008) suggests holding each level accountable through report cards similar to those that many districts are currently using, except that these report cards would contain federal, state, district, and school-level data. So for instance, under the section of the report card for the federal level, he provides a table that shows the percent of U.S. children in poverty, which is far above that of all European countries, and only six percentage points above that of Mexico. These report cards would help to legitimate a concern among school leaders for de-manding greater accountability at levels over their heads. Based on my analysis in chapter 3, I would add another category to Rogers's report card: corporate accountability, or to what extent corporations engage in productive, rather than speculative activities and take seriously their civic responsibility toward their local communities and their collective responsibility to provide jobs that pay a living wage and benefits.

Another way to think about reciprocal accountability is the ways that com-munities hold schools accountable and schools hold communities accountable. I will explore this notion of public accountability in more detail in the next section, but the school–community relationship ideally should be a reciprocal one. Parents, communities, and schools all have some responsibility for their children's education. Current literature on parent involvement and parent edu-cation largely places the onus on low-income parents. A reciprocal relationship would include forms of public accountability that I describe below. Ideally, this relationship would result in empowered communities and schools that could advocate together for social policies that better support their children's education and the quality of their daily lives.

Public Accountability One of the arguments for supporting high stakes testing, and for disaggregating scores by socioeconomic status, race, and disability was that test scores could be a resource for disenfranchised communities to hold schools accountable for better serving their children. When Deweyian colleagues criticized standardized tests from the perspective of progressive education principles, I too used to respond that, though far from ideal, they were often the only weapon low-income communities had to hold their schools accountable.

Having observed the reality of using tests in this way, I have changed by view. Many politically and educationally progressive friends, though, still argue that the benefits for an equity agenda outweigh the side effects of high stakes accountability models based on standardized tests (Skrla & Scheurich, 2004). However, until we have the kinds of assessments that encourage authentic and rigorous instruction, I believe other forms of community pressure have a better chance of bringing about not only better teaching, but also the kind of social movement that might eventually result in the paradigm shift I am promoting.

As I discussed in the previous chapter, we cannot be naïve about how parents and communities interface with schools. Questions of who represents the community, how community members are often co-opted by schools, and the traditional stand-offs between school professionals and community members over turf issues must all be taken into account. In New York City, anyone who knows the history of community control in the 1960s and 1970s can be forgiven for believing that policy options like high-stakes testing or school choice are "cleaner" than community involvement in school reform. In fact, Pedroni (2007) makes the case that key African-American leaders in Milwaukee only associated themselves with the right-wing Bradley Foundation and promoted a voucher plan *after* many years of organized, community-based attempts to impact public schools in Milwaukee had ended in failure.

Nevertheless, I will argue that we now have an impressive track record of using community organizing for holding schools accountable in more authentic ways than high-stakes testing does. Testing will likely always have some role to play in more authentic approaches to accountability. For instance, while organizations like the Industrial Areas Foundation (IAF) and the Association of Community Organizations for Reform Now (ACORN) have criticized high stakes testing, People Acting for Community Together (PACT), a community-organizing group in Miami-Dade County, is largely sympathetic to testing and direct instruction (Shirley & Evans, 2007). Nor can community organizing be viewed as a silver bullet. Public accountability through community organizing can only be one dimension—in alliance with school professionals—of school reform. But a growing body of research on community organizing and school reform is documenting many areas of success and great promise for this approach to school accountability and community empowerment.

Public accountability through community organizing is premised on the idea that public education is a collective responsibility. Its goal is to create a public space in which to bring together "differently positioned stakeholders—educators, parents, community members, elected and other public school officials, the private and non-profit sectors, and students themselves—to identify problems and develop solutions for improving schools in low—to moderate—income communities" (Gold, Simon, & Brown, 2004, p. 245).

A traditional problem with community control movements in low-income communities has been a lack of community capacity to launch an organizing effort. Gold et al. (2004) have developed a model that works to build community capacity through developing grassroots leaders, the building of social capital through networking and trust-building, and the creation of a strong organizational identity that can ensure big turnouts and ongoing stability. With an empowered community, schools will have to begin to pay attention. Advocacy leaders will welcome empowered communities as a source of solidarity and collective power, but all school leaders will have to deal with an empowered community one way or another, or risk confrontation. As schools and empowered communities build social trust, benefits begin to accrue to the school as the school and community work together. Among other things, they can use their power to garner greater resources for underserved schools, develop more authentic forms of joint ownership of schools and school decision making, increase safety in and around the school, and promote high quality instruction and curriculum in the school.

While most community organizing groups report more localized victories, as organizing groups become more coordinated, they are able to impact broader levels of the system. For instance, Brooklyn-Queens 4 Education Collaborative (BQ4E) is composed of several organizations including ACORN, Latin American Integration Center, Make the road by Walking, New York Civic Participation Project, and the Community Involvement Program at the Annenberg Institute for School Reform. Their mission is the following:

> The Brooklyn-Queens 4 Education Collaborative unites parents, community organizations, unions and a university in a collective effort to organize a powerful constituency for the improvement of the public schools in Region 4. This unique region includes the high immigrant neighborhoods of Bushwick in Brooklyn and Elmhurst, Corona, Jackson Heights, and Woodside in Queens. Together, we are working to build community power to ensure that every child in Region 4 receives a high quality, inclusive public education.

Stone, Henig, Jones, and Pierannunzi (2001) also argue that underinvestment in urban children can be challenged. In an 11-city study, they found that the higher the levels of civic capacity in urban areas, the more likely school improvement efforts were successful. High levels of civic capacity involved governmental and nongovernmental sectors, such as grassroots and community groups as well as the business community and civic leaders.

New accountability then brings greater balance to vertical forms of social engineering by adding horizontal forms of accountability that are more public or authentic. It is likely that both vertical and horizontal forms of accountability will be necessary, but vertical forms can be found that do not distort and hollow out the life world of schools and horizontal forms can provide the kind of support and pressure from communities that ensures a relevant and rigorous education for low-income students.

Enriching the Hollow School: New Pedagogies

Returning a focus onto the life world of schools will require a new kind of pedagogy that is rigorous, authentic, and additive, but also one that fosters empowered future political citizens. Rothstein, Jacobson, and Wilder (2008) have suggested one way to restore many of the noncognitive goals of schooling, although their proposal does not break with the current reform paradigm. They observe that high-stakes tests tend to determine what schools pay attention to. Their logic is a simple one: What if we identified an array of tasks we want schools to perform and find a way to assess them? For instance, if we are concerned that the hollow school addresses the cognitive development of students to the neglect of their physical development, then we could use a test of body mass index, or some other measure of physical fitness and make it high stakes. In such a case, schools would have to begin attending to the physical fitness of their students. In all likelihood we would see an abrupt interest in a return of physical education classes.

Rothstein and Jacobson (2007) report surveys in which Americans place such things as teaching values, preparing responsible citizens, teaching students to solve problems without violence, helping students to become economically self-sufficient, of greater importance than higher test scores. Preparing responsible citizens consistently comes in first. They suggest that the following educational goals should be assessed by our accountability system:

- Basic Academic Skills in Core Subjects (reading, writing, math, science, history).
- Critical Thinking and Problem Solving (analysis, interpretation, applying ideas to new situations).
- Social Skills and Work Ethic (communication skills, personal responsibility, getting along with others).
- Citizenship and Community Responsibility (readiness to vote responsibly, to volunteer, to become active in communities).
- Physical Health (good habits of exercise and nutrition).
- Emotional Health (self-confidence, respect for others, responsible behavior).
- Arts and Literature (participation in and appreciation of the arts, love of literature).
- Vocational Education (qualifying the non-college bound for skilled employment). (p. 39)

One problem with this approach is that it keeps us within the paradigm of social engineering. It assumes teachers, like Pavlov's dogs, will dutifully change their behaviors in line with a new incentive structure. While I made the case earlier that high stakes testing has succeeded in reaching behind the classroom door to narrow teacher's pedagogical options, the process has not resulted in

teachers massively abandoning all student-centered teaching practices and adopting strict teacher-centered practices. Cuban (2007) studied three districts and was
surprised to discover that teachers were still engaging in more student-centered,
progressive practices than he had expected. He concludes, however, that teachers,
in response to testing pressures, have retained the physical trappings of child-
centered pedagogy—desks in circles, learning centers, an air of informality—
while narrowing the content and skills they put into their daily lessons.

> The phrase *teacher-centered progressivism* points to the hybrid classroom
> practices and particular student-centered features that have been incorpo-
> rated into most teachers' repertoires over the decades as they adapted their
> practices to regulatory policies. Thus, what initially appeared as conflicting
> data drawn from evidence I collected in three urban districts and teacher
> reports across the nation of accountability, standards, and testing policies
> reshaping the content of their lessons turns out to be another instance over
> the past century of teacher adaptiveness in melding progressive classroom
> practices to fit current policies that sustain teacher-centeredness. (p. 22)

Delpit and others have warned that neither a Deweyian progressivism nor a
strict teacher-centered approach is what low-income students of color need. Nor
do the kinds of hybrid approaches that Cuban describes provide the answer because while teachers may retain some semblance of authentic interaction, curricula
are narrowed to please the test-makers. Nevertheless Rothstein and Jacobson's
(2007) proposal to expand the assessment of educational goals is far more promising than the far more limited tinkering with NCLB that some advocate.

A more holistic framework that was gaining popularity in the 1980s and focused on classrooms, schools, and communities was Cummins's (1986) widely
used framework for empowering minority students. Many of Cummins recommendations are the exact opposite of the direction NCLB eventually took schooling. Cummins model was focused on immigrant students, but contained many
elements of an effective school for low-income students of color. He attempted
to move research on immigrant children beyond an almost exclusive focus on
language and bilingual education, by exploring the ways the dominant culture
stigmatized low-income children and children of color. He also explored how
what he called *subtractive* education failed to build on the strengths of immigrant
children. His framework pushed attention beyond the classroom into the school
and community, much like the research on funds of knowledge that followed
(Gonzalez, Moll, & Amanti, 2005). Valenzuela (1999) provided ethnographic
documentation that subtractive education was alive and well years later. Cummins's work is particularly relevant to my analysis because he saw an advocacy
role for school professionals, in the sense that they could intentionally refuse to
legitimate practices that disempowered students. His attempt to address a shift
in professional role definitions (e.g., their mindset, attitudes, and expectations)
was what most intrigued me about his research:

An alternative role definition for psychologists or special educators can be termed an "advocacy" or "delegitimization" role. In this case, their task must be to delegitimize the traditional function of psychological assessment in the educational disabling of minority students by becoming advocates for the child on scrutinizing critically the societal and educational context within which the child has developed. This involves locating the pathology within the societal power relations between dominant and dominated groups, in the reflection of these power relations between school and communities, and in the mental and cultural disabling of minority students that takes place in classrooms. (Cummins, 1986, p. 652)

Cummins discussed four areas in which the role definitions of school professionals can either disable or empower minority students. First, he called for building on children's cultural and linguistic diversity, greater community participation, pedagogies that were more constructivist and less transmission oriented, and more authentic forms of assessment. The other area in which Cummins broke new ground was in insisting that while an immigrant child's language issues were important, even more important was how societal power relations were translated into the interpersonal space of classrooms. He argued that important messages about identity are communicated in classrooms that can either empower students or stigmatize them. From this he argued that "the ways that identities are negotiated between educators and students is at least as fundamental in determining student achievement as any of the myriad techniques for teaching reading or any other academic content" (Cummins, 2003, p. 51). Cummins's framework is still valid and should be included in any current framework for post-NCLB school reform.

While Cummins's work was more focused on English language learners, Lisa Delpit's research on low-income African Americans was widely read in the 1980s and 1990s. In the late 1980s, Delpit had two influential articles published in the *Harvard Educational Review* that were later collected in a 1995 book entitled, *Other People's Children: Cultural Conflict in the Classroom.* She argued that White teachers had much to learn from non-White teachers, and that the progressive methods that many White teachers found worked so well with middle-class children, were often inadequate for low-income, children of color. Her work was often misunderstood as supporting a "back to basics" approach, but was instead a sophisticated analysis of the role of cultural capital within the same student-teacher-community interactional space that Cummins explored with English language learners. Like Cummins, Delpit wanted school professionals to see themselves as advocates for children, but she saw advocacy as both teaching skills *and* critical and creative thinking.

Students need technical skills to open doors, but they need to think critically and creatively to participate in meaningful and potentially liberating work inside those doors. Let there be no doubt: a "skilled" minority person who is not also capable of critical analysis becomes the trainable, low-level functionary of the dominant society, simply the grease that keeps the institutions that orchestrate his or her oppression running smoothly. (Delpit, 1995, p. 19)

There is more recent work on culturally responsive pedagogies and culturally responsive schools that has continued to deepen our thinking about how to enrich students' learning and build equity throughout the school. I have chosen to highlight Cummins's and Delpit's work because early on they made links among classrooms, communities, and broader social forces. In crafting a post-reform agenda, we needn't reinvent the wheel. There are many discarded ideas that we can brush off and revitalize. While NCLB has made it exponentially more difficult for teachers to delegitimize practices that are harmful to children of color, there is still plenty of room to maneuver in many schools.

Grassroots Curriculum

Teachers around the country are finding ways to provide a rich and rigorous curriculum that treats students as future citizens of a country and planet in peril. For years schools have been inundated with curriculum materials that promote particular industries, such as teaching nutrition with materials sponsored by the beef or dairy industries. But now many different organizations are producing curricula for teachers aimed not at increasing profits, but rather at critical thinking about important social issues.

The Clean Air Campaign has produced clean air lesson plans written to meet the Georgia Performance Standards. These lessons are creative, interactive, and provide both students and educators with a comprehensive look at air quality. Lessons are interdisciplinary and cover several subject areas including health, physical science, life science, earth science, social studies, language arts, and chemistry. Gutstein and Peterson (2005) provide a collection of essays by math educators who teach math through social justice-oriented content.

The New York Collective of Radical Educators (NYCoRE) has produced a curriculum for educators to help middle and high school-aged students explore the role of the military in their lives and in their communities. *Camouflaged: Investigating How the US Military Affects You and Your Community* (2008) was generated by local New York City teachers to ensure that students have information from a variety of sources before they consider enlisting in the armed forces. NYCoRE also produced a curriculum guide for teaching about Hurricane Katrina entitled *An Unnatural Disaster: A Critical Guide for Addressing the Aftermath of Hurricane Katrina in the Classroom* (2006). These are a mere handful of the exciting array of grassroots efforts to counter a conservative and insipid curriculum provided by major textbook companies.

More important than the content of any curriculum is the pedagogy through which it is delivered. A potentially progressive curriculum delivered inauthentically will not be effective. An example from my experience as a high school principal is illustrative of this problem. From 1982 to 1984 I was principal of a Mexican "preparatorio" or academic high school. *Prepas,* as they are called, are not part of the Secretary of Education's (SEP) responsibility in Mexico: they are instead incorporated into the university system, and their curriculum, and often their exams, are determined by the local university. My prepa was incorporated into the local state university, La Universidad Autonoma de Puebla, which was strongly influenced by Marxist professors. A large portion of our curriculum was Marxist. The history of Mexico was taught from a historical materialist perspective. In philosophy classes, students got a heavy dose of Marxist dialectical thinking. Required readings included Engels, *The Origins of the Family, Private Property, and the State,* and Marx's *The German Ideology.*

As a young college student, I studied in Mexico City during the 1968 student movement and the Tlatelolco massacre in which hundreds of student protesters were killed or injured. While there, I had absorbed not only Marxist theory, but also a deep understanding of the power of social movements. When I returned to the United States in 1969, I joined Students for a Democratic Society, but my real political formation was with my Mexican roommates who let me tag along on city buses as they exhorted Mexican workers to join their movement. So I was not averse to students being exposed to Marxist thought so long as they were also exposed to the whole continuum of human thought.

I didn't totally win that battle with all of my Marxist teachers, just as I never was able to convince the chemistry teachers that learning the periodic table by using it in the laboratory was better than making students learn it by heart. But I soon discovered that those teachers who indoctrinated students in Marxist thought were largely ineffective. First, because their teaching practices were, much like the chemistry teachers', rigid and didactic. This was particularly ironic for those who were teaching Marxian dialectical and Freireian dialogic principles, but somehow not surprising. Second, the students did not respect these teachers because they viewed them as inauthentic. They wanted to radicalize their students without getting to know them first.

I would often hear students greeting some teachers as *compañero,* an expression of political solidarity. This puzzled me, since I knew many of these students were from affluent families and that many were not sympathetic to left politics. It soon became apparent to me—though apparently not to the teachers—that many students were using the term partly sarcastically and partly to curry favor with the teachers. For most of them, Marxism was just one more thing to take notes on, commit to short-term memory, and regurgitate on an exam.

I'm also reminded of a story a Hispanic friend in New Mexico told me. His son had a radical high school teacher who was known in the community as a political organizer for social justice causes. This teacher took his son to task for streaking his hair orange, critiquing him for being ashamed of his mestizo heritage. The student, who was merely following a fleeting fashion of the day, felt the teacher had insufficient knowledge of him to know what his motivation was. If this teacher thought she was winning hearts and minds among her students, she was as mistaken as the *compañeros* who taught Marxist philosophy in Mexico. The conclusion: advocacy without authenticity is problematic.

Advocacy teachers who are successful at teaching the *word* and the *world* (Freire, 1970), first get to know their students and build relationships with them, and second, engage, not in a pedagogy of answers, but rather in a pedagogy of questions; one that is problem-posing, and that isn't afraid to deal with controversial social issues. Anything short of this is indoctrination. For administrators, advocacy at the classroom level means fostering this kind of teaching, and defending teachers when the wolves are at the door, as they undoubtedly will be. But it also means developing authentic relationships with teachers and engaging with them in collective problem posing.

New Leadership: Working Within Dilemmas and Paradoxes.

At a recent meeting I attended, the New York City Department of Education officials presented their model of leadership development. They are seeking a linear, cause-and-effect pathway from leadership preparation to student achievement scores that is evidence-based. Given the success of the evidence-based practice movement in Washington, DC it is not surprising that there are several vendors hawking such wares. Perhaps the currently most popular vendor promising this evidence-based solution is called "Balanced Leadership" and many districts are contracting with Mid-Continent Research for Education and Learning, a company that provides professional development to districts based on what they claim is a meta-analysis of 30 years of leadership research (Waters, Marzano, & McNulty, 2003). Their claims are predictable: That effective leadership can be empirically defined and that it is—contrary to misconceptions—more science than art. In fact, their potential buyers will be happy to discover that they have identified 21 key leadership responsibilities that are significantly correlated with higher student achievement. Not surprisingly the company has a stable of consultants ready to fly to your school district and in-service your administrators in this cutting edge leadership science.

In most "scientific" approaches to leadership, more sophisticated understandings that leadership involves political, cultural, ethical, symbolic, and emotional, dimensions are marginalized. Nor is there much acknowledgment of important insights from neoinstitutional theory that sees leaders as managers of meaning and mediators of institutional legitimacy. Most importantly, there is little sense of leadership as anything but a series of behaviors and dispositions that lead to rising scores on standardized tests. A more narrow view of educational leadership is hard to imagine.

Leadership is essentially political and operates within a field of power. Like policy it involves the authoritative allocation of values and scarce resources. Traditional structural and human relations approaches to leadership fail to capture the idea that leadership is political and ideological at its very core, regardless of where the leadership is being exercised from. Power is relational and never unidirectional. Policy initiatives push downward onto the system, but resistant "street-level bureaucrats" push back in complex ways (Lipsky, 1983), creating the infamous unintended consequences as policies circulate among practitioners. This dilemma of the yin and yang of control and discretion has been the central dilemma of the organizational change and implementation literature for several decades.

Thus, many researchers and practitioners have framed leadership as a dynamic political process in which leaders resolve technical and ethical dilemmas (Cuban, 1992; Jacobson, Hickcox, & Stevenson, 1996; Shapiro & Stefkovich, 2005). Deal and Peterson (1994) call it a leadership paradox, viewing it as a leader's need to exercise both technical, hierarchical control and cultural, symbolic leadership, casting the leader as the engineer and the artist. They argue, "balancing these seemingly irreconcilable differences will require the attention of principals who can play the game impressively two ways, as technical problem-solvers and as symbolic culture shapers" (p. 98). These technical and cultural dimensions are common to leadership theories, but without a dimension that addresses advocacy, the shaping of the cultural level is too often viewed as an arena for the management of meaning through the manipulation of symbols toward greater control. While there is ample evidence that good transformational leaders effectively manage both technical and symbolic aspects of the organization, advocacy leaders are more likely to ask questions like who's steering the system and for whose benefit? What meanings are being managed and toward what ends?

Because advocacy leaders see themselves as part of a broader struggle to advocate for children in and out of school, they feel loyalty first and foremost toward the welfare of the children they are responsible for educating. This raises another common dilemma for leaders—to whom do they owe loyalty—or to put it more bluntly, who do they ultimately work for? Moller (1996) found this to be a central dilemma for the principals she studied,

> The dilemmas of loyalty were expressed in action where the principals found it difficult to decide to whom their loyalty should be in a conflict situation: students and parents, teachers, superiors, common curriculum, or personal pedagogical values? (p. 213)

Who has power at any point in time is often an open question. In complex policy ecologies (Weaver-Hightower, 2008), advocacy leaders are constantly making tactical and ideological calculations as they try to make sense of the dilemmas and contradictions they encounter and work toward moving their schools and districts in a more just and equitable direction.

What's a School Leader to Do?

There is little scholarship that describes how the neoliberal economic and discursive shifts I have described are playing out in the day-to-day lives of educational leaders. How can leaders be advocates if they are normalized by neoliberal discourses and limited in the time and effort they could give to resisting them. Having been a principal myself, I understand that there are never enough hours in a day to get even the most basic things done. Leaders arrive at work with a "to do" list that gets longer as the day goes on. And too often the "to do" list doesn't even include direct instructional support of teachers. However, the issue for advocacy leaders is not just what they do, but also how they make meaning of what they do and how they project that meaning to others. Sometimes leaders have to do things they don't believe in, but unless they make it clear to themselves and others that they are not happy about doing them, then sooner of later they may find it easier to defend such actions to themselves and others. The cognitive, sense-making process of leaders has been studied extensively, but seldom in terms of the ways in which they are disciplined—at least partially—by dominant discourses (Spillane et al., 2002; Weick, 1995).

Leaders who internalize these discourses and successfully resolve inner contradictions will feel little dissonance as they go about their work. They will be highly sought after as leaders because they legitimate the status quo with "authentic" conviction. That is, like Wolcott's (1973) informant, Ed Bell, they sustain current social arrangements through mundane, ritualistic interactions and discourses that make such social arrangements appear legitimate and commonsensical. Such leaders often develop mediatory myths that serve as sophisticated rationalizations for defending practices that sustain inequities.

Some school leaders believe that new forms of managerialism and high-stakes testing are not something to resist, but are rather the route to being an advocacy leader. Black (2008) provides a case study of Maria, a principal of an award-winning Texas elementary school that serves low-income immigrant children. From a test score standpoint, this is an excellent school and the showcase of the district. Maria's leadership can be best described as authoritarian, but her authoritarianism is mixed with a caring attitude toward her students, and, in her view, is necessary in order to defend the interests of her students. She sees herself as protecting the students against the low expectations of her students' parents and teachers.

In Maria's school a strong sense of urgency is fomented resulting in a high stress environment. Students are constantly (sometimes weekly) tested and teachers tightly monitored. Even bulletin boards are regimented and monitored. Parents are welcome in the school, but not consulted, and recess, much to some parents' chagrin, was eliminated to provide more time on task. Students are taught to compete with each other over test scores, which are publicly ranked from best to worst. They are also stringently disciplined "as reflected in the quiet, hands behind the back passage of lines of students walking through the hallways" (p.

12). Because students began showing signs of test anxiety, they are given lessons on relaxation and stress reduction techniques. While students' mother tongues were respected, an assimilationist ideology prevailed.

On paper, this is a good school, and while I don't see Maria as an advocacy leader, she is certainly running a tight ship in which students are "on task." Taking a page out of the Texas Accountability System and NCLB, Maria is a heroic leader, who does not tolerate excuses or any distraction from instruction aimed at raising test scores. While she is described as somewhat ambivalent about this level of control, she sees it as providing her students with the tools to be successful. There is little doubt that she cares about her students and sees herself as an advocate for them. And yet I will argue that Maria, with all due respect, is engaging in an inauthentic approach to advocacy. At best, she is an adversarial leader—closed, but transformative. At worse, she is merely authoritarian—closed and transactional. In its "tough love" approach and test-oriented instruction and curriculum, NCLB is hollowing out from schools the kind of authentic relationality and rich, relevant, and rigorous instruction that low-income children need and deserve.

Meanwhile, leaders who maintain cognitive dissonance, likely experience greater psychic costs and political liability. If they express reservations, they may not be promoted or they may chose to leave leadership positions to work for change elsewhere. Or they may internalize the contradictions and end up with ulcers. Isolated, with no guidance in managing these contradictions and lacking the solidarity of a larger social movement, they can become ineffectual. They may be neither effective legitimators of the status quo nor effective advocates.

Theoharis (2007) has documented the toll taken on leaders when they maintain this ideological dissonance and attempt to resist inequitable practices in their schools. Even though many of the principals he studied had modest successes to show for their efforts, they alluded to increased use of alcohol, weight gain, depression, illness, and even daily vomiting. One principal talked about the futility he felt trying to make changes in his school within an institutional and policy context that was unsupportive,

> This stuff (creating a more just school) is easier said than done. I mean, I have to tell you how hard it is. We try, but we're so far away from where I think we need to be. That's why I get discouraged. It gets to be too much, and I get discouraged…I think, man I'm a F-up, I'm no good at anything…. Why do I get discouraged? Because you care, you care and you try and you do and then you run up against the bureaucrats who tell you you can't do things, or you run up against a society that sometimes it's so unjust that whatever you do, you're not going to change it. You feel like what you're doing is futile. (Theoharris, 2007, p. 243)

I want to suggest a third possibility: Advocacy leaders might hold onto their fundamental beliefs and engage in apparently incongruent actions as a tactic or strategy that is part of a larger agenda for social justice. This third option, rather than seeking congruence or resolving ideological strain, views the development of what Dubois called a *double consciousness* as a desirable and intentional goal. Such an approach would need to link principals to other arenas for advocacy that could support their school-based efforts and provide a sense of solidarity. Some of these arenas might exist within their own low-income neighborhoods, but the dominant public relations orientation of educational leadership often makes those options invisible.

The achievement of this third option will require far different leader preparation and a new set of counterdiscourses to replace the mediatory myths currently on offer. It will require new leaders with a far more sophisticated analysis of the causes of low-income student failure than that offered by current neoliberal reformers and most administrator preparation programs. But it will also require a more nuanced understanding of the potential that already exists in many current leaders who have held onto their sense of dissonance, but are unclear as to how to fight back against dominant discourses. I came to this realization as I thought back on my own inchoate approach to being an advocacy leader and in reanalyzing data on a principal I had shadowed and interviewed during my dissertation study in the late 1980s.

This African-American urban principal, who I will call Seth, had grown up in a low-income neighborhood of a Midwestern city. He was principal of a comprehensive high school in a middle class neighborhood that bused in low-income students from the neighborhood he grew up in. He was particularly effective at building relationships and trust with many of the most "difficult" students, many of whom were involved in gang activity. The social networks he built with students meant he could usually get wind of possible disturbances or identify guilty parties after disturbances.

His public discourse at school assemblies was one in which he consistently evoked his own success as a local boy who worked hard and made it, in spite of the challenges. The entire student body knew that when he was a boy he awoke at 4:00 a.m. to deliver papers before going to school. He saw himself as a role model for his students and hopefully an inspiration for them to strive for success. He was a hard-working principal who deeply cared about his students, and ran a relatively safe school. Because of his understanding of the community his African-American students came from, he was able to mitigate the low expectations and pathologizing tendencies of some of the teachers. But he confided to me that he couldn't keep up this pace of work and its associated stress much longer, and the lack of the African-American students' academic success was clearly taking a toll on him. He told me that sometimes he would get so frustrated that he would just get in his car and drive somewhere to get away from the school.

I ended up not using my data on Seth and his school in my dissertation. I had other cases of principals who had learned to promote their schools without the sense of dissonance Seth experienced. My other principals were textbook legitimators of their schools—real public relations types who could make you think their schools were great even if they weren't. These other principals lacked Seth's sense of outrage at the injustices his students experienced. Seth was a dilemma for me, and reminded me of the sense of impotence I often felt working in similar contexts. It raised for me the question of what else principals might do to resist causes of inequality and discrimination that are institutional and structural. Seth saw himself as an advocate for the low-income, African-American students from his old neighborhood, and defended them when necessary, while also demanding their best effort. Nevertheless, he presided over a highly tracked school in which the high tracks were mostly White and the lower tracks were mostly African American.[1]

I can't say if Seth really bought into his narrative of hard work paying off. In other words, I don't know if his use of this mediatory myth was tactical or whether this was his real explanation of how the world worked. It was clear, however, that he was aware that in general the system was unfair and racist and the stress it caused him was evident.

I remember it was this question of whether he really believed his bootstrap narrative that seemed important to me at the time. As a doctoral student, somewhat in awe of this impressive man, I didn't feel it was appropriate to ask, "Do you really believe this bootstrap theory you're selling these kids?" My guess is that his answer to that question would have been that it gave the students hope, and that without at least hope, nothing is possible. I realized that my own double consciousness as a researcher and former principal were coming into play. As a researcher, I believed bootstrap narratives were myths that legitimated structural inequalities, but when I was a principal, I would have answered the question I never posed to Seth, in the same way I think he would have. So was Seth an advocacy leader? Was I?

While at the time there was little to no research on African-American principals, Seth clearly exhibited many of the positive qualities of African-American principals described by subsequent researchers (Dillard, 1995; Evans, 2007; Tillman. 2004). My sense though was that he had neither developed a simplistic, but coherent ideology that protected him from dissonance, nor viewed his actions as strategies toward a larger vision, which exposed him to emotional stress. He brought with him to the job many of the elements, such as community knowledge and experience of racism, that helped him advocate for students. But if, as I have argued, leaders are disciplined by discourse-practices and further pressured by role expectations to appear legitimate to a conservative institutional environment, then it is not surprising that many leaders are left alone to make sense of these lived contradictions.

Ironically, Seth is a prototype of principals of the 1970s and 1980s that have been deemed failures by the current reform. But the current reform hasn't addressed the institutional and structural causes of school failure. Instead this reform promotes the make-it-on-your-own policies of the competition state.

Its response is limited to school choice for poor kids and disaggregation of test scores by race and socioeconomic status. These are not necessarily bad ideas, but there is no evidence that they will make a dent in the vast social disparities we have created. The now discredited welfare state responded with an array of social programs that lifted people out of poverty. The current reform proposes no policies that would support families and communities. Instead, Under No Child Left Behind assumptions of individual student achievement and upward mobility are built into the reform and no alternative analysis is encouraged or permitted. The current reform has banished any larger analyses of student failure rates by labeling them as "making excuses" or believing that poor kids can't learn. Increasingly principals have even less freedom to pursue any other options, in spite of a rhetoric of increased autonomy. In this climate, it is difficult for advocacy principals to push back.

Advocacy Leadership and Double Consciousness

I have borrowed (and somewhat distorted) DuBois (1903/2007) notion of double consciousness to describe how aspiring advocacy leaders like Seth can deal with mediating conflicts within ideology as well as the discursive pressures from their institutional environment. In a larger sense, DuBois is talking about how the subaltern make sense of their world under conditions of social oppression—being American, while also being disenfranchised. While school leaders are middle managers, they are far from constituting an oppressed group. Nevertheless, the dual perspectivity that DuBois presents helps us think strategically about our outward performance.[2]

Double consciousness, the necessity of viewing one's self through the dominant group's eyes, provides members of nondominant groups with a set of insights into social institutions that the single consciousness of dominant group members lack. This is why members of dominant groups tend to be more susceptible to racial stereotyping and naïve notions of color-blindness. DuBois saw double consciousness as an ultimately painful predicament and warned that the danger of double consciousness resided in conforming or changing one's identity so that it was in accord with how others perceive the person. This tension of holding onto one's self, while striving for a world in which double consciousness is unnecessary, parallels the advocacy leaders' requirement of living in a dual world, one in which the leader holds onto his or her ideals for a more just world and the other in which one must act in ways that may, at least in the short run, appear contradictory.

In fact, it is more likely that members of subordinate groups are more comfortable with the apparent contradiction of encouraging students to strive for success, while knowing from experience that oppressed groups only find success though collective action. It is in fact this legacy of the collective achievement of civil rights that makes many African-American leaders instinctively know that one's fate is tied up with one's community and with changing inequitable laws and social policies.

Therefore advocacy leaders are leaders who can hold onto the idea that social justice for low-income students is much more than a question of raising test scores or even increasing authentic academic achievement. Improving academic achievement is a prerequisite for empowerment, but by itself is no guarantee. So an advocacy leader may avoid the dissonance between fundamental beliefs and operative consequences by thinking tactically. Telling students to work hard and achieve in the face of overwhelming institutional and structural constraints is not a contradiction if we are also teaching them about those constraints and working to change them.

For principals, however, change is easiest at the school level and there is a growing body of research that documents forms of advocacy that can be employed there (Frattura & Capper, 2007; Johnson, 2002; Meier, 1995). The logic of individual effort and hard work can be promoted side-by-side with an emphasis on collective empowerment. Individual success can be presented as an opportunity and an obligation to work for the common good. An advocacy leader promotes both individual and collective empowerment as students are taught to understand that historically achieving social justice has been the result of collective action.

At the community level advocacy leaders in low and mixed income communities view the community not as a threat, but rather as a source of power that can be leveraged to help reallocate resources to low-income schools (Fruchter, 2007). Not only can alliances with community organizations and social service agencies leverage political power and additional resources and services, but they also represent a form of public accountability that is more authentic than top-down forms of high-stakes testing.

Finally, while advocacy leaders at the school level may have less influence when it comes to social policy, they know that improving schools alone will not leverage social justice for their students. Educators, and urban educators in particular, are the canaries in the mine, when it comes to encountering social problems as they are manifested in schools and in the lives of our children. They know first hand that children need access to quality preschool programs and health care; their students' parents need living wages and affordable housing. And yet they don't use this as an excuse to maintain business as usual. On the contrary, they see social advocacy as part of their role. There is no reason that urban educators can't be the catalyst for the kind of social movement needed to demand social policies that support children, but they will have to think differently about their roles (Anyon, 2005).

While it may appear unrealistic to expect advocacy leaders to align with or participate in advocacy movements aimed at changing social policies, it may be more risky for them to be isolated. Collaboration with groups with a broader perspective may mitigate the internalization of dominant discourses that narrow the scope of leadership. The fact that social policy issues have largely been de-fined out of school leadership leaves school leaders few options other than to legitimate a school reform policy that suggests that school improvement alone will leave no child behind.

While NCLB has made advocacy leadership more difficult, there have always been and continue to be leaders who create authentic relationships within and without schools and who see themselves as activists at all levels of the system. A growing number of accounts of leadership in Brazil's citizen schools exempli-fies advocacy leadership (see Gandin, 2007). These are community-controlled schools strongly influenced by Paulo Freire's philosophy that focuses on teaching students to read the word and the world. Johanek and Puckett (2007) have pro-vided a detailed account of Leonard Covello's leadership in the 1940s and 1950s as principal of Benjamin Franklin High School in New York's East Harlem. His sweeping vision of a community school that honored students' cultural capital and provided a network of resources and civic engagement is exemplary of advocacy leadership. Deborah Meier and other Coalition of Essential Schools leaders share many characteristics with advocacy leaders. And in the United States, there are numerous historical and contemporary accounts of African-American advocacy leaders (Dillard, 1995; Johnson, 2006; Murtadha & Watts, 2005; Siddle Walker, 2003). The reason that so many African-American school leaders link school leadership with advocacy and activism no doubt has something to do with their traditional subaltern role and their view of school leadership as a legacy of the civil rights movement.[3]

And yet, too few master's and doctoral degree programs in educational administration, use the lives of advocacy leaders as case studies. Principals are increasingly being trained to comb through test data—to be CEOs in an audit culture. As administrator preparation leaves universities, its deacademiza-tion and paraprofessionalization will leave administrators less able to analyze policy or understand the legal, fiscal, philosophical, or historical foundations of schooling.[4]

I don't want to understate the growing interest in social justice leadership in educational administration programs in universities. There is a growing number of programs that include a focus on social justice and several theoretical models for social justice or ethical leadership have been proposed (Brown, 2004; Capper, Theoharris, & Sebastian, 2006; Enomoto, Kramer, & Starratt, 2007; Marshall & Oliva, 2005; Shapiro & Stefkovich, 2005; Starratt, 2007). However, there are still relatively few nuanced ethnographic accounts of the dilemmas school leaders face as they struggle with being advocates for low-income students and students of color. While there are many accounts of "successful" school leaders in practitioner journals, popular books, and even Hollywood movies, this tends to be a celebra-tory genre that glosses over the ways that leaders navigate the deep dilemmas they face and their victories, defeats, and compromises. More importantly we need more accounts like Evans's (2007) of the sense that school leaders make of the dilemmas and contradictions they face daily.

One would think that with the popularity of Practitioner Action Research and the number of school leaders engaged in doing applied doctoral degrees (EdD), that we would have many such accounts. Unfortunately, rather than being opportunities for deep and critical reflection on the daily dilemmas of being advocates for children, most of these dissertations end up being attempts to promote "successful" practices, engage in program evaluations, or please academic dissertation committees with little training in action research, and increasingly Human Subjects Review Boards are nervous about letting school practitioners study their own practice (see Anderson & Herr, 1999; Anderson & Jones, 2000; Herr & Anderson, 2008, for dilemmas related to producing deep knowledge about leadership in schools).

Marcus Foster: Presente!

A final illustration of advocacy leadership is the story of Marcus Foster, an African-American school leader in the 1960s and early 1970s, best known as principal of Simon Gratz High School in Philadelphia and Superintendent in Oakland, California. Foster illustrates the raw courage required of leaders who choose an advocacy role and the risk-taking this role requires. While, in reality, few advocacy leaders will risk death, Foster's tragic story highlights the importance of the work of school leaders and the impact they can have when they harness the power of their communities. In the turmoil of that period, Marcus Foster was viewed as too radical by some, but not radical enough by some others. The story of this courageous school leader did not have a happy ending. He was murdered in Oakland by members of the extremist Symbionese Liberation Army, better known for their abduction of Patty Hearst.

Foster's advocacy leadership provides a counterpoint to the contemporary managerial principal. Back in 1971, he advocated for something he called "new leadership," that saw principals as catalysts to empower those around them to engage in, not just leadership, but also advocacy. Rather than turn to business leaders as models, Foster viewed African-American clergy as providing an appropriate model.

> Ours is a time that requires leadership, not just administration. New ground will be broken by teachers, parents, community people, as well as by principals and others up the line.
>
> Fortunately, we can find some excellent examples of this "new leadership" in other realms of endeavor. I am thinking particularly of the clergymen [sic] who, in the last two decades [1950s and 1960s] have transformed their roles by extending the power of their faith beyond the church walls. Martin Luther King, Jr. preached love and hope as he marched through Southern towns. Father Groppi led his congregation in Midwest urban centers. These men came to believe that a meaningful ministry required them to bring religion to the places it was needed. It went beyond praying. When

political action was needed to move the spirit, they engaged in politics. When it was economics, as in the case of Rev. Leon Sullivan, who founded the Opportunities Industrialization Centers, the preaching led to jobs.

The kind of flexibility that characterized these leader-ministers has got to be built into our roles as leader-educators. In my own career I have sometimes played the salesman, the community organizer, the economist, the fund-raiser, and the speechmaker. One incident reported in the next chapter describes my role as producer of a guerrilla-theater play

I am not saying that everyone involved in education has to be a one-man band. What is important is that one comes to accept the diversity of tasks needed to make education work. One has to be open to working with people doing these unexpected things. This obviously is a very different attitude from sitting back while waiting for outsiders to get the job done. (Foster, 1971, pp. 17–18)

African-American principals like Marcus Foster often found themselves promoted to underresourced urban schools and districts that served children of color. This was often done as a symbolic gesture to the community in lieu of addressing serious resource inequalities between Black and White communities, or what critical race theorists call "interest convergence" (Bell, 1980). At Simon Gratz High School, Foster was brought in to replace a White principal who was under attack from community activists.

While Marcus Foster understood structural forms of oppression, he had no patience with teachers and principals who removed the onus on them to improve education by merely pointing a finger at unjust laws and social policies. But he didn't think the answer was to pressure them with punishments and humiliation. On the contrary, he saw teachers beaten down by bureaucracy and a "Don't rock the boat" mentality. His solution was not to gut the system of democratic participation, retool school leaders into entrepreneurs, and introduce market forces. In his initial speech as the new Oakland superintendent, he tried to set up a new incentive system based, not on fear of being punished for failure, but rather on encouraging risk-taking and mobilizing communities to demand more from their schools.

Another thing we want to do in Oakland is to send out a different signal about the reward system. In most bureaucracies, those who can keep their departments cool and running smoothly usually win the praise. Such systems work for those who get along with their immediate superiors. The watchword is: don't let anything exciting happen, don't do anything that might lead to negative publicity.

We are going to do it another way in Oakland. The reward system will work for those who dare to take risks. There may be failures, but if everything we do meets with success, we may not be reaching far enough beyond our grasp. We need to take risks even if turmoil is sometimes the result—as may happen when some of you try to establish meaningful relationships with your community. But given the insipidness of so many institutions, perhaps a little turmoil is not a bad thing.... Dare to be fluid, dare to be potent, dare to be powerful in bringing about the changes we need. (pp. 156–157)

Although Foster was himself an extraordinary and charismatic leader, his goal was to make leaders of others: teachers, students, and communities. His vision was a daring one, not limited to the kinds of platitudes one often finds in school mission statements. He had his pulse on the day-to-day operation of his school or district, but always with his eye on another horizon. He was not interested so much in keeping control of his constituencies, as in empowering them. What would Marcus Foster say were he to return today to see our segregated low-income urban high schools? What would he make of their metal detectors, their security cameras, and their roving police officers and military recruiters? He would likely not be totally surprised, but he would also likely ferret out those signs of hope in a growing community organizing and student activist movement.

Foster's vision harkens back to another all but forgotten educational leader, former scholar and president of the United Federation of Teachers, George Counts (1932), who asked the question: Dare the school build a new social order? Like Counts in the 1930s, Foster saw a society divided by haves and have-nots. I will end this section with a lengthy quote by Foster in which he provides a vision of how we might save our at-risk public institutions, and by extension, the authentic ideals of our society, through building social solidarity.

Traditionally, it has been possible to divide society up into two basic groups—the A's and the B's.

The A group is the historically dominant group. It holds the established, often legalized power. It makes and enforces the rules for its own members and those of the B-group.

The B-group is the traditionally subordinate group. Its members tend to be dependent and powerless. Any real power they might possess is considered illegitimate by the A-group and therefore has to be hidden or disguised.

In the traditional school situation, for instance, teachers and administrators comprise the A-group. They tell the students—the Bs—where they should go and what they should do. Rules cover not only educational matters such as what classes one attends or what materials are required, but also personal processes such as where and when one eats, goes to the bathroom, or under what conditions peers might talk to each other. There is no authentic student power in this kind of school. Student government is really a fiction, the purpose of which is to give students practice with certain political forms.

But things are changing. Minority or oppressed groups are no longer content to be submissive. The poor, the female, the black, the Army private, the student—all are unwilling to accept second-class citizenship no matter how the A-group rationalizes it.

The B-group members want to structure and direct their own lives; and they have discovered a source of power for making their demands real, not just rhetorical. Like the trade unionists of the nineteenth century, and the emerging nation-states of the post-World War II period, the Bs are realizing that their true power is in each other. As isolated groups, they have only the power to destroy. Together, they have the power to initiate action in directions compatible with their own goals.

The dominant groups have long understood the potency of united effort. What is known as "the weight of society" is nothing more than the various A-groups pulling together. Cooperative establishment power over the years has had little difficulty in pushing back the incessant revolts of individual B-groups. But facing a united front is something else again. The As have had to resort to new strategies for maintaining their dominant position.

This is the essence of the struggle that threatens to destroy the major institutions of our society. Nowhere is the pattern clearer than in the realm of urban education. (pp. 24–25)

Conclusion

At least in economic terms, the country is more conservative today than it was in the 1960s and 1970s. It is also more unequal and more segregated. Nevertheless, the pieces of a powerful social movement are lying around waiting for leaders, present-day Marcus Fosters, to pick up and galvanize. Common ground can increasingly be found across ideologically opposed groups. We can see growing pockets of activism around resistance to the wars in Iraq and Afghanistan and their "economic draft," control of Washington by corporate lobbyists, an inequitable private health care system, and lax environmental laws. Urban communities are better politically organized than in recent memory, taking on issues of housing, health care, community development, and education in low-income communities. This growing community activism provides school leaders with potential allies.

And yet, through complex processes that I have tried to describe in this book, school leaders are incorporated into a narrow testing paradigm that believes that a combination of high stakes testing and marketizing education provision will solve problems that are essentially social, not only educational. Unless, a paradigm shift occurs in which leadership is viewed as a form of advocacy, we can expect educational leaders to continue to be largely timid legitimators of an unequal status quo.

I have argued throughout this book that no amount of advocacy can replace building authentic and caring relationships with teachers and students. Teachers and students have amazingly nuanced antennae that easily distinguish authentic from inauthentic leaders. On the other hand, no amount of ethical caring, hard work, or even good teaching can make up for a society that does not support all of its families and children with adequate resources. A new generation of skilled leaders, able to combine authenticity with advocacy, can be the catalyst for the educational and social transformations that can realize, for the first time, the promise of public education.

Appendix A

The Interstate School Leaders Licensure Consortium developed the following Standards which can be accessed in more detail at the Council of Chief State School Officers' web page: http://www.cssoo.org

Standard 1. A school administrator is an educational leader who promotes the success of all students by facilitating the development, articulation, implementation, and stewardship of a vision of learning that is shared and supported by the school community.

Standard 2. A school administrator is an educational leader who promotes the success of all students by advocating, nurturing, and sustaining a school culture and instructional program conducive to student learning and staff professional growth.

Standard 3. A school administrator is an educational leader who promotes the success of all students by ensuring management of the organization, operations, and resources for a safe, efficient, and effective learning environment.

Standard 4. A school administrator is an educational leader who promotes the success of all students by collaborating with families and community members, responding to diverse community interests and needs, and mobilizing community resources.

Standard 5. A school administrator is an educational leader who promotes the success of all students by acting with integrity, fairness, and in an ethical manner.

Standard 6. A school administrator is an educational leader who promotes the success of all students by understanding, responding to, and influencing the larger political, social, economic, legal, and cultural context.

Notes

Introduction

1. Many school districts have replaced school business managers, certified in schools of education, with MBAs. Many departments of educational leadership in schools of education have ceased providing this certification. Business schools are likely to continue to play a larger role in the preparation of school leaders.
2. For instance, Michael Barber, a former education adviser to Tony Blair, who now works for the McKinsey consulting firm, was hired by Joel Klein to consult on the New York City reform. Richard Pring is a Cambridge professor and leader of the Nuffield Review, a major evaluation of education in England and Wales. A letter that Pring wrote to the *New York Times*, which was not published, appeared in the Huffington Post (quoted in Ravitch, 2007). It contained an assessment of British education under Barber's advisement:

   > The results of the "high stakes testing" are that teachers increasingly teach to the test, young people are disillusioned and disengaged, higher education complains that those matriculating (despite higher scores) are ill prepared for university studies, and intelligent and creative teachers increasingly feel dissatisfied with their professional work. I believe it is no coincidence that, according to the recent UNICEF Report, children in England are at the bottom of the league of rich countries in terms of happiness and feelings of well-being, or that England now criminalizes 230,000 children between 11 and 17 each year (the highest in absolute and relative terms in the whole of Europe), or that nearly 10% of 16–18 year olds belong to the Not in Education, Training and Employment group, despite the massive investment in that group over the last ten years. And why should one expect anything else as most of their daylight hours consist of preparing for tests, totally disconnected from their interests and concerns, present or future?

Chapter 2

1. While we are told that we need to raise our students' level of skills in order to compete in a global information economy, Felstead, Gallie, and Green's (2002) extensive survey of work skills in Britain showed that even if higher skill jobs (11 million) and intermediate skill jobs (13.3 million) were added together, they were still outnumbered by low-skill jobs. While this is not an argument for failing to prepare students for highly skilled jobs, there is a disconnect between the rhetoric of the information society and the reality of the current global workplace.
2. While I will use the 1983 *Nation at Risk* report as a kind of benchmark for the beginning of the current school reform movement, Engel (2000) argues correctly that the 1958 Nation Defense Education Act (NDEA) was a previous response to crisis language. When in October 1957, the Soviet Union launched *Sputnik*, the first orbiting space satellite, a mediocre American educational system was viewed as being the reason for America's lack of competitiveness.
3. Although I have critiqued the recent reforms implemented by the New York City Department of Education, the creation of small schools and even charter schools is a step in the right direction in terms of making schools more relational.

Chapter 3

1. While many progressive educators supported Caulkins work theoretically, many teachers complained that its implementation was far too scripted.
2. This Rumsfeld quote, reported by journalist Jeremy Scahill (2007) begins his account of the incredible growth of Blackwater USA, a secretive private army of soldiers subject to little public accountability. In fact, Bush's envoy in Iraq, Paul Bremer, decreed as he left Baghdad in 2004, that private contractors were immune from prosecution. While U.S. soldiers are being prosecuted by the Pentagon for killings and torture in Iraq, these private forces were declared immune. The morning after Rumsfeld's speech to his corporate deputies, the Pentagon was literally attacked as American Airlines Flight 77 crashed into one of its walls. Thus began a war on terrorism that has largely been outsourced to the private sector. Blackwater and other private security forces have also sought markets in the aftermath of disaster. The Department of Homeland Security paid $950 a day to Blackwater soldiers in the aftermath of Hurricane Katrina. "In less than a year, the company had raked in more than $70 million in federal hurricane-related contracts—about $243,000 a day.

Chapter 4

1. A previous version of this largely rewritten and updated chapter was published as: Anderson, G. L. (2001). Disciplining leaders. A critical discourse analysis of the ISLLC national examination and performance standards in educational administration. *International Journal of Leadership in Education*, 4(3), 199–216.

Chapter 5

1. A previous version of this largely rewritten and updated chapter was published as: Anderson, G. L. (1998). Toward authentic participation: Deconstructing the discourse of participatory reforms. *American Educational Research Journal*, 35(4), 571–606.
2. Some countries have been implementing participatory structures in school systems for some time. Beare and Boyd (1993) note that German schools have been required by the Potsdam agreement since the end of World War II to govern schools through a network of committees designed to make the system work along the lines of a participatory democracy. More recently countries which have experienced brutal dictatorships are utilizing participatory structures in schools as an attempt to democratize social institutions.
3. Shipps (1997), in an analysis of Chicago school reform during that period, argues that the corporate sector was always a key player, even during the "community control" period from 1988–1995.
4. Decentralization can have other "hidden" functions. Prawda (1993), a Mexican economist, argues that a nonpublicized (but widely known) function of Mexico's recent decentralization reform was to weaken the powerful Mexican teachers' union. In another case, the 1988 Education Reform Act in Britain dismantled the Inner London Education Authority (equivalent to the old Central Board of Education in New York City) and devolved authority to each of the 13 boroughs. A manifest function of this move was to remove a bloated and inefficient bureaucracy. A hidden agenda of the Thatcher administration was to eliminate an agency that was viewed as a hotbed of left-wing activity (Cooper, 1990).
5. See Malen (1994) for a more in-depth discussion of the links between legitimation and conflict management.

Chapter 6

1. Subsequent research has shown that detracking high schools, particularly when coupled with busing, is politically volatile and to be successful, requires staff development in teaching heterogeneous groups.
2. I could also have used James C. Scott's (1990) notion of hidden and public transcripts. Scott's work, like DuBois's work, looks at social conditions of extreme oppression. In both cases, the subaltern must develop creative tactics and strategies to survive, creating safe spaces in which

the necessary but humiliating public performances can be replaced by authentic communication and strategic plotting. The subalterns have lived in far more hopeless conditions than advocacy leaders, and still managed to hold onto utopian visions.

3. This doesn't mean African-American leaders all view advocacy in the same way. For instance, there are African-American leaders that I would not likely showcase as advocacy leaders, such as bat-welding Joe Clark of *Lean on Me* movie fame or Houston's Thaddeus Lott, with his support of a near military-style approach to teaching.

4. For instance, the New York City Department of Education's Leadership Academy, nicknamed the Jack Welsh Academy, is largely based on a nonacademic, problem-based curriculum and a year-long apprenticeship.

References

Abernathy, S. F. (2005). *School choice and the future of American democracy*. Ann Arbor: University of Michigan Press.

Abernathy, S. F. (2007). *No Child Left Behind and the public schools*. Ann Arbor: University of Michigan Press.

Abramowitz, M. (2001). Everyone is still on welfare: The role of redistribution in social policy. *Social Work, 46*(4), 297–308.

Abravenal, H. (1983). Mediatory myths in the service of organizational ideology. In L. R. Pondy, P. Frost, G. Morgan, & T. Dandridge (Eds.), *Organizational symbolism* (pp. 58–74). Greenwich, CT: JAI Press.

Altshuler, A. (1979). *Community control: The Black demand for participation in large American cities*. New York: Pegasus.

Anderson, G. L. (1990). Toward a critical constructivist approach to school administration: Invisibility, legitimation, and the study of non-events. *Educational Administration Quarterly, 26*(1), 38–59.

Anderson, G. L. (1991). The cognitive politics of teachers and principals: Ideological control in an elementary school. In J. Blase (Ed.), *The politics of life in schools* (pp. 120–138). Beverly Hills, CA: Sage.

Anderson, G. L. (2001). Promoting educational equity in a period of growing social inequity: The silent contradictions of Texas reform discourse. *Education and Urban Society, 53*(3), 320–332.

Anderson, G. L (in press). The politics of *Another Side*: Truth-in-military-recruiting advocacy in an urban school district. In J. Scott, C. Lubienski, & E. Debray-Pelot (Eds.), *The politics of advocacy in education: The politics of education yearbook*. Thousand Oaks, CA: Corwin Press.

Anderson, G. L., & Dixon, A. (1993). Paradigm shifts and site-based management in the United States: Toward a paradigm of social empowerment. In J. Smyth (Ed.), *A socially critical view of the self-managing school* (pp. 49–62). London: Falmer Press.

Anderson, G. L., & Grinberg, J. (1998). Educational administration as a disciplinary practice: Appropriating Foucault's view of power, discourse, and method. *Educational Administration Quarterly, 34*(3), 329–335.

Anderson, G. L., & Herr, K. (1999). The new paradigm wars. Is there room for rigorous practitioner knowledge in schools and universities? *Educational Researcher, 28*(5), 12–21.

Anderson, G. L., & Jones, F. (2000). Knowledge generation in educational administration from the inside-out: The promise and perils of site-based, administrator research. *Educational Administration Quarterly, 36*(3), 428–464.

Andre-Bechely, L. (2004). Public school choice at the intersection of voluntary integration and not-so-good neighborhood schools: Lessons from parents' experiences. *Educational Administration Quarterly, 39*(1), 1–38.

Andre-Bechely, L. (2005). *Could it be otherwise? Parents and the inequalities of public school choice*. New York: Routledge.

Annenberg Institute on School Reform. Brooklyn-Queens 4 Education Collaborative. Retrieved November 6, 2008, from http://www.annenberginstitute.org/CIP/nyco.html

Anyon, J. (2005). *Radical possibilities: Public policy, urban education, and a new social movement*. New York: Routledge.

Apple, M. (1996). *Cultural politics and education*. New York: Teachers College Press.

Apple, M. (2006). *Educating the "right" way: Markets, standards, God, and inequality*. New York: Routledge.

Apple, M. 2003). *The state and the politics of knowledge*. New York: Routledge.

Apple, M. W., Au, W., & Gandin, L. A. (Eds.). (2009) *Routledge international handbook of critical education*. New York: Routledge.

Apple, M. W., & Beane, J. A. (Eds.). (2007). *Democratic schools: Lessons in powerful education.* Portsmouth, NH: Heinemann.

Apple, M. W., & Buras, K. L. (Eds.). (2006). *The subaltern speak: Curriculum, power, and educational struggles.* New York: Routledge.

Argyris, C., & Schon, D. (1974). *Theory and practice: Increasing professional effectiveness.* San Francisco: Jossey-Bass.

Ayers, W., & Klonsky, M. (2006, February). Chicago's Renaissance 2010: The small schools movement meets the ownership society. *Phi Delta Kappan, 87*(6), 453–457.

Bacharach, S. B., Bamberger, P., Conley, S. C., & Bauer, S. (1990). The dimensionality of decision participation in educational organizations: The value of a multi-domain evaluative approach. *Educational Administrative Quarterly, 26,* 126–167.

Bachrach, P., & Botwinick, A. (1992). *Power and empowerment: A radical theory of participatory democracy.* Philadelphia: Temple University Press.

Baghban, M., & Li, H. (2007). "I thought I was a professional": Teachers and parents' reactions to NCLB in New York City. In H. Johnson & A. Salz (Eds.), *What is authentic educational reform? Pushing against the compassionate conservative agenda* (pp. 29–42). New York: Erlbaum.

Ball, S. (1987). *The micro-politics of the school: Towards a theory of school organization.* London: Methuen.

Ball, S. (1998). Big policies/small world: An introduction to international perspectives in educational policy. *Comparative Education, 34,* 119–130.

Ball, S. (2001). Performativities and fabrications in the education economy: Towards the performative society. In D. Gleason & C. Husbands (Eds.), *The performing school: Managing, teaching and learning in a performance culture* (pp. 210–226). London: Routledge/Falmer.

Ball, S. (2007). *Education plc: Understanding private sector participation in public sector education.* New York: Routledge.

Barber, B. (1975, April). Command performance. *Harper's Magazine, 250,* 51–54.

Barber, B. (1984). *Strong democracy: Participatory politics for a new age.* Berkeley: University of California Press.

Barker, J. (1993). Tightening the iron cage: Concertive control in self-managing teams. *Administrative Science Quarterly, 38*(3), 408–437.

Barlow, A. (2003). *Between fear and hope: Globalization and race in the United States.* Lanham, MD: Rowan & Littlefield.

Barnard, C. (1938). *The functions of the executive.* Cambridge, MA: Harvard University Press.

Bartlett, L., & Lutz, C. (1998). Disciplining social difference: Some cultural politics of military training in public high schools. *The Urban Review, 30*(2), 119–136.

Beare, H. (1993). Different ways of viewing school site councils: Whose paradigm is in use here? In H. Beare, & W. Boyd, (Eds.). *Restructuring schools: An international perspective on the movement to transform the control and performance of schools* (pp. 200–217). London: Falmer Press.

Begley, P. T. (2001). In pursuit of authentic school leadership practices. *International Journal of Leadership in Education, 4*(4), 353–366.

Bell, D. (1980). *Brown v. Board of Education* and the interest-convergence dilemma. *Harvard Law Review, 93,* 518.

Bellah, R., Madsen, R., Sullivan, W., Swidler, A., & Tipton, S. (1985). *Habits of the heart: Individualism and commitment in American life.* Berkeley: University of California Press.

Bensimon, E., & Marshall, C. (1997). Policy analysis for post-secondary education: Feminist and critical perspectives. In C. Marshall (Ed.), *Feminist critical policy analysis: Vol. 2. A perspective from post-secondary education* (pp. 1–21). London: Falmer Press.

Berliner, D. (2006). Our impoverished view of educational research. *Teachers College Record, 108*(6), 949–995.

Berliner, D. (2007). Investing in student lives outside of school, to increase achievement inside schools. In G. Rodrigues & A. Rolle (Eds.), *To what ends and by what means: The social justice implications of contemporary school finance theory and policy* (145–163). New York: Routledge.

Berliner, D., & Biddle, B. (1995). *The manufactured crisis: Myths, fraud, and the attack on America's public schools.* Reading, MA: Addison-Wesley.

Black, W. (2008). The contradictions of high stakes accountability "success": A case study of focused leadership and performance agency. *International Journal of Leadership in Education, 11*(1), 1–22.

Blanchard, J. (2008, April 22). Teacher shuns WASL, earns suspension—and praise. Seattlepi.com. Retrieved July 21, 2008, from http://seattlepi.nwsource.com/local/360031_wasl22.html

Blase J. (1989). The micropolitics of the school: The everyday political perspectives of teachers toward open school principals. *Educational Administration Quarterly, 25*(4), 377–407.

Blase, J., & Anderson, G. L. (1995). *The micropolitics of educational leadership: From control to empowerment*. New York: Teachers College Press.

Blase, J., & Kirby, P. (1992). *Bringing out the best in teachers: What effective principals do*. Newbury Park, CA: Corwin Press.

Boggs, C. (2000). *The end of politics: Corporate power and the decline of the public sphere*. New York: Guilford.

Borman, G. D., Hewes, G. M., Overman, L. T., & Brown, S. (2003). Comprehensive school reform and student achievement: A meta analysis. *Review of Educational Research, 73*(2), 123–139.

Bourdieu, P., & Passeron, J. (1990). *Reproduction in education, society and culture* (2nd ed.). London: Sage. (Original work published 1977)

Boyles, D. (2000). *American education and corporations: The free market goes to school*. New York: Falmer.

Brantlinger, E. (2003). *Dividing classes: How the middle class negotiates and rationalizes school advantage*. New York: Routledge.

Brantlinger, E., Majd-Jabbari, M., & Guskin, S. L. (1996). Self-interest and liberal educational discourse: How ideology works for middle-class mothers. *American Educational Research Journal, 33*(3), 571–598.

Brecher, J., Costello, & T. Smith, B. (2000). *Globalization from below: The power of solidarity*. Cambridge, MA: South End Press.

Brink, S. (2008, February 25). "Socialized medicine" loses much of its stigma. *Los Angeles Times*, A7.

Brown, K. (2004). Leadership for social justice and equity: Weaving a transformative framework and pedagogy. *Educational Administration Quarterly, 40*(1), 77–108.

Brunner, C. (1999). Taking risks: A requirement of the new superintendency. *Journal of School Leadership, 9*(4), 290–310.

Bryson, J., & Crosby, B. (1992). *Leadership for the common good: Tackling public problems in a shared-power world*. San Francisco: Jossey-Bass.

Buras, K. L. (2008). *Rightist multiculturalism: Core lessons on neoconservative school reform*. New York: Routledge.

Burch, P. E. (2005, December 15). The new educational privatization: Educational contracting and high stakes accountability. *Teachers College Record*, Retrieved January 21, 2006, from http://www.tcrecord.org ID Number: 12259

Burns, J. M. (1982). *Leadership*. New York: Harper.

California Nurses Association. (2006, November 8). Prop. 89: We've opened a door for reform that will never be closed. (Press release) Retrieved June 19, 2007, from http://www.calnurses.org/media-center/press-releases/2006/november/page.jsp

Callahan, R. (1962). *Education and the cult of efficiency*. Chicago: University of Chicago Press.

Campbell, J., & Neill, S. (1994). *Curriculum at stage one: Teacher commitment and policy failure*. Harlow, UK: Longman.

Capper, C., Theoharris, G., & Sebastian, J. (2006). Toward a framework for preparing leaders for social justice. *Journal Educational Administration, 44*(3), 209–224.

Carey, A. (1995). *Taking the risk out of democracy: Corporate propaganda versus freedom and liberty*. Urbana: University of Illinois Press.

Carnegie, D. (1936). *How to win friends and influence people*. New York: Simon & Schuster.

Carnoy, M. (2000). Globalization and educational reform. In N. Stromquist & K. Monkman (Eds.), *Globalization and education* (pp. 43–61). Lanham, MD: Rowman & Littlefield.

Carnoy, M., Elmore, R., & Siskin, L. (2003). *The new accountability: High schools and high stakes testing*. New York: Routledge Falmer.

Casanova, U. (1996). Parent involvement: A call for prudence. *Educational Researcher, 25*(8), 30–32.

Chapman, J., & Boyd, W. L. (1986). Decentralization, devolution and the school principal: Australian lessons on statewide educational reform. *Educational Administration Quarterly, 22*(4), 28–58.

Cherryholmes, C. (1988). *Power and criticism: Poststructural investigations in education*. New York: Teachers College Press.

Children's Defense Fund. (2004). *Robin Hood in reverse: Bush administration budget choices take from poor children and give to the rich*. Washington DC: Author.

Chubb, J., & Moe, T. (1990). *Politics, markets, and America's schools*. Washington, D.C.: The Brookings Institute.

Clark, B. (2004). Exam privatization threatens public schools. *CorpWatch*. Retrieved August 9, 2008, from http://www.corpwatch.org/article.php?id=11543

Clegg, S. R. (1989). *Frameworks of power*. London: Sage.

Cohen Ross, D. (1999). How schools can help link children to free and low-cost health insurance programs. Center on budget and policy priorities. Retrieved August 24, 2008, from http://www.cbpp.org/11-1-99health.htm.

Coleman, J., Campbell, E., Hobson, C., & McPartland, J. (1966). *Equality of educational opportunity*. Washington DC: U.S. Government Printing Office.

Cooper, B. (1990). Local school reform in Great Britain and the United States: Points of comparison—Points of departure. *Educational Review, 42*(2), 133–149.

Cooper, C. W. (2007). School choice as "motherwork": Valuing African American women's educational advocacy and resistance. *International Journal of Qualitative Studies in Education, 20*(5), 491–512.

Covey, S. (1989). *The 7 habits of highly effective people*. New York: Free Press.

Counts, G. (1932). *Dare the school build a new social order?* New York: Day.

Cuban, L. (1990). Reforming again, again, and again. *Educational Researcher, 19*(1), 3–13.

Cuban L. (1992). Managing dilemmas while building professional communities, *Educational Researcher, 21*(1), 4–11.

Cuban, L. (2004). *The blackboard and the bottom line: Why schools can't be businesses*. Cambridge, MA: Harvard University Press.

Cuban, L. (2007). Hugging the middle: Teaching in an era of testing and accountability. *Education Policy Analysis Archives, 15*(1). Retrieved May 26, 2008, from http://epaa.asu.edu/epaa/v15n1/

Cummins, J. (1986). Empowering minority students: A framework for intervention. *Harvard Educational Review, 56*(4), 649–657.

Cummins, J. (2003). Challenging the construction of difference as deficit: Where are identity, intellect, imagination, and power in the new regime of truth? In P. Trifonas (Ed.), *Pedagogies of difference: Rethinking education for social change* (pp. 41–59) New York: Routledge.

Dahl, R. (1961). *Who governs? Democracy and power in an American city*. New Haven, CT: Yale University Press.

Dahlberg, L., & Siapera, E. (Eds.). (2007). *Radical democracy and the internet: Interrogating the theory and practice*. New York: Palgrave Macmillan.

Darling-Hammond, L. (2001). *The right to learn*. San Francisco: Jossey-Bass.

Darling-Hammond, L., & Wood, G. (Eds.). (2008). *Democracy at risk: The need for a new federal policy in education*. Washington, DC: The Forum for Education and Democracy.

Davies, S., Quirke, L., & Aurini, J. (2006). The new institutionalism goes to market: The challenge of rapid growth in private k-12 education. In H. D. Meyer & B. Rowan (Eds.), *The new institutionalism in education* (pp. 103–122) Albany, NY: SUNY Press.

Deal, T., & Peterson, K. (1994). *The leadership paradox: Balancing logic and artistry in schools*. San Francisco: Jossey-Bass.

Debord, G. (1995). *The society of the spectacle* (D. Nichelson-Smith, Trans.). New York: Zone Books. (Original work published 1967)

Debray, E. (2006). *Politics, ideology and education: Federal policy during the Clinton and Bush administrations*. New York: Teachers College Press.

de Jong, E. J. (2008). Contextualizing policy appropriation: teachers' perspectives, local responses, and English-only ballot initiatives. *Urban Review, 40*(2), 1–23.

Delpit, L. (1995). *Other people's children: Cultural conflict in the classroom*. New York: New Press.

Deming, W. E. (1993). *The new economics for industry, government, and education*. Cambridge: MA: MIT.

Derber, C. (1998). *Corporation nation*. New York: St. Martin's Press.

Dewey, J. (1929). *Individualism: Old and new*. New York: Putnam.

Dillard, C. B. (1995). Leading with her life: An African American feminist (re)interpretation of leadership for an urban high school principal. *Educational Administration Quarterly, 31*(4), 539–563.

Donmoyer, R. (2005). Scientists as scriptwriters: A study of educational researchers' on educational decision-making. In B. Alexander. G. L. Anderson, & B. Gallegos, (Eds.), *Performance theories and education: Power, pedagogy, and the politics of identity* (pp. 239–261) Mahwah, NJ: Erlbaum.

Dorn, S. (2007). *Accountability Frankenstein: Understanding and taming the monster*. Charlotte, NC: Information Age.

Driscoll, M. E. (1998). Professionalism versus community: Is the conflict school and community about to be resolved? *Peabody Journal of Education, 73*(1), 89–127.

DuBois, W. E. B. (2005) *The souls of Black folk*. New York: Simon & Schuster. (Original work published 1903)

Duggan, L. (2003). *The twilight of equality: Neoliberalism, cultural politics, and the attack on democracy*. Boston: Beacon Press.

Duignan, P., & Bhindi, N. (1997). Authenticity in leadership: An emerging perspective. *The Journal of Educational Administration, 35*(3), 195–209.

Dunbar, C., & Villarruel, F. (2002). Urban school leaders and the implementation of *zero-tolerance* policies: An examination of its implications. *Peabody Journal of Education, 77*(1), 82–104.

Easton, D. (1953). *The political system: An inquiry into the state of political science*. New York: Knopf.

Edelman, M. (1978). *Political language: Words that succeed and policies that fail*. New York: Academic Press.

Edelman, M. (1988). *Constructing the political spectacle*. Chicago: University of Chicago Press.

Edmonds, R. (1979). Some schools work and more can. *Social Policy, 9,* 28–32.

Education Queensland. (2001). *Queensland school reform longitudinal study*. Brisbane, Australia: Queensland Government.

Education Schools Project. (2005). Educating school's leaders. Retrieved April 5, 2007, from http://www.edschools.org/reports_leaders.htm

Educational Testing Service. (1999). *School leaders' licensure assessment: 1999–2000: Registration Bulletin*. Princeton, NJ: Author.

Egan, T. (2007, June 28). Red state welfare. *New York Times*, A23.

Ehrenreich, B. (1990). *Fear of falling: The inner life of the middle class*. New York: Perennial.

Elliott, A., & Lemert, C. (2006). *The new individualism: The emotional costs of globalization*. New York: Routledge.

Elliott, J. (2002). Characteristics of performative cultures. In D. Gleason & C. Husbands (Eds.), *The performing school: Managing, teaching and learning in a performance culture* (pp. 192–209) London: Routledge/Falmer.

Elmore, R. (2002). *Bridging the gap between standards and achievement*. Washington D.C.: Albert Shanker Institute.

Engel, M. (2000). *The struggle for control of public education: Market ideology vs. democratic values*. Philadelphia: Temple University.

Enomoto, E., Kramer, B., & Starratt, R. (2007). *Leading through the quagmire: Ethical Foundations, Critical methods, and practical applications for school leaders*. Lanham, MD: Rowan & Littlefield.

ETS (1999). School Leaders Licensure Assessment: 1999–2000. *Registration Bulletin*. Princeton, NJ: Educational Testing Service.

Evans, A. (2007). School leaders and their sense-making about race and demographic change. *Educational Administration Quarterly, 43*(2), 159–188.

Fairclough, N. (1992). *Discourse and social change*. Cambridge, UK: Polity Press.

Fairclough, N. (2003) *Analysing discourse: Textual analysis for social research*. London: Routledge.

Fairclough, N. (2005). Critical discourse analysis. *Marge Linguistique, 9,* 76–91.

Foucault, M. (1979). *Discipline and punish: The birth of the prison.* New York: Vintage.

Fege, A. (2006). Getting Ruby a quality public education: Forty-two years of building the demand for quality public schools through parental and public involvement. *Harvard Education Review, 76*(4), 570–586.

Felstead, A., Gallie, D., & Green, F. (2002). *Work skills in Britain 1986–2002*. Nottingham, UK: DfES.

Ferguson, K. (1984). *The feminist case against bureaucracy*. Philadelphia: Temple University Press.

Feuerstein, A. (2001). Selling our schools? Principals' views on schoolhouse commercialism and school-business interactions. *Educational Administration Quarterly, 37*(3), 322–371.

Forgacs, D. (Ed.) (2000). *The Antonio Gramsci reader: Selected writings, 1916–1935*. New York: NYU Press.

Foster, M. (1971). *Making schools work: Strategies for changing education*. Philadelphia: Westminster Press.

Foucault, M. (1972). *The archeology of knowledge*. New York: Random House.

Foucault, M. (1977). *Discipline and punish: The birth of the prison*. New York: Vintage Books.

Fowler, F. (2008). *Policy studies for educational leaders*. Upper Saddle River, NJ: Prentice-Hall.

Frank, T. (2000). *One market under God: Extreme capitalism, market populism, and the end of economic democracy*. New York: Doubleday.

Fraser, N. (1997). *Justice interruptus: Critical reflections on the "postsocialist" condition*. New York: Routledge.

Frattura, E., & Capper, C. (2007). *Leading for social justice: Transforming schools for all learners.* Thousand Oaks, CA: Corwin Press.

Freire, P. (1970). *The pedagogy of the oppressed.* New York: Seabury Press.

Friedman, M. (1962). *Capitalism and freedom.* Chicago: University of Chicago Press.

Fruchter, N. (2007). *Urban schools, public will: Making education work for all our children.* New York: Teachers College Press.

Fuller, H. (1997, April). *The crisis in urban education.* Paper presented at the Annual Meeting of the American Educational Research Association, Chicago.

Galbraith, J. (1998) *Created unequal: The crisis in American pay.* New York: Simon & Schuster.

Gandin, L. (2007). The construction of the citizen school project as an alternative to neoliberal educational policies. *Policy Futures in Education, 5*(2), 179–193.

Gardner, W, Avolio, B., &Walumbwa, F. (Eds.). (2005). *Authentic leadership theory and practice: Vol. 3. Origins, effects and development.* Greenwich, CT: JAI Press.

Gee, J. P., Hull, G., & Lankshear, C. (1996). *The new work order: Behind the language of the new capitalism.* Boulder, CO: Westview Press.

Gelberg, D. (1997). *The "business" of reforming American schools.* Albany, NY: SUNY Press.

George, B. (2003). *Authentic leadership: Rediscovering the secrets to creating lasting value.* San Francisco: Jossey-Bass.

Gewirtz, S. (2002). *The managerial school: Post-welfarism and social justice in education.* London: Routledge.

Gewirtz, S., Ball, S., & Bowe, R. (1995). *Markets, choice, and equity in education.* London: Open University Press.

Giddens, A. (1994). *Beyond left and right: The future of radical politics.* Stanford, CA: Stanford University Press.

Gilbert, N. (2002). *Transformation of the welfare state: The silent surrender of public responsibility.* Oxford, UK: Oxford University Press.

Gintis, H. (1994). School choice: Discussion with Herbert Gintis. *Educational Policy Analysis Archives, 2*(6), 1–8.

Ginwright, S., Noguera, P., & Cammarota, J. (Eds.). (2006). *Beyond resistance! Youth activism and community change: New democratic possibilities for practice and policy for America's youth.* New York: Routledge.

Gitlin, A., & Margonis, F. (1995). The political aspect of reform: Teacher resistance as good sense. *American Journal of Education, 103,* 377–405.

Glass, G. (2008). *Fertilizers, pills, and magnetic strips: The fate of public education in America.* Charlotte, NC: Information Age.

Gold, E., Simon, E., & Brown, C. (2004). A new conception of parent engagement: Community organizing for school reform. In F. English (Ed.), *Handbook of educational leadership: New dimensions and realities.*(pp. 237–268). Thousand Oaks, CA: Sage.

Goldstein, J. (in press). Distributed accountability: How district leaders create structures to ensure teaching quality. *Journal of School Leadership.*

Gonzalez, N., Moll, L., & Amanti, C. (2005). *Funds of knowledge: Theorizing practices in households and classrooms.* Mahwah, NJ: Erlbaum.

Goodlad, J. (1970). *Behind the classroom door.* New York: Jones.

Goodsell, C. T. (2004). *The case for bureaucracy: A public administration polemic.* Washington, DC: Congressional Quarterly Press.

Gorostiaga, J., & Paulston, R. (2004). Mapping perspectives on school decentralization: The global debate and the case of Argentina. In P. Ninnes & S. Metha (Eds.), *Re-imagining comparative education: Postfoundational ideas and applications for critical times* (pp. 255–284). London: Routledge Falmer.

Gronn, P. (1983). Talk as the work: The accomplishment of school administration. *Administrative Science Quarterly, 28*(1), 1–21.

Grossman, R., & Adams, R. (1995). *Taking care of business: Citizenship and the charter of incorporation.* Cambridge, MA: Charter.

Grubb, N., & Lazerson, M. (2004). *The education gospel: The economic power of schooling.* Cambridge, MA: Harvard University Press.

Gutmann, A., & Thompson, D. (2004). *Why deliberative democracy?* Princeton, NJ: Princeton University Press.

Gutstein, E., & Peterson, B. (Eds.). (2005). *Rethinking mathematics: Teaching social justice by the numbers.* Milwaukee, MN: Rethinking Schools.

Haas, E. (2007). False equivalency: Think tank references on education in the news media. *Peabody Journal of Education, 82*(1), 63–102.

Habermas, J. (1975). *Legitimation crisis*. Boston: Beacon Press.

Habermas, J. (1987). *The theory of communicative action: Vol. 2. Lifeworld and system: A critique of functionalist reason* (Thomas McCarthy, Trans.). Boston: Beacon Press.

Hardt, H. (1993). Authenticity, communication, and critical theory. *Critical studies in mass communication, 10*, 49–69.

Hargreaves, A. (1994). *Changing teachers, changing times: Teachers' work and culture in the postmodern age*. New York: Teachers College Press.

Harley, B. (1999). The myth of empowerment: Work organization, hierarchy and employee autonomy in contemporary Australian workplaces. *Work, Employment and Society, 13*, 314-328.

Harvey, D. (2005). *A brief history of neoliberalism*. New York: Oxford University Press.

Hayes, D., Mills, M., Christie, P., & Lingard, B. (2006). *Teachers and schooling making a difference: Productive pedagogies, assessment and performance*. Crows Nest, NSW: Allen & Unwin.

Henry, M. (1996). *Parent-school collaboration: Feminist organizational structures and school leadership*. Albany, NY: SUNY Press.

Herr, K.. & Anderson, G. L.(2005). *The action research dissertation: A guide for students and faculty*. Thousand Oaks, CA: Sage.

Herr, K., & Anderson, G. L. (2008). Teacher research and learning communities: A failure to theorize power relations? *Language Arts, 85*(5), 382–391.

Herszenhorn, D. (2004, March 25). Not so long out of school, yet running the system. *New York Times*, p. A25.

Herszenhorn, D. (2006, February 10). Parent council to boycott city's lobbying trip to Albany. *New York Times*, p. B1.

Hoover-Dempsey, K., & Sandler, H. (1997). Why do parents become involved in their children's education? Review of *Educational Research, 67*(1), 3–42.

Howard, R., & Preisman, J. (2007). The bankrupt "revolution": Running schools like businesses fails the test. *Education and Urban Society, 39*(2), 244–263.

Hu, W. (August 6, 2008). Demand rising, New York private schools expand. *New York Times*, p. C10.

Illich, I. (1972). *Deschooling society*. New York: Perennial.

Jacobs, B., & Levitt, S. (2002). *Rotten apples: An investigation of the prevalence and predictors of teacher cheating*. John F. Kennedy School of Government, Harvard University. Unpublished manuscript.

Jacobson, S., Hickcox, E., & Stevenson, R. (Eds.). (1996). *School administration: Persistent dilemmas in preparation and practice*. Westport CT: Praeger.

Johanek, M. C., & Puckett, J. (2006). *Leonard Covello and the making of Benjamin Franklin High School as if citizenship mattered*. Philadelphia: Temple University Press.

Johnson, M., & Pajares, F. (1996). When shared decision-making works: A 3-year longitudinal study. *American Educational Research Journal, 33*, 599–630.

Johnson, R. (2002). *Using data to close the achievement gap: How to measure equity in our schools*. Thousand Oaks, CA: Corwin Press.

Johnson, S. (1998), *Who moved my cheese?* New York: Putnam.

Johnston, D. C. (2007). *Free lunch: How the wealthiest Americans enrich themselves at government expense*. New York: Portfolio.

Kallick, D. D. (2002). *Progressive think tanks: What exists, what's missing. Report for the Program on Governance and Public Policy, Open Society Institute*. Retrieved June 18, 2008, from http://www.soros.org/initiatives/gov/articles_publications/publications/progressive_20020115

Kantor, H., & Lowe R. (2006). From New Deal to no deal: No Child Left Behind and the devolution of responsibility for equal opportunity. *Harvard Education Review, 76*(4), 474–502.

Katz, M. B. (1995). *Improving poor people: The welfare state, the "underclass," and urban schools as history*. Princeton, NJ: Princeton University Press.

Kerr, N. D. (1964). The school board as an agency of legitimation. *Sociology of Education, 38*, 34–59.

Kim, J. (2004). Summer reading and the ethnic achievement gap. *Journal of Education For Students Placed At Risk, 9*(2), 169–188.

Klein, N. (2007). *The shock doctrine: The rise of disaster capitalism*. New York: Metropolitan.

Knight Abowitz, K. (1997). Neglected aspects of the liberal-communitarian debate and implications for school communities. *Educational Foundations, 11*(2), 63–82.

Kumashiro, K. (2008) *The seduction of common sense: How the right has framed the debate on America's schools*. New York: Routledge.

Kuttner, R. (1999). *Everything for sale*. Chicago: The University of Chicago.

Labaree, D. (1997). *How to succeed in school without really learning: The credentials race in American education*. London & New Haven, CT: Yale University Press.

Laczko-Kerr, I., & Berliner, D. (2002). The effectiveness of "Teach for America" and other under-certified teachers on student academic achievement: A case of harmful public policy. *Education Policy Analysis Archives, 10*(37). Retrieved July 2002, from http://epaa.asu.edu/epaa/v10n37/

Ladson-Billings, G. (1995). Toward a theory of culturally relevant pedagogy. *American Educational Research Journal, 32*, 465–492.

Ladson-Billings, G. (1997). *Dreamkeepers: Successful teachers of African-American children*. San Francisco: Jossey-Bass.

Lakoff, G. (2004). *Don't think of an elephant: Know your values and frame the debate*. New York: Chelsea Green.

Lakoff, G. (2008). *The political mind*. New York: Penguin Books.

Lareau, A. (1989). *Home advantage: Social class and parental intervention in Elementary education*. New York: Falmer Press.

Larson, C., & Murtadha, K. (2002). Leadership for social justice. In J. Murphy (Ed.), *The educational leadership challenge: Redefining leadership for the 21st century* (pp. 134–161). Chicago: University of Chicago.

Lasch, C. (1995). *The revolt of the elites: And the betrayal of democracy*. New York: Norton.

Lavelle, L. (2005, April 18). A payday for performance. *Business Week*, p. 14.

Lemann, N. (2000). *The big test: The secret history of the American meritocracy*. New York: Farrar, Straus & Giroux.

Levin, H. (1998). Educational performance standards and the economy. *Educational Researcher, 27*(4), 4–10.

Levin, H. (2001). Studying privatization in education. In H. Levin (Ed.), *Privatizing education: Can the marketplace deliver choice, efficiency, equity, and social cohesion?* (pp. 3–19). Boulder, CO: Westview Press.

Levine, J. (2007). *Sobol v. Sobol. TC Today, 32*(1), 9–13, 32, 33.

Lewis, J., & Surrender, R. (2004). *Welfare state change: Towards a third way*. Oxford: Oxford University Press.

Lingard, B., Hayes, D., Mills, M., & Christie, P. (2003). *Leading learning: Making hope practical in schools*. London: Open University Press.

Lipman, P. (1997). Restructuring in context: A case study of teacher participation and the dynamics of ideology, race, and power. *American Educational Research Journal, 34*(1), 3–37.

Lipman, P. (2004). *High stakes education: Inequality, globalization, and urban school reform*. New York: Routledge.

Lipsky, M. (1983). *Street-level bureaucracy: Dilemmas of the individual in public services*. New York: Russell Sage Foundation.

Lugg, C. (2007). *Kitsch: From education to public policy*. New York: Taylor & Francis.

Luke, A. (2003). Literacy and the other: A sociological approach to literacy research and policy in multilingual societies. *Reading Research Quarterly, 38*(1), 132–141.

Lukes, S. (2005). *Power: A radical view* (Rev. ed.). London: Macmillan.

Malen, B. (1994). Enacting site-based management: A political utilities analysis. *Educational Evaluation and Policy Analysis, 16*(3), 249–267.

Malen, B., & Ogawa, R. (1988). Professional-patron influence on site-based governance councils: A confounding case study. *Educational Evaluation and Policy Analysis, 10*(4), 251–20.

Marcuse, H. (1964). *One-dimentional man*. Boston: Beacon Press.

Market (2007). New York City Department of Education, p.1. Retreived January 18, 2007, from http://print.nycenet.edu/Offices/ChildrenFirst/Empowerment/Market/default.htm

Marshall, C., & Oliva, M. (2005). *Leaders for social justice: Making revolutions in education*. New York: Allyn & Bacon.

Mayo, E. (1933). *The human problems of an industrial civilization*. New York: Macmillan.

McGrath, D., & Kurillof, P. (1999) "They're going to tear the doors off this place": Upper-middle-class parent school involvement and the educational opportunities of other people's children. *Educational Policy, 13*(5), 603–629.

McNeil, L. (2000). *Contradictions of school reform: The educational costs of standardized testing*. New York: Routledge.

McQuarrie, M. (2007). *From backyard revolution to backyard reaction: Protest, development, and the anti-politics machine in Cleveland, 1975–2005*. Unpublished doctoral dissertation, New York University, New York.

Mead, G. H. (1967). *Mind, self, and society*. Chicago: University of Chicago Press.

Mediratta, K., Lewis, A. C., & Fruchter, N. (2002). *Organizing for school reform: How communities are finding their voices and reclaiming their public schools*. New York: Institute for Education and Social Policy.

Mehan, H. (1993). Beneath the skin and between the ears: A case study in the politics of representation. In S. Chaiklin & J. Lave (Eds.), *Understanding practice: Perspectives on activity and context* (pp. 241–268). Cambridge, UK: Cambridge University Press.

Meier, D. (1995). *The power of their ideas: Lessons from a small school in Harlem*. Boston: Beacon Press.

Meier, D. (2002). *In schools we trust: Creating communities of learning in an era of testing and standardization*. Boston: Beacon Press.

Merritt, J. (2004, April 26). A syllabus way beyond the SATs: Nonprofit Educational Testing Service plans to expand by creating for-profits. *Business Week*. Retrieved September 20, 2007, from http://www.businessweek.com/magazine/content/04_17/b3880102.htm

Meyer, H. D. (2006). The rise and decline of the common school as an institution: Taking myth and ceremony? Seriously. In H. D. Meyer & B. Rowan (Eds.), *The new institutionalism in education* (pp. 51–66). Albany, NY: SUNY Press.

Meyer J., & Rowan, B. (1977). Institutionalized organizations: Formal structure as myth and ceremony. *American Journal of Sociology, 83*(2), 341–363.

Mickelson, R. (1999). International business machinations: A case study of corporate involvement in local educational reform. *Teachers College Record, 100*(3), 476–506.

Miller, J. (1990). *Creating spaces and finding voices: Teachers collaborating for empowerment*. Albany, NY: SUNY Press.

Mills, C. W. (1961). *The sociological imagination*. New York: Grove Press

Minkler, M., & Wallerstein, N. (Eds.). (2003). *Community-based participatory research for health*. San Francisco: Jossey-Bass.

Minow, M. (2002). *Partners, not rivals: Privatization and the public good*. Boston: Beacon Press.

Miron, G., & Nelson, C. (2002). *What's public about charter schools? Lessons learned about choice and accountability*. Thousand Oaks, CA: Corwin Press.

Moller, J. (1996). Reframing educational leadership in the perspective of dilemmas. In S. Jacobson, E. Hickcox, & R. Stevenson (Eds.), *School administration: Persistent dilemmas in preparation and practice* (pp. 207–225) Westport CT: Praeger.

Molnar, A. (2005). *School commercialism*. New York: Routledge.

Murphy, J., Jost, Y., & Shipman, N. (2000). Implementation of the Interstate School Leaders Licensure Consortium Standards. *International Journal of Leadership in Education, 3*(1), 17–39.

Murtadha, K., & Watts, D. M. (2005). Linking the struggle for education and social justice: Historical perspectives of African-American leadership in schools. *Educational Administration Quarterly, 41*(4), 591–608.

Naipaul, V. S. (1992). *A bend in the river*. Gloucester, MA: Peter Smith.

National Center on Education and the Economy. New Commission on the Skills of the American Workforce. (2006). *Tough choices or tough times: The report of the New Commission on the Skills of the American Workforce*. San Francisco: National Center on Education and the Economy.

National Commission on Excellence in Education. (1983). *A nation at risk: The imperative for educational reform*. Washington, DC: Government Publishing Office.

National Council of Churches. (1999). The churches and the public schools at the close of the twentieth century. Retrieved August 3, 2008,from http://www.ncccusa.org/about/edpol.html

National Council of Churches. (2003). *Ten moral concerns in the implementation of the Child Left Behind Act*. Retrieved June 20, 2007, from http://www.ncccusa.org/pdfs/LeftBehind.pdf

National Education Association. (January, 2003). *Protecting public education from tax giveaways to corporations: Property tax abatements, tax increment financing and funding for schools* (Research Working Paper). Washington, DC: Author.

National Priorities Project. (2007). *The cost of war*. Retrieved August 7, 2007, from http://national-priorities.org

National Research Council. (2002). *Scientific research in education*. (Committee on Scientific Principles for Education Research; R. J. Shavelson, & L. Towne, Eds.). Washington, DC: National Academy Press.

New York Collective of Radical Educators. (2006). *An unnatural disaster: A critical guide for addressing the aftermath of Hurricane Katrina in the classroom*. New York: NYCORE.

New York Collective of Radical Educators. (2008). *Camouflaged: Investigating how the U.S. military affects you and your community*. New York: NYCORE.

Newman F., & Associates (1996). *Authentic achievement: Restructuring schools for intellectual quality*. San Francisco: Jossey-Bass.

Nichols, S., & Berliner, D. (2007). *Collateral damage: How high stakes testing corrupts America's schools.* Cambridge, MA: Harvard Education Press.

Novicevic, M., Harvey, M., Buckley, M. R., Brown, J., & Evans, R. (2006). Authentic leadership: A historical perspective. *Journal of Leadership and Organizational Studies, 13*(1), 64–77.

Oakes, J. (1985). *Keeping track: How schools structure inequality.* New Haven, CT: Yale University Press.

Orfield, G. (2001). *Schools more separate: Consequences of a decade of resegregation.* Cambridge, MA: The Civil Rights Project, Harvard University.

Ospina, S., & Foldy, E (2005, September). *Toward a framework for social change leadership.* Paper presented at the Annual Meeting of the Public Management Research Association, Los Angeles.

Ouchi, W. G. (2004, August). Tilting the balance: A management consultant's prescription for changing the equilibrium between central office and schools. *TheSchool Administrator.* Retrieved April 4, 2006, from http://www.aasa.org /publications/sa/2004_08/ouchi.htm

Parent involvement in the 1990s: Beyond pizza sales. (1993, April 14). *Rethinking Schools, 1,* 5.

Parker, L., & Margonis, F. (1996). School choice in the U.S. urban context: Racism and policies of containment. *Journal of Education Policy, 11*(6), 717–728.

Peale, N. V. (1956), *The power of positive thinking.* New York: Fawcett Books.

Pear, R. (2005, October 1). Buying of news by Bush aides is ruled illegal. *New York Times,* pp. A1, A13.

Pedroni, T. C. (2007). *Market movements: African American involvement in school voucher reform.* New York: Routledge.

Perlstein, D., Sadovnik, A., & Semel, S. (2004). *Justice, justice: School politics and the eclipse of liberalism.* New York: Peter Lang.

Peters, M. (2001). *Poststructuralism, Marxism, and neoliberalism.* Lanham, MD: Rowman & Littlefield.

Peters, T., & Waterman, R. (1982). *In search of excellence: Lessons from America's best-run companies.* New York: Collins.

Pinkney Pastrana, J. (2007). Subtle tortures of the neo-liberal age: Teachers, students, and the political economy of schooling in Chile. *Journal of Critical Education Policy Studies, 5*(2). 1–19.

Plank, D., & Boyd, W. L. (1994). Antipolitics, education, and institutional choice: The flight from democracy. *American Educational Research Journal, 31*(2), 263–281.

Pope, D. C. (2001). *Doing school: How we are creating a generation of stressed out, materialistic, and miseducated students.* New Haven, CT: Yale University Press.

Popkewitz, T. (1979). Schools and the symbolic uses of community participation. In C. Grant (Ed.), *Community participation in education* (pp. 79–90). Boston: Allyn & Bacon.

Prawda, J. (1993). Educational decentralisation in Latin America: Lessons learned. *International Journal of Educational Development, 13*(3), 253–264.

Putnam, R. (2000). *Bowling alone: The collapse and revival of American community.* New York: Simon & Schuster.

Queensland Department of Education, Training and the Arts. Retrieved November 6, 2008, from http://education.qld.gov.au/corporate/newbasics/

Radin, B. (2006). *Challenging the performance movement: Accountability, complexity, and democratic values.* Washington, D.C.: Georgetown University Press.

Ramage, J. (2005). *Twentieth-century American success rhetoric: How to construct a suitable self.* Carbondale: Southern Illinois University.

Ravitch, D. (2005, May 12). Where the mayor went wrong. *The Wall Street Journal,* p. 15.

Ravitch, D. (2007). The unprinted letter about changes in U.S. education. *The Huffington Post.* Retrieved June 16, 2008, from http://www.huffingtonpost.com

Rebell, M., & Wolf, J. (2008). *Moving every child ahead: From NCLB hype to meaningful educational opportunity.* New York: Teachers College Press.

Reich, R. (1991). *The work of nations.* New York: Knopf.

Reitzug, U. C., & Capper, C. (1996). Deconstructing site-based management: Possibilities for emancipation and alternative means of control. *International Journal of Educational Reform, 5*(1), 56–59.

Riesman, D., Glazer, N., & Denney, R. (1954). *The lonely crowd.* New Haven, CT: Yale University Press.

Rogers, T. (2008, January 13–14). *Education is a civil right.* PowerPoint presentation at the midwinter conference of the New York Council of School Superintendents, Albany, NY.

Rothstein, R. (2004). *Class and schools: Using social, economic and educational reform to close the black–white achievement gap.* New York: Teachers College Press.

Rothstein R., & Jacobson, R. (2007). A test of time: Unchanged priorities for students' outcomes. *School Administrator, 64*(3), 36–40.

Rothstein, R., Jacobson, R., & Wilder, T. (2008). *Reassessing the achievement gap: Fully measuring what students should be taught in school.* New York: The Campaign for Educational Equity, Teachers College, Columbia University.

Rowan, B. (2006a). The new institutionalism and the study of educational organization: Changing ideas for changing times. In H. D. Meyer & B. Rowan (Eds.), *The new institutionalism in education* (pp. 15–32). Albany, NY: SUNY Press.

Rowan, B. (2006b). The school improvement industry in the United States: Why educational change is both pervasive and ineffectual. In H. D. Meyer & B. Rowan (Eds.), *The new institutionalism in education* (pp. 67–86). Albany, NY: SUNY Press.

Ryan, J. (2006). *Inclusive leadership.* San Francisco: Jossey-Bass.

Salinger, J. D. (1951). *The catcher in the rye.* New York: Little, Brown and Co.

Saltman, K. (2005). *Edison schools: Corporate schooling and the assault on public education.* New York: Routledge.

Saltman, K., & Gabbard, D. (Eds.). (2003). *Education as enforcement: The militarization and corporatization of schools.* New York: Routledge.

Scahill, J. (2007). *Blackwater: The rise of the world's most powerful mercenary army.* New York: Nation.

Schemo, D. (2003, July 11). Questions on data cloud luster of Houston schools. *The New York Times,* p. A1.

Scott, J. (Ed.). (2005). *School choice and diversity: What the evidence says.* New York: Teachers College Press.

Scott, J., & DiMartino, C. (in press). Public education under new management: A typology of educational privatization applied to New York City's restructuring. *Peabody Journal of Education.*

Scott, J., & Fruchter, N. (in press). Community resistance to school privatization: The case of New York City. In R. Fischer (Ed.), *'The people shall rule': ACORN, community organizing, and the struggle for economic justice.* Nashville, TN: Vanderbilt University Press.

Scott, J. C. (1990). *Domination and the arts of resistance: Hidden transcripts.* New Haven, CT: Yale University Press.

Scott, W. R. (2001). *Institutions and organizations.* Thousand Oaks, CA: Sage.

Seliger, A. (1976). *Ideology and politics.* London: George Allen & Unwin.

Sennett, R. (1998). *The corrosion of character: The personal consequences of work in the new capitalism.* New York: Norton.

Sennett, R. (2006). *The culture of the new capitalism.* New Haven, CT: Yale University Press.

Sergiovanni, T. (1999). *Building community in schools.* San Francisco: Jossey-Bass.

Sergiovanni, T. (2000). *The lifeworld of leadership: Creating culture, community, and personal meaning in our schools.* San Francisco: Jossey-Bass.

Shane, S., & Nixon, R. (2007, February 4). In Washington, contractors take on biggest role ever. *New York Times,* p. A1.

Shapiro, J., & Stefkovich, J. (2005). *Ethical leadership and decision-making in education: Applying theoretical perspectives to complex dilemmas.* Mahwah, NJ: Erlbaum.

Shipps, D. (1997). The invisible hand: Big business and Chicago school reform. *Teachers College Record, 99,* 73–116.

Shirley, D. (1997). *Community organizing for urban school reform.* Austin: University of Texas Press.

Shirley, D., & Evans, M. (2007). Community organizing and no child left behind. In M. Orr (Ed.), *Transforming the city: Community organizing and the challenge of political change* (pp. 109–133). Lawrence: University of Kansas Press.

Shuman, M. (1998). *Going local: Creating self-reliant communities in a global age.* New York: The Free Press.

Shutz, A. (2006). Home is a prison in the global city: The tragic failure of school-based community engagement strategies. *Review of educational Research, 76*(4), 691–743.

Siddle Walker, V. (2003). The architects of Black schooling in the South: The case of one principal leader. *Journal of Curriculum and Supervision, 19*(1), 54–72.

Siddle Walker, V. (2005). Organized resistance and Black educators' quest for school equality, 1878–1938. *Teachers College Record, 107*(3), 355–388.

Sierra Club. (2007) Clear skies proposal weakens the Clean Air Act. Retrieved July 7, 2007, from http://www.sierraclub.org/cleanair/clear_skies.asp

Singer, P.W. (2003). *Corporate warriors: The rise of the privatized military industry.* Ithaca, NY: Cornell University Press.

Skrla, L., & Scheurich, J. (2004). *Educational equity and accountability.* New York: Routledge.

Smith, M. L., Miller-Kahn, L., Heinecke, W., & Jarvis, P. (2004). *Political spectacle and the fate of American schools.* New York: Routledge Falmer.

Smith Richards, J. (2006, October 22). Cheating is up—among teachers: Pressure for state-test success driving some to break the rules. *The Columbus Dispatch*, p. 4.

Soros, G. (1998). *The crisis of global capitalism: Open society endangered.* London: Little, Brown.

Soros, G. (2002). *On globalization.* New York: Public Affairs.

Spillane, J., Diamond, J. Burch, P., Hallet, T., Jita, L., & Zoltners, J. (2002). Managing in the middle: School leaders and the enactment of accountability policy. *Journal of Educational Policy, 16*(5), 731–762.

Spring, J. (2000). *The universal right to education: Justification, definition, and guidelines.* Mahwah, NJ: Erlbaum.

Stanger, A., & Omnivore (2007, October 5,). Foreign policy, privatized. *New York Times*, p. A25.

Starratt, R. J. (2007). *Building an ethical school.* New York: Taylor & Francis.

Stiglitz, J., & Bilmes, L. (2008). *The three trillion dollar war: The true cost of the Iraq conflict.* New York: Norton.

Stone, C., Henig, J., Jones, B., & Pierannunzi, C. (2001). *Building civic capacity: The politics of reforming urban schools.* Lawrence: University Press of Kansas.

Stullberg, L. (2008). *Race, schools, and hope: African-Americans and school choice after Brown.* New York: Teachers College Press.

Sunderman, G., & Kim, J. (2004). *Inspiring vision, disappointing results: Four studies on implementing the No Child Left Behind Act.* Cambridge, MA: Civil Rights Project, Harvard University.

Sunderman, G., Tracey, A., Kim, J., & Orfield, G. (2004) *Listening to teachers: Classroom realities and No Child Left Behind.* Cambridge, MA: Civil Rights Project, Harvard University.

Sutton, M., & Levinson, B. A. (2000). Introduction: Policy as/in practice—A sociocultural approach to the study of educational policy. In M. Sutton & B. A. U. Levinson (Eds.), *Policy as practice. Toward a comparative sociocultural analysis of educational policy* (pp. 1–22). Westport, CT: Ablex.

Sweetland, S. R. (2001). Authenticity and sense of power in enabling school structures: An empirical analysis. *Education, 121*(3), 581–588.

Terry, R. W. 1993. *Authentic leadership: Courage in action.* San Francisco: Jossey-Bass.

Theoharis, G. (2007). Social justice educational leaders and resistance: Toward a theory of social justice educational leadership. *Educational AdministrationQuarterly, 43*(2), 221–258.

Thompson, P. (2008). Head teacher critique and resistance: A challenge for policy and leadership/management scholars. *Journal of Educational Administration and History, 40*(2), 85–100.

Tillman, L. (2004). African American principals and the legacy of Brown. *Review of Research in Education, 28,* 101–146

Tomasevski, K. (2003). *Education denied: Costs and remedies.* London: Zed Books.

Torres, C. A. (1996). State and education revisited: Why educational researchers should think politically about education. *Review of Research in Education, 21,* 255–331.

Tyack, D., & Cuban, L. (1997). *Tinkering towards utopia: A century of public school reform.* Cambridge, MA: Harvard University Press.

Valenzuela, A. (1999). *Subtractive schooling: U.S. Mexican youth and the politics of caring.* Albany, NY: SUNY Press.

Valenzuela, A. (Ed.). (2005). *Leaving children behind.* Albany: SUNY Press.

Ware, L. (1994). Contextual barriers to collaboration. *Journal of Educational and Psychological Consultation, 5*(4), 339–357.

Warren, M. (1996). What should we expect from more democracy? Radically democratic responses to politics. *Political Theory, 24*(2), 241–270.

Waters, J. T., Marzano, R. J., & McNulty, B. A. (2003). *Balanced leadership: What 30 years of research tells us about the effect of leadership on student achievement.* Aurora, CO: Mid-Continent Research for Education and Learning.

Weaver-Hightower, M. (2008). An ecology metaphor for educational policy analysis: A call to complexity. *Educational Researcher, 37*(3), 153–167.

Weick, K. (1995). *Sensemaking in organizations.* Thousand Oaks, CA: Sage

Weiler, H. (1990). Comparative perspectives on educational decentralization: An exercise in contradiction? *Educational Evaluation and policy analysis, 12*(4), 433–448.

Weiner, L. (2008). Building the international movement we need: Why a consistent defense of democracy and equality is essential. In M. Compton & L. Weiner (Eds.), *The global assault on teaching, teachers, and their unions: Stories for resistance* (pp. 251–265). New York: Palgrave Macmillan.

Weiss, L., & Fine, M. (2005). *Beyond silenced voices.* Albany, NY: SUNY Press.

Welch, A. R. (1998). The cult of efficiency in education: Comparative reflections on the reality and the rhetoric. *Comparative Education, 34*(2), 157–175.

West, C. (2005). *Democracy matters.* New York: Penguin Books.

Westheimer, J. (Ed.). (2007). *Pledging allegiance: The politics of patriotism in America's schools.* New York: Teachers College Press.

Wexler, P., Crichlow, W., Kern, J., & Martusewicz, R. (1992). *Becoming somebody: Toward a social psychology of school.* London: Falmer.

Whitaker, S. (2007). *Advocacy for school leaders: Becoming a strong voice for education.* Lanham, MD: Rowman & Littlefield.

Whitfield, D. (2001). *Public services or corporate welfare.* London: Pluto Press.

Whyte, W. (1956). *The organization man.* Garden City, NY: Anchor.

Wolcott, H. (1973). *The man in the principal's office: An ethnography.* New York: Holt, Rinehart, & Wilson.

Wohlstetter, P., Smyer, R., & Mohrman, S. (1994). New boundaries for school-based management: The high involvement model. *Educational Evaluation and Policy Analysis, 16*(3), 268–286.

Ylimaki, R. (2005). Political risk-taking: Leading literacy education in an era of high-stakes accountability. *The Journal of School Leadership, 15*(1), 1–23.

Zimet, M. (1973). *Decentralization and school effectiveness: A case study of the 1969 decentralization law in New York City.* New York: Teachers College Press.

Index